Testir

Historical Urban Studies

Series editors: *Richard Rodger* and *Jean-Luc Pinol*

Titles in this series include:

Culture and Class in English Public Museums, 1850–1914
Kate Hill

European Cities, Youth and the Public Sphere in the Twentieth Century
Edited by Axel Schildt and Detlef Siegfried

City Status in the British Isles, 1830–2002
John Beckett

Resources of the City
Contributions to an Environmental History of Modern Europe
Edited by Dieter Schott, Bill Luckin and Geneviève Massard-Guilbaud

The European City and Green Space
London, Stockholm, Helsinki and St Petersburg, 1850–2000
Edited by Peter Clark

Property, Tenancy and Urban Growth in Stockholm and Berlin, 1860–1920
Håkan Forsell

Civil Society, Associations and Urban Places
Class, Nation and Culture in Nineteenth-Century Europe
Edited by Graeme Morton, Boudien de Vries and R.J. Morris

The Transformation of Urban Liberalism
Party Politics and Urban Governance in Late Nineteenth-Century England
James R. Moore

Paris-Edinburgh
Cultural Connections in the Belle Epoque
Siân Reynolds

The City and the Senses
Urban Culture Since 1500
Edited by Alexander Cowan and Jill Steward

Some of the contributors

Testimonies of the City

Identity, Community and Change in a Contemporary Urban World

Edited by
Richard Rodger
and
Joanna Herbert

Routledge
Taylor & Francis Group
LONDON AND NEW YORK

First published 2007 by Ashgate Publishing

2 Park Square, Milton Park, Abingdon, Oxon OX14 4RN
711 Third Avenue, New York, NY 10017, USA

Routledge is an imprint of the Taylor & Francis Group, an informa business

First issued in paperback 2016

British Library Cataloguing in Publication Data
Testimonies of the city: identity, community and change in
a contemporary urban world.– (Historical urban studies)
1.Sociology, Urban
I. Rodger, Richard II. Herbert, Joanna
307.7'6

Library of Congress Cataloging-in-Publication Data
Testimonies of the city: identity, community, and change in a contemporary urban world / edited by Richard Rodger and Joanna Herbert.
p. cm. – (Historical urban studies series)
Includes bibliographical references and index.
ISBN: 978-0-7546-5560-2 (alk. paper)
1. Cities and towns – Europe – History – 20th century. 2. Social change – Europe –History – 20th century. 3. Sociology, Urban – Europe. 4. Oral history – Europe. 5. Europe – Social conditions – 20th century. 6. Social history – 20th century. I. Rodger, Richard. II. Herbert, Joanna. III. Series: Historical urban studies.

HT131.T474 2007
307.7609409'04 – dc22

2006017123

ISBN 13: 978-0-7546-5560-2 (hbk)
ISBN 13: 978-1-138-25932-4 (pbk)

Contents

Historical Urban Studies General Editors' Preface

Density and proximity are two of the defining characteristics of the urban dimension. It is these that identify a place as uniquely urban, although the threshold for such pressure points varies from place to place. What is considered an important cluster in one context – may not be considered as urban elsewhere. A third defining characteristic is functionality – the commercial or strategic position of a town or city that conveys an advantage over other places. Over time, these functional advantages may diminish, or the balance of advantage may change within a hierarchy of towns. To understand how the relative importance of towns shifts over time and space is to grasp a set of relationships that is fundamental to the study of urban history.

Towns and cities are products of history, yet they themselves have helped to shape history. As the proportion of urban dwellers has increased, so the urban dimension has proved a legitimate unit of analysis through which to understand the spectrum of human experience and to explore the cumulative memory of past generations. Though obscured by layers of economic, social and political change, the study of the urban milieu provides insights into the functioning of human relationships and, if urban historians themselves are not directly concerned with current policy studies, few contemporary concerns can be understood without reference to the historical development of towns and cities.

This longer historical perspective is essential to an understanding of social processes. Crime, housing conditions and property values, health and education, discrimination and deviance, and the formulation of regulations and social policies to deal with them were, and remain, among the perennial preoccupations of towns and cities – no historical period has a monopoly of these concerns. They recur in successive generations, albeit in varying mixtures and strengths; the details may differ.

The central forces of class, power and authority in the city remain. If this was the case for different periods, so it was for different geographical entities and cultures. Both scientific knowledge and technical information were available across Europe and showed little respect for frontiers. Yet despite common concerns and access to broadly similar knowledge, different solutions to urban problems were proposed and adopted by towns and cities in different parts of Europe. This comparative dimension informs urban historians as to which factors were systematic and which were of a purely local nature: general and particular forces can be distinguished.

These analytical and comparative frameworks inform this book. Indeed, thematic, comparative and analytical approaches to the historical study of towns and cities is the hallmark of the Historical Urban Studies series, which now extends to over 30 titles, either already published or currently in production. European urban historiography has been extended and enriched as a result and this book makes another important addition to an intellectual mission to which we, as General Editors, remain firmly committed.

Richard Rodger, University of Leicester
Jean-Luc Pinol, Université de Lyon II

Illustrations and Table

Illustrations

Table

Notes on Contributors

Leen Beyers studied history and anthropology and holds a PhD in History from Leuven University (KUL, Belgium). She is a postdoctoral fellow sponsored by the Fund for Scientific Research Flanders-Belgium and has published on the history of Italian migration, on ethnic boundaries in neighbourhood life, and on oral history.

Wladimir Fischer is a Research Associate at the University of Vienna and specializes in the modern history and cultures of South-Eastern Europe. He is currently concerned with migrants' history in the metropolises of Central and Eastern Europe since the late nineteenth century. Communication and modernization in the development of Eastern and South-Eastern European nation states is the area on which his doctoral thesis was based, and which will appear in the series *Studien zur Geschichte Südosteuropas*, published by Lang. Other publications include 'Minorities, belongings and citizenship' (2004) and 'Traveling tunes' in S. Ingram et al., *Ports of Call. Central European and North American Culturels in Motion* (2003), a study of migrant musical practices.

Joanna Herbert is a Research Fellow in the Department of Geography, Queen Mary University of London. She is currently researching migrants who work in low-paid employment in London and has worked on several research projects concerned with the experiences of minority ethnic groups. Her doctorate used oral histories and life stories to explore the experiences of South Asians in Leicester and the perceptions of white inhabitants in response to their settlement. This won the Michaelis-Jena Ratcliff Prize 2005 'for an important contribution by an individual to the study of Folk Lore and Folk Life in Great Britain and Ireland' and will be published as a book *Negotiating Boundaries in the City: Migration, Ethnicity, and Gender in Britain* (Ashgate).

Sándor Horváth is a Research Fellow in the Institute of History of the Hungarian Academy of Sciences, Budapest. His research interests include social identities, youth history, and everyday life in socialist cities, and this last area was the subject of his dissertation and book on the everyday life and cultural history of the first Hungarian socialist city, Sztálinváros. Currently, Horváth is working on the 'generational gap' of the 1960s from a micro-historical perspective. Recent publications include: 'Everyday life in the first

Hungarian socialist city', *Journal of International Labor and Working-Class History* (2005); 'A kapu és a határ: mindennapi Sztálinváros' ['The Gate and the Border: Everyday Stalintown'] (2004); and 'Pubs and "hooligans" in a socialist city in Hungary: the public sphere and youth in Stalintown', in A. Schildt and D. Siegfried (eds), *European Cities, Youth and the Public Sphere in the Twentieth Century* (2005).

Ronnie Johnston is a Reader in History at Glasgow Caledonian University, Scotland. He has published extensively on the history of occupational health and industrial relations in the UK and is the author of *Clydeside Capital, 1870–1920* (2000) and (with Arthur McIvor) of *Lethal Work* (2000) and *Miners' Lung: A History of Dust Disease in British Coal Mining* (2006). He is Deputy Editor of the *Journal of Scottish Historical Studies* and Deputy Director of the Centre for the Social History of Health and Healthcare, a joint venture of Glasgow Caledonian University and Strathclyde University.

Arthur McIvor is a Reader in History and Director of the Scottish Oral History Centre at the University of Strathclyde, Glasgow, Scotland. He has published extensively on the history of work, industrial relations and occupational health in the UK and is the author of *Organised Capital* (Cambridge 1996), *A History of Work in Britain, 1880–1950* (2001), and (with Ronald Johnston) *Lethal Work* (2000) and *Miners' Lung: A History of Dust Disease in British Coal Mining* (2006). He serves on the Editorial Board of the *Labour History Review*.

Verônica Sales Pereira teaches sociology in the International Relations Program of the *Centro Universitário de Belas Artes* of São Paulo, Brazil. She obtained her BA, MA and PhD in Sociology from the University of São Paulo and attended a doctoral programme at the École des Hautes Études en Sciences Sociales in Paris. Her research focuses primarily on the relation between individual and social memory in the urban experience. She published 'Urbanização de favelas: duas experiências em construção' ['Urbanization of slums: two experiences under construction'] and 'Família, mentiras e um gravador' ('Family, lies and a tape-recorder') in the *Pólis* and *Plural* reviews, respectively. Pereira has also presented papers in sociology and oral history congresses, both in Brazil and abroad. Currently she is investigating the construction of urban memory in de-industrialized areas in São Paulo city.

Maria Raluca Popa trained as an art historian at the Art Academy of Bucharest, Romania, and then studied for MA and PhD degrees in Central and Eastern European history at the Central European University, Budapest.

A former fellow of New Europe College – Institute for Advanced Studies, Bucharest, she has collaborated in projects with the Romanian Institute of Recent History and the Open Society Archives, Budapest. In addition to her art history interests, Maria Popa has specialized in architectural and urban history, which also encompasses cultural studies, intellectual and comparative history. She has published articles for Romanian journals, yearbooks and cultural newspapers, and is at present translating her PhD thesis, preparing the results of her research for publication, and organizing a specialist session for the European Urban History Association conference (2006).

Richard Rodger is Professor of Urban History and previously, Director of the Centre for Urban History, University of Leicester. His efforts to encourage the study of urban history have resulted in books on *European Urban History: Prospect and Retrospect* (1993), *A Consolidated Bibliography of Urban History* (1994), *Teaching Urban History in Europe* (2006) (with Denis Menjot) and, since 2000, as Director of the East Midlands Oral History Archive – a project to collect oral testimony as a means to develop contemporary urban history. As Editor of *Urban History* and General Editor (with Jean-Luc Pinol) of 30 books in the series Historical Urban Studies, Rodger has continued to encourage new work and innovative approaches to urban history. His most recent books have been *The Transformation of Edinburgh: Land Property and Trust in the Nineteenth Century* (2001) and *Cities of Ideas: Civil Society and Urban Governance in Britain 1800–2000* (2004). In 2004, he was elected to membership of the British Academy of Social Sciences.

Estzer Zsófia Tóth is a Research Fellow at the Institute of Political History, Budapest where she teaches an introductory course on oral history within the doctoral programme of the Department of Economic and Social History at the ELTE University of Budapest. Her research focuses on everyday life and the formation of workers' identity under socialism. She has a particular interest in oral history, gender studies, and migration, all of which are evident in her PhD thesis (2004) on the 'Micro-history of a State Prize-winning brigade of unskilled female workers'. Estzer Toth's other publications include: '"I do not worship Kádár but he was such a great man …": the memory of a State Award in the life narratives of women workers' in I. Feitl and B. Sipos (eds), *Regimes and Transitions. Hungary in the Twentieth Century* (2005), and 'Aus Bauerntöchtern – Arbeiterinnen? Sozial- und Erfahrungsgeschichte von Akkordarbeiterinnen in Ungarn', in I. Miethe et al., *Ost und West. Biografische Perspektiven* (2004).

Caroline Varlet teaches architectural and urban history at the Ecole d'architecture de Paris-la-Villette, and also contributes to the Masters programme 'Territories, Spaces, Societies' at the Ecole des Hautes Etudes en Sciences Sociale. Varlet's research interests are principally concerned with housing history and women's identities. These themes formed central elements of her PhD thesis at the EHESS in 2006, 'La femme dans l'espace domestique, 1919–1939', as well as 'Portrait d'une classe moyenne: les immeubles à Loyer Modéré et le confort moderne à Paris, 1923–1933', U. Kuhl (ed.), *Le socialisme municipal en Europe* (2002), and some 15 papers published in various journals, including *Histoire Urbaine, Cahiers d'Histoire*, and *Pages Paysages*.

Ruth Wallach is the head of the Architecture and Fine Arts library at the University of Southern California. She is a co-author of a photographic history of *The Historic Core of Downtown Los Angeles* (Arcadia 2004). Most of her scholarly activities are in two different areas: current trends in academic libraries, specifically in collection development and related services, and the role of public art in the rethinking of American city spaces.

Valentina Gulin Zrnić is a Research Associate at the Institute of Ethnology and Folklore Research, Zagreb, Croatia. She graduated in history (Central European University, Hungary, 1997) and ethnology (Zagreb 1999) dealing with historical anthropology, literary anthropology, and Mediterranean studies, and obtained a PhD in ethnology and anthropology (Zagreb 2004). Zrnić's research interests focused on urban anthropology, specifically relating to urban communities, narrative accounts of urban life under socialism, community and identity, and the symbolic and social construction of space, and contemporary social and cultural transformation of the post-socialist city.

Acknowledgements

This book developed from a panel session 'Constructing urban memories: the role of oral testimony' at the Seventh International Conference on Urban History in Athens, October 2004. It would not have been possible without the willing cooperation of the participants, and of others who could not be present at the meeting but who contributed in different ways to the final version.

For the research support on which their chapters are based, Joanna Herbert, Leen Beyers, Veronica Pereira and Maria Luca Popa would like to acknowledge the contributions respectively of the Economic and Social Research Council, Fund for Scientific Research Flanders–Belgium, Centro Universitario Belas Artes, and the Central European University.

We gratefully acknowledge the following individuals and organizations for their permission to reproduce illustrations: Ronnie Johnson and Arthur McIvor (2.1); Józsefné Staffel (3.1); Eszter Zsófia Tóth (3.2, 3.3); László Csengodi (3.4, 3.5, 3.7); György Kiss (3.6); Károlyné Takács (3.8, 3.9); Jánosné Tasnádi (3.10); Budapest City Archives (4.1, 4.2, 4.4, 4.5); Kálmán Tolnai (4.3); Zagreb City Council (5.1); S.T.E.F. (5.2); Geofote (5.3); Valentina Gulin Zrnić (5.4); Željko Horvatek (5.5); Alexandru Beldiman (8.1); *Monuments Historiques* (8.2, 8.7); Maria Luca Popa (8.3, 8.9); Constantin Jugurică (8.4); Andra Panait and Maria Luca Popa (8.5); Copyright Locke Science Publishing Co., Inc. (8.6); Mariana Celac (8.8); Carlos Vergara (9.1); Verônica Sales Pereira (9.2, 9.3, 9.4); Ruth Wallach (10.1, 10.2, 10.3, 10.4, 10.5); Initiative Minderheiten, Austria (11.2).

We would like to dedicate this book to generations of graduate students in the Centre for Urban History, Leicester and in research institutes elsewhere who study the enduring and fascinating changes in towns and cities through time. Though this book captures some testimonies of the city, ongoing graduate work is a testament to the importance of understanding cities and historical urban studies more generally.

Richard Rodger

Queen Mary College,
Leicester, August 2006

Joanna Herbert
Centre for Urban History,
University of London
London, August 2006

CHAPTER ONE

Frameworks: testimony, representation and interpretation

Joanna Herbert and Richard Rodger

Academic interest in oral testimonies has grown significantly in the last twenty years, as is evident by the expansion in the study of oral history internationally and the biographical and narrative turn in the social sciences.[1] Accordingly, oral testimonies have attracted interest from a range of disciplines. Indeed, oral history itself has been influenced by a diverse number of fields, including anthropology, ethnology and folklore, sociology, cultural studies, psychology and linguistics and has developed by fusing ideas, concepts and methodological issues from these fields to provide fresh insights and sophisticated tools for analysis and interpretation. The collection of chapters presented here reflects this multi-disciplinary approach and includes authors from a diversity of disciplinary backgrounds, whose research focuses on a broad range of international cities. The breadth of oral testimonies is also evident and the volume incorporates spoken recollections of contemporary events recorded in an interview and then transcribed, otherwise known as oral history, but also includes a chapter that draws on personal accounts published in newspapers and another that explores the representation of oral materials in public urban spaces.

Despite this growing popularity of oral sources within and across various disciplines, there remains some resistance among historians to oral testimonies as a viable research method. This resistance is not new. In the second half of the twentieth century, the importance of oral testimonies as

---

[1] The biographical turn refers to the renewed interest in biographical methods and research, such as oral accounts, that is seen to represent a paradigm shift in the social sciences away from positivism and social constructivism. See P. Chamberlayne, J. Bornat, and T. Wengraf (eds), *The Turn to Biographical Methods in Social Science: Comparative Issues and Examples* (London 2000). An example of the growth in oral history internationally is the formation of the International Oral History Association in 1996, which represents a 'worldwide network of oral history scholars, professionals and researchers'.

a valuable resource gradually gained recognition; yet in late 1970s and early 1980s, criticisms came to the fore that these sources were essentially unreliable, consisting merely of 'old men drooling about their past.'[2] The inaccuracy of people's opinions due to nostalgia, forgetfulness, or unconscious and conscious attempts to present false information were seen as major failings. These criticisms sparked intense and critical debates.[3] Initially, oral historians attempted to defend these attacks by rectifying this bias and it was not until the 1980s that the subjectivity of oral testimonies, once at the root of such criticisms, was hailed as an advantage. Those who used oral testimonies in their research argued that oral history was a specific type of historical evidence that did not necessarily produce factually accurate details but offered a lens to view the narrators' world view, their emotions and feelings, and their visions and desires. It enabled an exploration of the psychological impact of events and meanings that individuals themselves attributed to episodes in their lives as they attempted to assess and make sense of their past in the context of the present day. To reiterate the words of Portelli, 'the diversity of oral history consists in the fact that "untrue" statements are still psychologically "true" and that these previous "errors" sometimes reveal more than factually accurate accounts.'[4] From this perspective, the notion of an inaccurate or untrue oral source was immaterial. In short, oral testimonies offered a unique perspective on aspects of history that conventional sources not only ignored, but could not capture. The role of the interviewer was also revised and was no longer seen as detached and omniscient but was implicated in the process and crucial to its construction. The spoken testimony came to be viewed as the result of a collaborative experience. A greater understanding of these issues, of both the potential of oral testimonies and their complex and problematic nature, underscored the vital need for consistent critical analysis and reflexivity on behalf of the researcher.

While the collection of first hand accounts has had a marked impact on the *practice* of history, oral history still tends to be viewed as marginal and secondary within mainstream academic history.[5] Possible explanations for this have included the notion that historians prefer the written source to engaging with living people, perhaps based on the presumption that the written source is more objective and, therefore, superior. Other explanations

---

[2] P. Burke, *New Perspectives on Historical Writing* (London 1993), 114.

[3] R. Grele, L. Passerini, A. Portelli and P. Thompson were influential in these debates. For a review, see D.K. Dunaway and W.K. Baum (eds), *Oral History: An Interdisciplinary Anthology* (London 1996).

[4] A. Portelli, 'The peculiarities of oral history', *History Workshop Journal*, 12, 1981, 100.

[5] For the impact of oral history on history see R. Perks and A. Thomson, 'Introduction' in R. Perks and A. Thomson (eds), *The Oral History Reader* (London 1998), ix–xiii.

blamed historical topics heavily weighted towards studies of previous centuries and on training that traditionally focused on empirical and quantitative methods.[6] The latter may explain why reservations concerning oral testimonies continue to stem from issues relating to reliability, validity and representativeness despite the debates and developments in the 1980s.

Key concepts

Within this context, this book attempts to illuminate the insights that oral testimonies can offer to the urban historian. As the following chapters will show, oral accounts can open up new ways of thinking about and understanding the city. Firstly, oral sources can aid a deeper and richer understanding of the *experience* of urban life. They can provide detailed descriptions of particular social settings, which help to reconstruct a picture of daily life in the city from the respondents' perspective. While earlier oral history studies conducted in the 1960s and 1970s have since been criticized for their naïve idealism in aiming to recover the raw and authentic experience, the focus on the realm of experiences remains important, particularly in the context of traditional social history that has typically centred on legislative and administrative aspects or the pursuit of aggregate data.[7] It also reminds us that the city is not simply lived as a spectacle, a site of aesthetic pleasure as featured in post-modern writings of the city, but is an embodied experience that is often mundane and repetitive. These aspects are key features of Varlet's chapter, which shows how daily life for Parisians during the interwar period was remembered as a series of rhythms and rituals that structured everyday life. The intimate details of the organization and performance of laundry tasks, bathing rituals and the provision and preparation of food creates a vivid impression of the arduous and habitual nature of daily life, a cluster of routines and schedules from which Sunday, a day of pleasure, offered brief respite. Yet this 'essence of the city' was also evoked through memories of the senses, such as the warmth and condensation associated with laundry work, the anticipation of cherries at the beginning of the summer, or the pot-au-feu left to stew for hours on laundry day. Thus, while a dominant theme was how urban life for Parisians during the interwar period was experienced as highly routinized, difficult and subject to constraints, oral testimonies also reveal the many layers of the urban experience.

---

[6] C. Brown 'What's the point?', paper presented at the Centre for Urban History, Leicester, Seminar Series, November 2002. J. Sangster 'Telling our stories: feminist debates and the use of oral history', in Perks and Thompson, *The Oral History Reader*, 93

[7] P. Thompson, 'The voice from the past', in Perks and Thomson, *The Oral History Reader*, 23.

Oral testimonies also allow an insight into human agency. Advocates of oral testimonies often claim that oral accounts, particularly life story approaches that aim to encapsulate the whole life story, restore some of the agency to the narrator. That is, the interview allows the narrators the central stage to construct their own story so that they are not positioned as objects of the research but are fully engaged in the interview process of interpreting and evaluating their lives.[8] In the context of urban history, oral testimonies also show how people's experience of the city is not a passive one; rather, they are active agents that attribute meanings to and invest in the urban landscape. This theme underpins many of the chapters presented here yet it is also at the crux of Zrnić's chapter, which reveals how the individual's relationship to the city is a dynamic and creative process. This is illustrated by an exploration of how inhabitants of housing communities built in the second half of the twentieth century in the new city of New Zagreb participated in creating their own sense of community and belonging by, for example, forging networks with neighbours and participating in local organizations. These actions fostered a particular culture and consciousness on each estate. Official discourses stigmatized the housing estates as dreary and nameless, but the local inhabitants did not share this perception and attributed positive meanings to the area. This focus on the subjective perceptions of particular areas, particularly the discrepancy between official views and the opinions of the actual inhabitants has been an enduring theme of oral histories of urban working class life.[9] It highlights a further value of oral testimony to elucidate how and in what ways spaces have different meanings for different social groups.

Oral testimony can reveal how groups create mental maps of the city and in essence create spaces for themselves that are typically distinct from dominant cultures.[10] This insight is most important considering the recent spatial turn in the humanities and social sciences. That is, developments in new cultural geography have reasserted space and place into critical theory.[11] Influenced by

---

8 M.G.W. Bamberg and A. McCabe, 'Editorial', *Narrative Inquiry*, 8, 1, 1998, iii.

9 See for instance, C. Brown, *Wharf Street Revisited: A History of the Wharf Street Area of Leicester* (Leicester 1995).

10 K. Lynch, *The Image of the City* (Cambridge, Mass. 1960); and K. Lynch (ed.), *Growing up in Cities: Studies of the Spatial Environment of Adolescence in Cracow, Melbourne, Mexico City, Salta, Toluca, and Warszawa* (Cambridge, Mass. 1977).

11 D. Harvey, 'The geography of capitalist accumulation: a reconstruction of the Marxian theory', in R. Peet (ed.), *Radical Geography* (Chicago 1977), 263–92; S. Daniels, *Fields of Vision: Landscape Imagery and National Identity in England and the United States* (Cambridge 1992).

theorists such as Lefebvre[12] there has been a critical rethinking and privileging of space and a consequent appreciation that human life does not simply have a temporal and social dimension, but is also spatial.[13] This, of course, was a key element in the early development of urban history in Britain[14] in the 1960s and 1970s, which has drawn further strength from cultural geographers, leading to a renewed focus on the importance and role of space, particularly the spatial context of identities.[15] In Johnston's and McIvor's paper, the masculine spaces of the pub, the football ground and the bookmakers featured heavily in the narratives of working class men in Glasgow and helped to create and reinforce a masculine identity.[16] In Horváth's chapter, which focuses on the micro street level, a group of hippies in Budapest in the 1960s and 1970s transformed a space by a particular tree into a key meeting place where they could freely express their utopian identity. This illustrates how seemingly mundane and taken-for-granted landscapes are saturated with meanings. When the hippy gang walked along the streets and casually decided to visit the American Embassy to pay tribute to a musician, this was interpreted by the police as 'agitating the state'. The oral testimonies show how groups have their own geographies, and the importance of understanding mental maps of the city. They highlight how identities were constructed in particular spaces and how these spaces were highly contested.

Yet Horváth's chapter also offers a unique insight into the values, perceptions and motivations of the youths that were reported by the police

---

[12] H. Lefebvre, *The Production of Space* (Paris 1974, trans. Oxford 1991).

[13] R. Sennett, *The Conscience of the Eye: Design and Social Life of Cities* (New York 1993); R. Samuel, *Theatres of Memory. Vol.1, Past and Present in Contemporary Culture* (London 1994); D. Hayden, 'The power of place', *Journal of Urban History*, 20, 1994, 466–85; D. Hayden, 'The meaning of place in art and architecture', *Design Quarterly*, 122, 1983, 18–20; S. Zukin, *Landscapes of Power* (Los Angeles 1991).

[14] See H.J. Dyos and M. Wolff (eds), *The Victorian City: Images and Realities*, vol. 2 (London 1974) for early examples of this development. For a more extensive overview of recent modern British urban history, see M.J. Daunton (ed.), *Cambridge Urban History of Britain vol. 3, 1840–1950* (Cambridge 2000).

[15] According to Soja this development is one of the most important intellectual and political advances of the late twentieth century. See E.W. Soja, *Thirdspace. Journeys to Los Angeles and Other Real-And-Imagined Places* (Oxford 1999), 2. See also D. Cosgrove and S. Daniels (eds), *The Iconography of Landscape* (Cambridge 1988); J. Wolff and J. Seed (eds), *The Culture of Capital: Art, Power and the Nineteenth-century Middle Class* (Manchester 1988); R. Colls, 'When we lived in communities: working class culture and its critics', in R. Colls and R. Rodger (eds), *Cities of Ideas: Civil Society and Urban Governance in Britain 1800–2000* (Aldershot 2004), 283–307.

[16] By way of comparison with a non-oral testimony version of the topic see J. Tosh, *A Man's Place: Masculinity and the Middle Class Home in Victorian England* (New Haven 1999).

as threatening and criminal. This highlights how oral narratives enable us to shift focus and attention away from dominant groups in society to explore and understand the perspectives of the marginalized, stigmatized or excluded.[17] This focus on uncovering the histories of 'hidden' groups has been a longstanding feature of oral histories. Since the 1960s, academics have endeavoured to 'give a voice' to marginalized groups, such as women and the working classes and while these proclamations of 'giving a voice' are now deemed as patronizing, oral testimonies are still crucial to accessing the experiences of groups who are simply not available through conventional written sources. For instance, recent developments have included the growing use of oral testimonies to explore the experiences of lesbians and gay men, as few relevant written sources exist.[18] As Thompson predicted, oral histories have proved invaluable for those researching migrant groups, particularly migrants who may not be well educated, do not speak (or may not be proficient in) the dominant language of the host society and who are depicted in the files of the local record office simply as a problem.[19]

The importance of oral testimonies to those interested in migrant groups is reiterated by Fischer who highlights that it is most significant for those groups that may not be formally organized, are invisible in the public sphere, and who have consequently been ignored from mainstream historiography.[20] As Tóth shows, oral testimonies are also invaluable for research on migrant women, particularly as academics continue to claim that, despite increasing attention in recent years, the paucity of gender as a fundamental organizing principle within migration studies still remains.[21] Alongside providing access to otherwise neglected groups, oral testimonies also enable an exploration of previously uncharted and contentious topics of social history, such as the detrimental effect of working in heavy industries on employees' health.[22]

---

[17] The group would also include asylum seekers and refugees, criminals and patients, and all instances where Data Protection prevents access to personal information.

[18] G. Brown, 'Listening to queer maps of the city: gay men's narratives of pleasure and danger in London's East End', *Oral History*, 29, 1, 2001, 48–61.

[19] P. Thompson, 'The voice from the past', 25.

[20] There has been an abundance of studies in recent years. For an overview see A. Thomson, 'Moving stories: oral history and migration studies', *Oral History*, 27, 1, 1999, 24–37. In this volume, see also Herbert and Wallach.

[21] For the gap on women see K. Willis and B. Yeoh 'Introduction: Gender and Migration', in K. Willis and B. Yeoh (eds), *Gender and Migration* (Cheltenham 2000), xi. For recent work, see M. Barber, 'Hearing women's voices: female migration to Canada in the early twentieth century', *Oral History*, 33, 1, 2005, 68–87.

[22] See Johnston and McIvor in this volume. See also M. Abendstern, C. Hallett and L. Wade, 'Flouting the law: women and the hazards of cleaning moving machinery in the cotton industry, 1930–1970', *Oral History*, 33, 2, 2005, 69–78.

Oral testimonies not only offer an alternative perspective or fill in the gaps in our knowledge left by traditional histories; they can go beyond this and have the potential to actually challenge the categories and assumptions of official history. This is a distinct strength of oral accounts and is a theme interwoven in many of the chapters presented here. For instance, oral histories of migrant women have served as an important counterpoint to the presumption that female migrants were disempowered victims who simply followed the pioneering men as dependant wives and mothers. Tóth's chapter in this volume contributes to this growing body of literature by showing how the women in her interviews portrayed themselves as independent and self sufficient.[23] Meanwhile, Popa's paper challenges the conventional notion that equated the reconstruction of Bucharest in the 1980s with the actions of a dictator by highlighting how the transformation of the Romanian city was influenced by a multitude of factors.

In challenging traditional histories, oral testimonies draw our attention to the complexity of urban life. They remind us that there was no single static determinant, but a host of dynamic factors at work. Popa's interviews elucidate the processes behind the urban reconstruction, which involved continuous negotiation between different social groups. This insight into processes and negotiation also features in Wallach's chapter on the use of oral histories as public art. Wallach shows that while the art served to fix history in a public setting, behind this was a complex process whereby the artists negotiated both the views of the community leaders and the contested histories within the immigrant communities, which included generational fissures. This emphasis on the complexity of urban processes and relationships within communities is a unique feature of oral testimonies and is a dimension that simply cannot be gleaned from quantative methods.

Method, analysis and representation

The chapters presented in this volume provide fresh insights into methodological issues. The need to discuss methodology is most pertinent. Interviews are not neutral tools for acquiring information and a number of issues demand careful consideration. Oral testimonies draw from memory, but memories are not static, individualistic items that are stored away and then brought to the fore in the interview. Rather, as Pereira explains in her chapter, personal memories are entwined with the histories of the group, that is, as collective memories, and these interrelate in complex and dynamic ways. For instance, a collective history such as a the Second World War may

---

[23] See also L. Ryan, 'Family matters: (e)migration, familial networks and Irish women in Britain', *The Sociological Review*, 52, 3, 2004, 351–70.

be used to frame and give meaning to more recent events that were also associated with a loss or trauma.

Moreover, oral testimonies are essentially based on what people *decide* to tell. The result is a simplification of reality and a process of editing whereby certain details are selected, prioritized and ordered while others are suppressed and omitted. What is told is not necessarily all that is remembered and the process of selecting and relaying information may depend on the nature of the relationship and interaction between the researcher and the teller. Critical attention to the role of the researcher has been influenced by developments in anthropology, autobiographical work and feminist analysis and has helped to dispel the illusion of an objective researcher who maintains adequate distance from the 'subject' of the research.[24] This awareness of the role of the interviewer was also highlighted by Portelli who compared the oral historian to a stage director: 'If others speak instead [of the historian], it is still the historian who makes them speak; and the 'floor', whether admittedly or not, is still the historian's.'[25] The interviewer is the first person to speak on the recorded interview and continues to ask the questions, thus defining and establishing the roles of the interview and shaping the respondents responses. However, this relationship is often erased from the written text, as the author selects the respondent's answers from the dialogue and presents them as quotes to support his or her argument. In Portelli's words, 'a personal exchange becomes a public statement', and 'a performance is turned into a text'.[26]

The social location of the researcher has also been problematized. The extent to which the researcher and respondent share the same cultural background and world view has been noted as an important factor in gaining access to the respondents and also securing their trust. As Zrnić discusses, her insider status ensured that the respondents were more relaxed and open to discussion, particularly when they realized that she had shared many of their experiences. The interviewer's self-presentation and their performance are also influential factors. It has been contended that if the interviewer chooses not to reveal aspects of their identity, or their values, opinions and experiences, the respondent may in turn be unwilling to disclose private information, or discuss contentious issues and instead may convey

---

24 See for example, M.L Pratt, 'Fieldwork in common places', cited in J. Clifford and G. Marcus, *Writing Culture: The Poetics and Politics of Ethnography* (California 1986), 32–3; J. Fabian, *Time and The Other: How Anthropology Makes it Objects* (New York 1993), xi; S. Reinharz, *Feminist Methods in Social Research* (Oxford 1992).

25 Portelli, 'The peculiarities of oral history', 105.

26 A. Portelli, 'Oral history as genre', in M. Chamberlain and P. Thompson (eds), *Narrative and Genre* (London 1997), 32.

a superficial or public account of their culture.[27] This is supported by Zrnić who explains that when her interviews developed into conversations and exchanges, the testimonies were far richer compared to her initial approaches when she assumed the role of the distanced interviewer. Tóth also avoided the role of the omnipresent interviewer and assumed an informal stance in an attempt to prevent the respondent from simply relaying what they thought the interviewer wanted to hear.

The phrasing of questions is also important and has a significant bearing on what the respondent decides to tell. Life story approaches, as adopted by Tóth in this volume, follow the principles of encouraging the narrator to relay the story of their life, prioritizing all events and experiences that have been personally important to them. In the second interview phase, the interviewer typically attempts to gain more details about the topics raised in the initial session, resisting the temptation to interrupt the narrative even when the respondents' stories may seem peripheral to the research agenda.[28] Several authors in this volume have noted the importance of asking indirect, rather than direct questions to elicit information. This may be most useful if a direct question seems too intrusive or deals with a sensitive issue. For instance, asking minority ethnic groups directly if they have experienced racism often provokes a defensive response. But this can be overcome by asking them to recall actual episodes in their lives such as their experiences of a locality or workplace. It is worth reiterating here the observations of Hollway and Jefferson who claim that researchers often ask the question of their research to the person they are interviewing, yet this typically results in the respondent resorting to superficial and clichéd answers. They therefore urge researchers to ask open-ended questions about actual lived events rather than probing for opinions.[29] Another fruitful approach discussed in this volume is to ask comparative questions. According to Beyers, this is particularly applicable for research on ethnic identities as it enables the respondents to draw distinctions and differences between themselves and others. Furthermore, negative or positive comments about 'others' shows how self identities are defined and constructed.

---

27 Portelli, 'Oral history as genre', 31.

28 See for example, T. Wengraf, *Qualitative Social Interviewing: Biographic Narrative and Semi-Structured Methods* (London 2001), 111–51. Rosenthal has also been influential here. See G. Rosenthal, 'Reconstruction of life stories: principles of selection in generating stories for narrative biographical interviews', in R. Josseleson and A. Lieblich (eds), *The Narrative Study of Lives*, I. (London 1993),59–91.

29 They term this approach 'free association narrative interview method'. For further discussion, see W. Hollway and T. Jefferson, 'Biography, anxiety and the experience of locality', Chamberlayne, Bornat, and Wengraf (eds), *The Turn to Biographical Methods in Social Science*, 167–80.

When considering the context of the interview, it is also important to reflect on how the respondent brings their own agendas to the interview. The respondent may feel impelled to tell particular stories and communicate their message, regardless of the interview questions. They may want to express their moral outrage concerning a particular event or convey their feelings of discontentment. For instance, Gardner has discussed how stories told by Bengalis in East London about illness and suffering can be read as attempts to communicate their general dissatisfaction about living in Britain and their sense of powerlessness and exclusion.[30] As Tonkin reminds us, stories can be construed as 'purposeful social actions' that may have a rhetorical power.[31] This theme is evident in Herbert's chapter, which shows that while the researcher's role is certainly influential, the respondents are not simply passive and the interview itself may be a contested and negotiated process.

The analysis of the oral sources also warrants attention, particularly as Beyers notes the discipline of oral history has tended to neglect this aspect. Several chapters in this volume draw on narrative analysis and show how these techniques can serve as a valuable research tool for the urban historian. Influenced by literary criticism, there has been a recent surge of interest in narrative within many disciplines. In contrast to content analysis, whereby common themes are identified and in this process individual stories are dissected and the coherence of the original story is often lost, narrative analysis shows how meanings can be gleaned not only through the *content* of texts but through a close reading of the *form.* This shifts attention away from what is being said to *how* things are said. Thus, the focus is on the linguistic nuances of an interview, which signal how the narrative should be interpreted.

The definition of narrative is most important as not all oral accounts can be classified as narratives. Narratives can be broadly defined as accounts of events across time that contain a beginning, middle and an end.[32] Narratives refer to how someone describes events that have happened. They take the viewpoint of the teller and are always in the past tense. Events are a crucial element of narratives. A story follows a chronological sequence of events and a narrative is the way in which these events are reordered into a plot. Hence a plot does not need to follow a linear sequence. The process of reordering events is imperative as without it there would simply be a

---

30 K. Gardner, *Age, Narrative and Migration: The Life Course and Life Histories of Bengali Elders in London* (Oxford 2002).

31 E. Tonkin, *Narrating Our Past: The Social Construction of Oral History* (Cambridge 1992), 51–2.

32 For various definitions see R. Franzosi, 'Narrative analysis – or why (and how) sociologists should be interested in narrative', *Annual Review Sociology*, 24, 1998, 517–54.

random conglomeration of incidents, yet this process may also involve the teller attempting to make sense of their past. As a result, they may bestow particular meanings to an incident where, when it occurred, the event had several meanings or even none. Narratives can, therefore, help to give meaning, unity and composure to the past, although this composure may never be absolute.

Narratives also have a trajectory. That is, the temporal sequence of events involves a development or alteration in situations, perhaps ending in a resolution or conclusion. So the events in the story may lead to a change in fortunes from bad to good, or from good to bad, as in a tragedy, but the situation at the end of the story is always different from the outset. Put simply then, a narrative is composed of time, events, order and transformation. These characteristics are most important as they have implications for the interpretation of narratives. For instance, the ways in which elements in a story are organized, or the date when a person decides to 'start' their narratives, may have particular significance. So, for instance, in interviews with South Asians, the respondents invariably began their story with the exact date when they arrived in the UK, perhaps emphasizing how the event of migration was a pivotal point in their lives.[33]

There are a number of different features of narratives that can be analysed ranging from individual phrases or images to the overall format and shape of the narrative. Beyer's chapter in this volume illustrates the range of narrative features that can be analysed in her interviews with indigenous respondents living in a mining town in Belgium. The narrative dimensions included the use of passive and active verbs, the selection of information, and evaluative statements to describe 'outsiders'. Indeed, the depiction of characters in a narrative offers important clues to understanding the respondent's perspective and self identity. Beyers discusses how negative labels of ethnic 'others' can be traced in her interviews, yet in other areas of research, characters may not be given explicit positive or negative character traits; rather their character is often inferred. For example, the teller may present themselves as the victim in a relationship, and with whom we may therefore sympathize; as a result, the audience may deduce that the other character is the aggressor and should be blamed.

Genre has emerged as an important field of study in narrative research. A genre can be defined as a type of narration that is characterized by particular norms and expectations. They have recognizable conventions that signal how the audience should interpret the words. Portelli identified a variety of genres in interviews with Italians such as the worker standing up to the

---

[33] This refers to the research in J. Herbert, 'Contested terrains: negotiating ethnic boundaries in the city of Leicester Since 1950', University of Leicester PhD thesis, 2004.

big boss – a representation of personal courage – or political resistance and war stories that signalled men's active role in the public sphere. Portelli also noted 'hospital stories', a genre evident in women's narratives, which, although less well known compared to familiar tales of war, offered women the opportunity to discuss their effect on the public sphere.[34] 'Migrant stories' may also represent a particular genre. This includes the classic tale of the migrant's rise to success and stories of the migrant adventurer. Both are typically male narratives.[35] Johnston and McIvor in this volume identified two distinct genres in the narratives of Glasgow men who worked in heavy industries. One was underpinned by a rhetoric of solidarity and focused on the collective responses of the workers to their working conditions, while the other was individualistic and depicted a heroic personal struggle. In the latter narrative, the workers were characterized as the victims and the employer was cast as the villain. However, Johnston and McIvor deduce that this characterization may have been shaped by the growing awareness of the effects of asbestos in recent decades. This observation is most important as it reminds us that the recalling of past events cannot be disentangled from present day concerns.

Metaphors can also be analysed in narratives. In narratives of migration, clothes have been identified as a recurring image used to articulate the experiences of transition, movement and independence, but also to highlight poverty and a sense of difference.[36] Metaphors are, therefore, commonly used to communicate sentiments that may be difficult to put into words. In Johnston and McIvor's chapter, hell was a prominent metaphor used in the respondent's depictions of their workplace, providing an unequivocal message about how they felt about and perceived their working conditions. In Pereira's chapter, the inhabitants of the Brás district in Sáo Paulo used the shared image of the cemetery in their narratives to articulate and comprehend the profound sense of 'urban emptiness' they felt as a result of transformations in their urban environment.

Clearly narrative analysis helps us to tap into subjective experiences and social identities, but the approach is not without its pitfalls. Criticisms have included that it may lead to a narrow focus, a search for the respondent's 'real' intentions or privileging the form of the interview over the actual content.[37] However, as Beyers persuasively argues in her chapter, these limitations can

---

[34] Portelli, 'Oral history as genre'.

[35] See, for instance, P. Werbner, 'Rich man poor man – or a community of suffering', *Oral History*, 8, 1, 1980, 43–8.

[36] L. Ryan, '"I'm going to England": women's narratives of leaving Ireland in the 1930s', *Oral History*, 30, 1, 2002, 42–53.

[37] See, for example, Franzosi, 'Narrative analysis', 527; Sangster, 'Telling our stories'.

be avoided if narratives are analysed with the aid of secondary sources, not only in an attempt to check the factual bias but most importantly to anchor the narrative in its historical and social context. Moreover, rather than favouring one form of analysis over another, content and narrative analysis can be used in conjunction, as featured in many of the chapters presented here.

A final consideration is the representation of the interviews. This theme is most pertinent to research involving minority ethnic groups or migrants, for as Puwar has argued, the new voices cannot simply be added in as part of an attempt to rectify their previous marginalization or exclusion. This is because they are invariably interpreted in the context of dominant categories such as the victim-hood of migrants or alternatively the celebration of their difference, a dichotomy that fails to encapsulate the complexity of their experiences.[38] Thus issues of power inequalities remain and the new voices cannot be divorced from the understanding and interpretations of the researcher.

The problems associated with representations are clearly highlighted in Wallach's chapter, which explores two works of public art in Los Angeles. One project signified a celebration of Japanese Americans in the city from 1890–1945 and included recollections of those who lived there. However, there were numerous conflicts concerning how the history should be depicted. Debates centred on the choice of quotes, the choice of language used to convey the experiences, as well as which aspects of history should be remembered and forgotten. The issue of representation is also a theme of Herbert's chapter, particularly the issue of arranged marriages, which was a recurring theme in the accounts of South Asian women, but is also a highly contentious topic that has been subject to racist interpretations. The need to reflect on the range of issues relating to the methodology, interpretation and representation does not detract from the particular strengths of oral testimonies; rather, it highlights how it is essential to engage with these issues to avoid naïve interpretations and to gain as full an understanding as possible.

The chapters and central themes

This book offers rare insights into the minds and strategies of individuals as they sought to cope with the challenges of urban life as they experienced

[38] N. Puwar, 'Memory work for revisioning Britishness', paper presented at the conference 'Immigration, History and Memory in Britain', De Montfort University, Leicester, September 2003. For further discussion, see also G.C. Spivak, 'Can the subaltern speak?', in C. Nelson and L. Grossberg (eds), *Marxism and the Interpretation of Culture* (London 1988), 271–313.

it. Unlike *The Myths We Live By*[39] in which recorded life stories based on the memories of Australian soldiers, Swedish concentration camp survivors, native American storytellers, and Italian schoolchildren provided insights into recent memory and transient myths, *Testimonies of the City* addresses the stark realities and perceptions of urban life. In this sense, it is a wider-ranging, more theoretically informed collection based on interviews, which, though obtained in the period *c.* 1980–2000, straddle topics that range across the human condition in the course of the second half of the twentieth century.

If 'space' and 'aliens' might be thought to be futuristic rather than historical, these themes are shown by the authors to be of enduring significance to human experience. While a web of bureaucratic red tape is considered characteristic of modernity, then individual strategies to cope with authority is a theme that permeates several chapters. This individualism and the plurality of modern lifestyles and values – cultural, sexual, political, and social – links the chapters through an analysis of the respondents 'voices'. Many were young, dispossessed economically or educationally, or constrained institutionally and by force of personal circumstances. Their insights, however, are not of those living on the 'edge' of society. To marginalize their voices would be an arrogant labelling and degrading to their testimonies. Indeed, the strength of the accounts presented here is how the respondents' views shed light on the functioning of authority – on police, planners, professionals, and policy-makers. The interviewees' 'take' on how society *really* functioned is what binds the collection together. Individuals' pragmatism and realism, their unglamorous and unacknowledged contributions, and their resolution in the face of difficulty is a far cry from *The Myths We Live By,* though there is one common element: a recognition that oral testimony is the only historical source likely to inform some recent human issues.

Without exception, each author engages actively with issues of method and theory. Indeed, because the sociologist, anthropologist, and ethnologist join forces with social, architectural and art historians in their consideration of oral testimony, the outcome is a penetrating assessment of how much testimonies reveal of the contemporary city. Though the final section of the book is formally called 'Migration and Methods', the systematic and sensitive acknowledgment by each author of their methods is evident throughout the book. This meticulous attention to sources, how they are compiled, how the source and the scholar interact, what filters need to be applied to unravel meaning, all contribute to the subtle use of testimony

---

39 R. Samuel and P. Thompson (eds), *The Myths We Live By* (London 1990) based on papers presented at the Sixth International Oral History Conference on Myth and History, Oxford September 1987

gathered in the home, workplace, on the street, and in the community – in fact, in everyday situations.[40] The authors demonstrate how important it is to be aware of 'spin' and how fragile and fickle memory is as a historical source. The customary defence of oral testimony as a historical source occasionally intrudes in the chapters, more as part of the historiography of the subject than as a belief that it is necessary any longer to mount a defence of its use as a means to explore historical change.

From the multiple disciplinary perspectives adopted there is an overwhelming sense of testimony as a testament or tribute to the vitality of city living. The dynamic daily rhythms of urban life, survival skills among socialist city-dwellers, the tense cultural negotiations between migrants and the indigenous society, and the imagery that contributed to and resulted from the clash of cultures as traditional values were confronted with those of modernity are themes present in virtually all of the chapters. In this sense, and from different geographical, political and cultural perspectives, the chapters reveal much about the problems common to urban populations in the second half of the twentieth century.

In addition, three specific points should not go unnoticed. Firstly, and to return to that old favourite, written sources, the primacy once afforded to text in historical writing will never again be achieved. This is not just because the argument about authenticity and subjectivity has been become passé, but because in a digital age that has emerged from one in which telephone messages and faxes preceded the electronic file, much of the decision-making in the late twentieth century either went unrecorded in a physical sense of a document, or has not found its way into archives. The home video will, no doubt in the future, also gain a degree of ascendancy to complement the oral interview as a fruitful historical source. In short, we *need* recorded testimony because in many cases we have no other sources. It may, with video, prove to be our *only* historical source in many instances. Even the most reluctant historian will come to rely on such sources, particularly as archive holdings increasingly accumulate such items.

Secondly, which of us, in an unguarded moment at least, would not plead guilty to some of the deadly sins – pride, envy, gluttony, lust, anger, greed, and sloth? Yet, do these not inform our daily lives? Decisions are tinged with such human failings and, similarly, coloured by personal virtues. Prudence, temperance, courage, justice, love, hope and faith, humility, kindness, abstinence, chastity, patience, liberality and diligence are qualities that govern our lives and, in a modern world, often come under intense pressure. *Testimonies of the City*, therefore, brings out many of these qualities and

---

[40] The importance of different perspectives is provided in L. Stopes, 'The Baltimore Neighborhood Heritage Project: oral history and community involvement', *Radical History Review*, 25, 1981, 27–44.

shortcomings. Generous neighbours in Leicester's South Asian communities, solidarity amongst the youth of Budapest and sensitivity towards the Japanese residents of Los Angeles are particular examples of these personal qualities revealed in this volume, but every chapter is saturated with strong emotions and human characteristics. Far from confessing to the arbitrary nature of the chapters, this is to stress how interconnected the chapters are and, gently, to remind readers that even if it was not their principal purpose, the authors indirectly have provided many insights into shared topics that affect the contemporary city. Indeed, human qualities bind the chapters together, not exactly through the seven deadly sins or an overabundance of virtue, but through shared experiences and emotions. The insights are genuinely 'unique and precious'.[41]

Thirdly, since few of us are multi-lingual, and even fewer are able to pick up the coded references and colloquialisms of other languages, then oral testimony presents a major barrier to the development of comparative historical analysis. This is all the more so with a multiplicity of 'minority' European languages. So to draw on testimony based, for example, on Flemish, Hungarian, Serbo–Croat, and Romanian provides most readers with rare insights and valuable counterpoints to experiences elsewhere. Thus a Central and South-Eastern European perspective on urban life since 1960 informs the Western European perspectives presented here. In terms of responses to power and authority, the interviews from Brazil, Romania and Croatia make for intriguing comparisons across continents. Despite the emphasis on individual responses to urban conditions, the structured and ritualistic nature of daily life in socialist and westernized cities, and the rhythms that defined these patterns, also emerges from the interviews. By these means, a genuinely comparative urban historical perspective emerges, as authors and linguists fuse their knowledge and expertise. Place is important to urban historians; geographies and spatial dimensions suffuse the literature on towns and cities through time. However, place is subordinate to process, in the sense that understanding the mechanics of urban change in a historical setting is fundamental to an appreciation of how towns and cities evolve. To undertake comparative and contemporary urban history, therefore, must inevitably rely on teamwork and a consideration of a shared agenda. This is what the authors of each chapter seek to do.

Through the lens of urban dwellers, identities are seen to be forged through an iterative process between in-coming and 'host' populations in Zagreb, Bucharest, Budapest, Vienna, and Paris, as well as in Glasgow, Leicester, Sáo Paulo, Los Angeles, and Belgian mining communities of Limburg. This focus on identity is particularly important as several new

---

41 A. Portelli, 'What makes oral history different?', in Perks and Thomson (eds), *The Oral History Reader,* 67.

states have been created in Europe, while others have re-emerged from a period of isolationism and repression under communist rule, and yet more are coming to terms with a re-examination of the relationship between regional identities and the central state. 'What does it mean to be British?' or French, Hungarian or Austrian has, thus, come under intense scrutiny, just as the same nationalist question has posed questions over identities in Baltic and Balkan states, and in the former Soviet Union Republics. The unit of analysis commonly considered, the state, and the relationship citizens have with the geographical and political boundaries within which they find themselves, is increasingly recognized as bound up with cultural, linguistic, and behavioural characteristics, many of which are determined at a local, urban unit of analysis.[42] Thus the geography of the nation state is undergoing re-examination in much the same way that cultural geography induced a new spatial awareness with questions raised concerning the nature, production and ownership of space, the construction of divisions between public and private spheres, and the regulation of the social life of streets and households, particularly in relation to gender and class. Therefore, testimonies that explore these relationships and how residents relate to the civic state contribute to an understanding of community and neighbourhood. Identity and loyalty are entwined. Localism, participation and stake-holding, key elements in the formation of identity, are themes to which the contributors return frequently, and on which many testimonies are based.

The volume is organized into parts that address particular themes within urban history.[43] Indeed, each of the four themes – 'Social Identities', 'Community Neighbourhood and Daily Life', 'Responses to Urban Change', and 'Migration and Methodology' – around which the chapters are deliberately organized, relate to earlier works on towns and cities so as to

---

[42] See for example, S. Zimmermann (ed.), *Urban Space and Identity* (Budapest 1995); R. Colls, *The Identity of England* (Oxford 2002) especially, 5–6 for references *c.*1980–2000 on the emerging interest on the nation state; A. Schildt and D. Siegfried (eds), *European Cities, Youth and the Public Sphere in the Twentieth Century* (Aldershot 2005) for essays on Amsterdam, Naples, Vienna, and Manchester; D. Pomfret, *Young People and the European City: Age Relations in Nottingham and St. Etienne 1890–1940* (Aldershot 2004); S. Gunn and R.J. Morris (eds), *Identities in Space: Contested Terrains in the Western City since 1850* (Aldershot 2001); M.J. Miller, *The Representation of Place: Urban Planning and Protest in France and Great Britain 1950–80* (Aldershot 2003), 321–38 for a useful bibliography on the subject of negotiated spaces.

[43] These themes in urban history would require a very long bibliography. By way of introduction, see J.-L. Pinol (ed.), *Histoire de l'Europe Urbaine*, 2 vols. (Paris 2003). Each contributor has provided a select list of references that are considered useful background to the chapter.

complement and extend previous approaches. In each of these four theatres of urban experience, the contributors are concerned methodologically with the construction and deconstruction of memory, though each chooses a different historical stage on which to present their work so as to reveal the social pathology of the city. Despite this focus on a specific place, the meaning and significance of their urban testimonies crosses boundaries of time and space with relative ease – an indicator of its relevance to the formation of identity and even to the universality of some aspects of human behaviour and experience. Thus, chapters that focus on European experiences have implications for the Americas, and vice versa. Urban experiences in totalitarian states, or of migrants who seek to come to terms with the dominant cultures have commonalities despite the particularities of place.

Part 1 'Social Identities' draws on oral sources to examine how identities are constructed within particular urban settings and shows how identities are shaped by a host of variables such as work, gender, class, ethnic origin, and age, within particular spatial contexts. The chapters also use oral testimonies to explore the world views of particular social groups and elucidate how social identities impacted and shaped the respondents' lives.

In Part 2 'Community, Neighbourhood and Daily Life', Beyers and Zrnić highlight the complex ways in which communities are imagined and constructed, both through a common history of shared experiences, but also in responses to newcomers, who are essentially defined and therefore, rejected as 'outsiders'. Crucially, in the process of drawing symbolic boundaries and demarcating who belonged to their community, the more established groups also reveal how they perceive themselves. Varlet's chapter meanwhile focuses more closely on the experiences of the neighbourhood and daily life and uses oral testimonies to reconstruct daily practices and living conditions to show how city life was organized.

In Part 3 'Responses to Urban Change' Popa and Pereira explore interpretations and responses to urban redevelopment, Popa from the perspective of the agents involved in the reconstructions, such as the architects and planners and Pereira from the view of the local inhabitants who experienced the changes to their locality. Wallach's chapter examines how the redevelopment of Los Angeles' city centre has involved works of public art that used oral testimonies of minority ethnic communities. The chapters in this section also contribute to an understanding of the nature of memory by revealing how people try to 'make sense' of, and come to terms with, their past and highlighting the role of public memories. Popa's research not only revises the official and dominant memory of the redevelopment of Bucharest, but also shows how public memory was instrumental in the reconstruction of the city by helping to define what should be preserved. Pereira highlights how public and private memories intersect, while Wallach shows how oral testimonies have been transformed into public memories in the form of commemorate public art. However, the problems involved in fixing memories in public and presenting in effect, one history, also underscores how public memories may often fail to capture the complexity and diversity of the lived experience.

Finally, Part 4 'Methods and Migration' brings together two papers that focus on oral testimonies to explore the experiences of immigrant groups, particularly the dilemmas and difficulties that this entails. The chapters explore methodological issues such as the power of the researcher in relation to the 'researched' and grapple with questions concerning the influence of identity, such as gender and ethnicity, on the interview process. They also discuss the difficulties of representing minority ethnic groups, and demonstrate Puwar's concerns that new voices cannot simply be added in. Ultimately, these last chapters elucidate the complexities involved in oral history research and highlight the need for reflexive analysis.

Taken as a whole, the chapters presented here engage with important debates in urban history, enhance our understanding of oral testimonies as a particular source, and illustrate how oral testimonies offer new insights into conceptualizing and comprehending the contemporary city. By highlighting the unique perspectives and value that oral sources offer, it is hoped that this will encourage those that remain resistant to oral sources to critically rethink their reservations and assumptions.

PART 1

SOCIAL IDENTITIES

CHAPTER TWO

Narratives from the urban workplace: oral testimonies and the reconstruction of men's work in the heavy industries in Glasgow

Ronnie Johnston and Arthur McIvor[1]

This chapter explores the utility of oral history in relation to our understanding of twentieth century urban workplace culture. As will be illustrated, oral testimonies can help us penetrate deep into hidden urban spaces including the workplace. Consequently, oral history methodology can be a powerful tool with which to sharpen our understanding of the dynamics of the working environment, and the identities that these complex dynamics forge. Also discussed are some of the difficulties inherent in oral testimony, including the problems of grappling with contradictory evidence, inter-subjectivity and multiple discourses. The focus of the study is male workers in the so-called heavy industries in Glasgow, a city that in 1950 had a population of around one million. The city and its surrounding industrial conurbation (see Figure 2.1) known as Clydeside, was one of the most industrialized regions in the world in the first half of the twentieth century and has been compared with the Ruhr region of Germany. It was also one of the most proletarianized, a consequence of a local economy characterized by a heavy concentration of employment in shipbuilding, the docks, heavy engineering, iron and steel and other manufacturing. Frequently labelled 'Red Clydeside' because of a legacy of volatile industrial relations and socialist political activity from the first quarter of the twentieth century, the tough working environment in this region helped to incubate a heavily masculinized working-class culture, often associated with the idea of the 'hard man'. These features of Glasgow working-class life came to assume

[1] We are particularly grateful to Neil Rafeek (Research Fellow in the Scottish Oral History Centre, University of Strathclyde) for assistance with some interviews and transcription. Thanks also to David Walker and Hilary Young for providing leads and permission to cite from interviews.

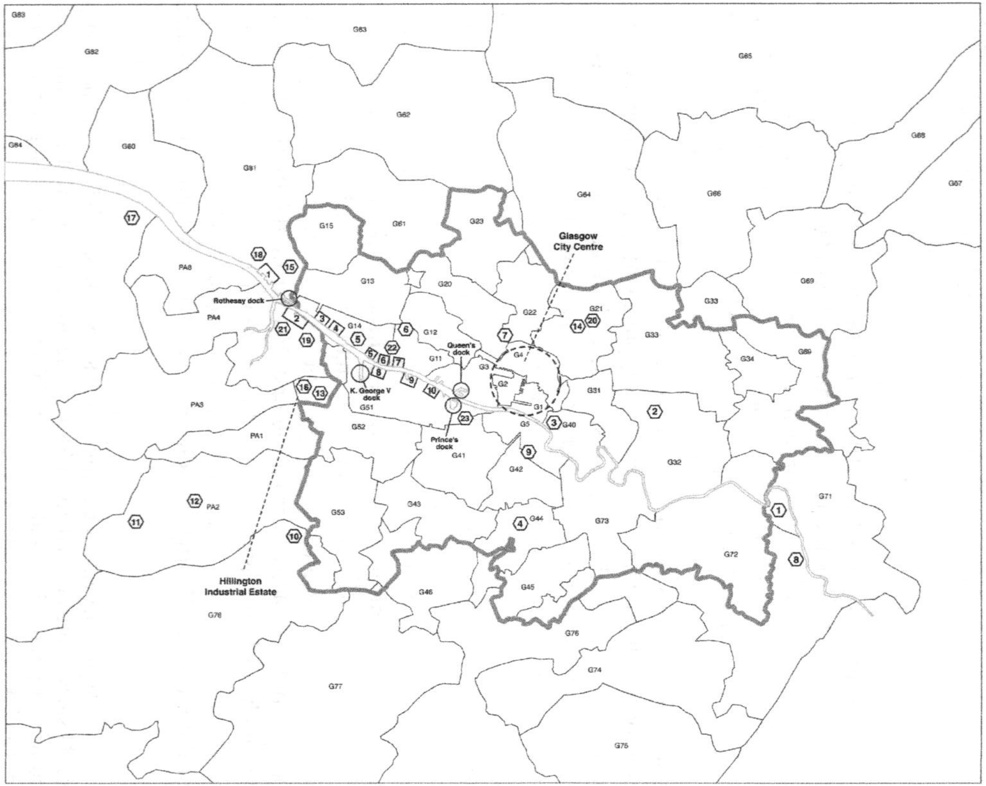

○ Major docks

□ Upper Clyde shipbuilding & shiprepairing yards

1. John Brown's
2. Simon Leibnitz
3. Barclay Curle 1
4. Yarrow's
5. Blythswood
6. Connell's
7. Barclay Curle 2
8. Blythswood (repair)
9. Fairfield's
10. Harland & Wolff

⬡ Other Industrial sites

1. Clydebridge Steel Wks
2. Parkhead Forge
3. Templeton's Carpet Factory
4. G & J Weir's Engineering
5. Albion Motors
6. Barr & Stroud
7. Bryant & May
8. Hoover Ltd
9. Dixons Iron Works
10. Shank's
11. John Lang & Sons
12. J & P Coats
13. Rolls Royce
14. North British Locomotive Co.
15. Singer Co. Ltd
16. Babcock & Wilcox
17. Royal Ordnance Wks
18. Turners' Asbestos
19. Clyde Rubber Works
20. Marinite Co.
21. Renfrew Power Station
22. North British Diesel Engine Works
23. MacLellan's Iron Wks

— City boundary

2.1 Glasgow: major industrial sites *c.* 1950

almost cult status, and especially so after the publication of McArthur and Kinsley Long's *No Mean City* in the mid-1930s. From the 1950s onwards, deindustrialization saw Clydeside's staple industries go into atrophy, and high unemployment was to dog Glasgow and its hinterland from the 1970s onwards. However, the cult of the Glasgow 'hard man' persisted for some time to come.

The oral history project

The urban environment consists of a wide variety of functional spaces, but only very rarely have urban and social historians infiltrated the world of work – where bodies constituted the biological core of an ecological system.[2] Therefore, a lack of attention by historians on the interaction between employment and health constituted the main rationale for an oral history project focusing on the body at work. Interviews were conducted with 33 male Clydeside workers, whose experiences embrace the shipyards, docks, iron and steel works, heavy engineering, construction and other manufacturing. The respondents' jobs ranged from skilled craftsmen to labourers, from the lowest grades through to charge-hands and foremen. However, interviewees did not constitute a representative sample of the male Glasgow workforce. Indeed, tested against the decennial census, our cohort under-represents several categories of Glaswegian male workers, including those in transport, chemicals, paper and printing, food and drink, and woodworkers. However, the group exemplifies a reasonable range of male occupations in Glasgow, with a good coverage of the three most male-dominated occupations according to the census: that is, shipbuilding, construction and metals. The average age of those interviewed was 68, with birth dates ranging from 1917 to 1948, while the employment histories of respondents ranged from the early 1930s to the present.

Most of the interviews were conducted as part of the research undertaken for our book on the history of the asbestos tragedy in Scotland.[3] The interviewees were told beforehand of our main interest and the project's aims. This is vital so the potential respondent can make an informed decision about whether or not they wish to consent to being interviewed and to transfer the copyright of their testimony to an archive. Most interviewees completed a pre-interview questionnaire. The respondents were recruited in a number of ways, including contacting the Glasgow offices of the charity Clydeside

---

[2] A.F. McEvoy, 'Working environments: an ecological approach to industrial health and Safety', in R. Cooter and B. Luckin (eds), *Accidents in History: Injuries, Fatalities and Social Relations* (Amsterdam 1997), 62.

[3] R. Johnston and A. McIvor, *Lethal Work: A History of the Asbestos Tragedy in Scotland* (East Linton 2000).

Action on Asbestos (CAA), an organization which has done tireless work as an advocate for the disabled community in Glasgow. It was realized, though, that depending upon CAA clients could 'skew' the sample and efforts were made to address this by extending recruitment, including approaching the Transport and General Workers' Union (T&G) in Glasgow. However, because around half of our final cohort of respondents had some connection with CAA (and many had been or were involved in compensation litigation), this undoubtedly had significant effects upon the discourses embedded in the narratives we accumulated. This theme will be returned to later.

The interviews were mainly conducted by Ronnie Johnston, with several undertaken by a colleague, Neil Rafeek. In most cases, the interviews took place on a one-to-one basis in the respondents' homes. However, there were two 'group' interviews at the Glasgow offices of the T&G, with two and three respondents respectively, and two interviews where the respondents' wives were present. One respondent, the 'exemplar' highlighted in a later section, was interviewed twice. Recently, some oral historians have identified and elucidated the inter-subjective nature of the oral interview, and noted how testimony can be affected by a range of factors. The work of Summerfield and Thomson stands out here.[4] Clearly, as far as the present project was concerned, there were different dynamics operating in the 'group' interviews compared to the single ones. In the former, for example, a 'dominant' individual could influence the testimony of the others. On the other hand, memories were sometimes 'triggered' and frequently contradicted within the group interview, leading on occasions to more in-depth and insightful recollections.

Undoubtedly the interviewer also had an influence, however subtly, upon the process of recollection. Ronnie Johnston is an educated (at one time a mature student), working-class Glasgow male brought up in a shipyard community (Govan), whose father was a joiner who worked in both shipbuilding and construction. Ronnie Johnston used his background, local knowledge and awareness of dialect to good effect in the interviews, empathizing with respondents, creating rapport and 'locating' himself, sometimes through his father's experiences, alongside them. This proved fruitful, with several respondents opening up to an 'insider' in a way they would perhaps not have done to another interviewer, offering, for example, intimate personal information about relationships. Ronnie Johnston's age (around 40 at the time) and gender, may well have had further effects, in that respondents felt comfortable with their largely 'traditional' male identities. This relationship was indicated starkly in another recent oral history project on masculinity in Glasgow by Hilary Young, where several elderly male

---

4 P. Summerfield, *Reconstructing Women's Wartime Lives* (Manchester 1998); A. Thomson, *Anzac Memories: Living with the Legend* (Melbourne 1994).

respondents 'reconfigured' their male identities because the interviewer was female, in her early 20s, educated and perceived to be 'feminist'.[5]

The other interviewer, Neil Rafeek, is slightly younger than Ronnie Johnston and is another highly experienced oral historian. While his family background is middle-class (father a town planner; mother a teacher), Neil Rafeek was brought up in the heavy industry community of Sunderland in the north-east of England, and has been actively involved in trade union and labour politics. He has developed an informed, well-honed, non-patronizing interview technique, drawing upon his experience and background to empathize and 'bond' with his subjects, creating a comfort zone that encouraged the free flow of recollections.

The testimonies tell us much about the experience, culture and attitudes of industrial workers, facilitating the reconstruction of identities, and probing what it meant to be a man working in heavy industry in the 1950s and 1960s. The neglected interaction between the workplace and the body is also explored. The interviews are both interpretive and informative. When reflecting, workers are trying to make sense of their working lives; and are reviewing, and in some cases coming to terms with, the processes that damaged their bodies. This was especially evident, for example, in the case of mesothelioma suffers (the most serious of the asbestos-related diseases) where the testimony constituted a trauma narrative. Some respondents had particular agendas they wished to pursue, such as attaching blame for their diseased bodies to the employers, management and the government. Only rarely was any individual culpability conceded.

'It was hell': remembering and reconfiguring the work environment

The oral testimonies of male Glaswegian workers reflect the essential dualism of work in the urban environment. On the one hand, a consistent theme in the oral evidence was the enjoyment and satisfaction that male workers extracted from their work experience. For some respondents, paid employment was remembered in a rosy, nostalgic and positive light, with the camaraderie of workmates, the banter and black humour, and the rewarding experience of the labour process itself frequently to the fore. A Glasgow lagger (insulation engineer) reflected in this fashion:

---

5 Young argues that her male respondents 'softened' their historical masculine identities in interviews with her compared to a previous set of interviews with a male interviewer: 'The image of the stereotypical Glaswegian hard man has been endangered by the emergence of a more liberated feminine existence and has shocked men into redefining and reconstructing their own masculinity'. See H. Young, 'New men, hard men: an oral history of masculinity in Glasgow, from 1950–2000' (Honours Dissertation, History, University of Strathclyde, 2001), 59.

> Oh good comradeship you know, you always get good squads, good patter, och aye it was – it was *a great job* … Oh I loved … even the noo' when you go onto sites and you've got a good squad of guys, your day goes in, you're working away …[6]

The skilled craftsmen were most likely to represent this positive vision of work, though in some cases this was tinged with regret at the erosion of craft skill and discretion with technological change and the reorganization of work. A 72-year-old retired Glasgow boilermaker plater commented:

> You had tae depend on the workmanship of the men too. And it was remarkable how they built ships. It was all through experience. The likes of the noo there, I don't think they would be able to build ships noo, because the tradesmen are not there noo.

He continued, describing his work thus:

> And once you got it up there, and you got it tae fit – and it did fit – it was a great satisfaction. That's when tradesmen gets the satisfaction, when everything works. Because you put a lot intae the job. And everybody else, you know people who don't really know the job … You've got tae be a mathematician an a'. You've got tae dae sines, tangents, and a' the different degrees. At that time there were no, there were no calculating machines. All you had was a log book, a wee log book. You got your, you know, your numbers and you calculated.[7]

Such oral testimonies undoubtedly elucidate urban work spaces that have all but disappeared, illustrating labour processes, describing work environments and conditions, and shedding insights into relationships, attitudes and rituals that once characterized the heavy industries. The rites of passage of apprenticeship and on-the-job training, where youths were socialized into a dangerous and macho environment would be a good example. In the shipyard insulation trades, the way that workplace camaraderie dissected and negated sectarianism also comes across strongly.[8] Oral history provides rich, 'thick' description which helps us to evoke the workplace, providing a conduit to the past that places us shoulder to shoulder with the docker, the plater, the fitter, the builders' labourer and the asbestos insulator.

---

6 Interview, Neil Rafeek with Jim O'Donnell, 26 March 2005 (for the Scottish Oral History Centre and archived at SOHC, University of Strathclyde). For those not fluent in contemporary Scots vernacular, the following glossary may prove useful: noo = now; wee = little; tae = too; nai = no; dain = doing; doon = down; hadnae = hadn't; couldnae = couldn't; wernae = weren't; wasnae = wasn't.

7 Scottish Occupational Health Oral History Project (subsequently cited as SOHOHP), SOHC Archive Deposit 016, Interview A3.

8 Interview, Neil Rafeek with Hugh Cairney, 26 March 2005 (SOHC).

On the other hand, many of our respondents interpreted a primary 'task' in the interview as 'educating' us about how grim work was in the past and in the process marking their own manliness in contrast to the 'easy life' of today (and perhaps indirectly of the 'academic'). There was a tendency to recall later dates when key changes in occupational health knowledge and practice occurred, and to over-generalize, failing to differentiate between the varying practices and occupational health standards of firms across Glasgow. In some cases, commenting that there was absolutely no state presence, no union involvement and no protection at all at work seems hardly plausible, given the weight of evidence to the contrary. However, what is important here is how such workers *perceived* their working lives. There was a propensity, moreover, in some testimonies, to paint the work experience as universally grim, indicated, for example, in the recurrent use of the 'hell' metaphor in describing the work environment.

Nonetheless, the oral evidence sheds many important insights into the social history of the heavy industry workplace in Glasgow. Several points might be briefly highlighted. Firstly, the oral testimony illuminates the intimate relationship between employment and the body, and, connected to this, the many and varied ways that those with power in the workplace, the employers, managers and foremen – evocatively described by one shipyard worker as 'the bastards in bowlers' – exploited those lacking such power.[9] This was invariably so even where statutory provision existed to 'protect' workers' rights, as amply illustrated in the case of workers exposed to asbestos in the Glasgow shipyards and construction sites. Cutting corners on managerial instruction was endemic on Clydeside, including stripping asbestos without first soaking it to curtail dust. Removing asbestos without protective clothing or apparatus, often with the inducement of a hefty bonus, was also common well into the 1970s. Certainly, it was the most insecure workers who were most vulnerable, as was the case with several workers known for their attraction to alcohol being 'persuaded' by the carrot of a few extra pounds to illegally strip asbestos.[10] Bashir Maan, a leader in the Asian community in Glasgow, has also noted how it was the dirtiest and dangerous jobs in the chemicals factories in Glasgow that were among the first to be occupied by migrant male Pakistanis in the 1950s and 1960s. Immigrant labour such as this was primarily utilized because of the hazardous nature of the work process.[11] As de-industrialization deepened, the volatile and insecure nature of the Glasgow labour market from the 1960s further empowered the employers. A reflection of this came through two

---

[9] See A. McKinlay, *Making Ships; Making Men* (Clydebank 1991).

[10] SOHOHP, Interview A9.

[11] Interview, Neil Rafeek with Bashir Maan, 12 May 2003 (SOHC), University History Project.

testimonies of Glasgow labourers who took work in the Turner's Asbestos Factory in Clydebank in the 1960s, despite their awareness of the risks to their health that such an occupation entailed.[12] One described the working conditions in the plant in 1964 thus:

> I'll never forget till the day I die the first impression of that place. It was like walking into Dante's Inferno without the fire. It was just hell. The noise was unbelievable ... Dust was flying through the air everywhere, clouds of dust. And there were wee men walking about – I ended up dain it for the first two or three days I was there – sweeping the floor. Nae masks, just overalls. Clouds of stoor [dust] everywhere it just filled the air.[13]

An industrial nurse described conditions in the North British Locomotive works in Springburn, Glasgow in a similar way:

> They took me into the foundry and I was frightened. The air was very black, the men were *absolutely* black and they said 'hello hen' or whatever was the Glasgow way. I was absolutely shocked and I said to somebody 'it's like Dante's Inferno'.[14]

The shipyards were also notoriously dangerous and dirty places in which to toil. This is what one shipyard trade union convenor had to say:

> Some of the conditions that these men were working in was really atrocious ... When you see the conditions in the Clyde it was like fighting an atomic war with a bow and arrow, you know. You hadnae a chance. In the yard there, if you were working at the stern of the ship ... The only way you could work round the rudder post and round the screw and that was when the tide went right out. And when the tide did come in and then went out it left all this residue. All rotting fruit that had fallen off ships and dead dogs and what have you. And the men had to go down and work amongst that you know. And you can imagine the conditions in the middle of winter.[15]

A riveter employed in John Brown's Clydebank shipyard recalled of the 1930s: 'You couldnae get a dirtier job ... you were black from head to foot; grime and sweat. Every riveter's shirt was torn – we walked about the shipyard like ratbags'.[16] Moreover, conditions worsened in the heavy industries as employers faced contracting markets. An industrial hygienist noted of the steelworks at Ravenscraig in the late 1970s:

---

[12] SOHOHP, Interview A19; A26.

[13] SOHOHP, Interview A19.

[14] Interview, Neil Rafeek with Dorothy Radwanski, 22 October 2001.

[15] SOHOHP, Interview A18.

[16] A. McKinlay, *Making Ships*, 28.

> A lot of the time for the old plants you were really patching up problems. You weren't really addressing the real problems, I mean plants where you had massive problems of fumes and dust and noise etc., you knew very well that the only real solution was to start again.[17]

Some of the smaller concerns were the most penny-pinching, prioritising profit over health, as these comments from a sheet-metal worker indicate:

> Interviewer: What was the occupational health facilities like? Was there ever an occupational health nurse?
>
> Never in my day unless you were in some of the big [ship] yards. If they were in some of the big yards they carried a nurse. The dockers carried two nurses. And we used to go over to them for, sometimes, serious cuts, like. And eh, that was stopped because it was costing them half a crown for a dressing. I remember I got my elbow cut just across the joint there. Hit a plate. And they sent me down the tunnel at plantation, through the tunnel, up Finnieston Street, on to Great Western Road, walk along to the Western, to get it stitched. I could have got a penny ride from the front door to the Southern General. They wouldnae give you the penny, or the penny-halfpenny I think it was, actually. That was the type of firm that you were working with right enough. *Terrible*.[18]

The interviews indicate the persistence in Glasgow of a vibrant popular workplace culture in the heavy industries which could in itself act as a drag anchor, slowing the pace of improved occupational health and safety standards. Peer pressure operated to induce workers to eschew safety measures and protective clothing such as helmets in the 1950s and 1960s. In the North British Locomotive Works, for example, an industrial nurse noted how the men would not wear their goggles, with the result that men were getting 'terrible eye accidents'.[19] As the heavy industries declined, moreover, competitive pressures and the increasing age-profile of the workforce led to the fossilization of attitudes and stagnation in occupational health and safety standards. As one respondent noted:

> The oil refineries were the start of us getting a wee bit more safety conscious you know ... overalls, water to wash ourselves. But the shipyards have carried on the same old way for a long number of years when the places like Grangemouth and the ICI were settling down a bit to give you canteen facilities. Well you never had that in the shipyards.[20]

---

17 Interview, Neil Rafeek with Ian Kellie, 5 December 2001 (SOHC).

18 SOHOHP, Interview A9. Ian Kellie had also noted how the smallest iron and steel firms invariably had the worse occupational health and safety standards.

19 Interview, Neil Rafeek with Dorothy Radwanski, 22 October 2001.

20 SOHOHP, Interview A22.

Secondly, oral testimony provides a view from the point of production which tells us much about the influence and the limitations of state regulation of the workplace. The twentieth century has been characterized by a revolution in government intervention in employment, with legislation affecting most areas of working life, from wages, hours, union recognition and rights, to health and safety on the job.[21] However, what comes strongly through workers' recollections is the existence of a considerable gulf between statutory control and the reality of actual workplace practice. In short, legislation continued to be widely ignored or subverted. One Clydeside asbestos factory worker summed this up evocatively:

> When you went in the door of Turner's asbestos there was a factory act with all the stuff. The only problem was that you couldnae see through it with the layer of asbestos cement on the glass you know.[22]

Thirdly, the oral evidence facilitates engagement with debates on the role of the trade unions in the workplace. This links in to the prevailing urban myth about 'Red Clydeside', in which it is held that the trade unions in this region were militant and all-powerful up to the late 1970s. We argued in *Lethal Work* that the role of the trade unions on asbestos was uneven.[23] On the one hand, the union leadership failed to prioritize occupational health in general, and this included the dangers of asbestos. Consequently, they were unwilling to sanction strike action *specifically* on the asbestos issue. Indeed, the dominant strategy, although perhaps understandable in the context of de-industrialization, was to protect jobs and maximize wages. Certainly, the oral testimonies of male Glaswegians who worked in the heavy industries contained a significant amount of criticism of their trade unions, and this was especially the case with the accounts of industrial disease victims.[24] Indeed, for one respondent, the unions were 'as bad as the employers'.[25] However, some of the more 'solidaristic' discourses emphasized the positive role of the unions, especially noting how much was done to protect workers at the local branch level. As might be expected, this was especially marked in the two 'group' interviews undertaken at the offices of the T&G in Glasgow. One of these respondents (who later became Secretary of the Glasgow Laggers' Branch) recalled how he was barred from employment as an insulator in six Clydeside firms prior to 1960 as a consequence of his outspoken attitude

---

[21] See A. McIvor, *A History of Work in Britain, 1880–1950* (Basingstoke, 2001), 148–73.

[22] SOHOHP, Interview A19.

[23] Johnston and McIvor, *Lethal Work*, 158–72.

[24] See, for example, SOHOHP, Interviews A5; A9; A14; A19.

[25] SOHOHP, Interview A9.

on working conditions.[26] Others spoke with pride of their long struggle for recognition, and the insulating engineers' fight for skilled craft status and improved conditions. Such contradictory stories regarding the role of the trade unions illustrate the interpretive nature of oral evidence, and underline the inter-subjective aspect of the interview testimonies.

Being critically reflexive about such testimony is important, and this raises the question of whether or not respondents were 'laying it on thick', exaggerating the bleaker and more dangerous aspects of their employment in Glasgow, perhaps to enhance their own masculinity. Several related how you had to be 'real men' to survive in this tough environment and perhaps in the process embellished, to some extent, the 'hellish' nature of such work. Undoubtedly the perspective of these men regarding their own work has been influenced by the improvement in work conditions they had experienced. Views expressed *at the time* would have been markedly less critical. In the process of recalling past work experience, respondents informed us about material circumstances and prevailing attitudes, while also re-interpreting their working lives, not least in the light of what has happened since the events being recalled.

The 'hard man' at work

Oral testimony comes into its own in probing prevailing attitudes and defining identities, and such evidence is particularly insightful in reconstructing male identities. Glasgow developed something of a reputation as an especially patriarchal city, with high levels of male crime, violence (including domestic violence) and alcohol abuse – a 'mean city' of tough men, sectarianism and gang warfare.[27] The city was also associated with poverty and ill-health. These negative images of the city persisted into the last quarter of the twentieth century, as Mike Pacione's survey of Glasgow indicates.[28]

The issue of masculinity and occupational health has been explored by the present authors elsewhere.[29] Undoubtedly, in their heyday, the heavy industries in Glasgow 'toughened up' workers and de-sensitized them to

---

[26] SOHOHP, Interview 23.

[27] See A. McArthur and H. Kingsley Long, *No Mean City* (London 1935); Annmarie Hughes, 'Popular pastimes and wife assault in inter-war Glasgow' (Honours dissertation, History, University of Strathclyde, 1996).

[28] M. Pacione, *Glasgow; The Social-Spatial Development of the City* (Chichester 1995).

[29] R. Johnston and A. McIvor, 'Dangerous work, hard men and broken bodies: masculinity in the Clydeside heavy industries, *c*1930–1970s', *Labour History Review*, 69, no. 2, 2004, 135–51.

2.2 Representing masculinity

danger through a long process of socialization and acculturation. A high tolerance of danger and a propensity to take risks was part-and-parcel of machismo work culture. The one-time communist agitator Jimmy Reid famously noted during the 1971 Upper Clyde Shipbuilders' work-in: 'we don't only build ships on the Clyde, we build men'.[30] A cult of toughness characterized the heavy industries and young male workers adapted to this and absorbed it through peer pressure. Glasgow oral testimonies contain many examples where *machismo* attitudes of both management and men exposed workers to overstrain and more serious risks that undermined health and safety. In effect, these generations of men whose lives were ordered by productionist values in the heavy industries were a party to the erosion of their own resources of health.

Elements of male behaviour in the Glasgow heavy industries include the deeply entrenched work ethic and the emphasis men laid upon the wage packet. A consistent thread running through the oral evidence was the stress men placed upon 'never being idle' and maximizing their own earnings, even to the detriment of their own health and longevity.[31] In this brutal, unforgiving and often insecure work environment, an intensely competitive spirit prevailed, and workers gained much pride and esteem from their ability to earn high wages. This is illustrated in the testimony of a boilermaker plater who narrated how he held out for weeks against the management to secure £22 for a job for his squad.[32] The initial offer was £5. Moreover, within this culture, being able to tolerate the toughest work conditions, take the greatest risks and hold one's alcohol were celebrated as praiseworthy male attributes. This is how one retired west-Scotland steel maker described his work in the furnaces in the 1930s:

> About one steel worker in every ten could stand up to them successfully, which was one reason why the furnacemen were looked up to in the world of heavy industry. That they got the biggest pay packets was another reason. They also had the biggest thirsts and that too was a prideful possession in that part of the world ... A legend grew up about the steel smelters.[33]

Another recalled the environment of the Hallside Steelworks on Clydeside in the 1960s:

> It was a very macho culture ... It could also be quite violent too. But it was, you would say, very much an old-fashioned west of Scotland man's world, definitely ... You had to be able to look after yourself ...

---

[30] Cited in M. Bellamy, *The Shipbuilders* (Edinburgh 2000), 199.

[31] For a good example, see SOHOHP, Interview A6.

[32] SOHOHP, Interview A3.

[33] R. Fraser, *Work* (London 1969), 56–7.

> had to be prepared to stand up and say you were prepared to fight … if you backed down, that would be it. Everyone, everyone would stamp on you from then on, so you had to do that. But once you'd done that, that was OK.[34]

Standing up to management was also a much revered masculine attribute. As one Clydeside miner noted: 'If you were a *weak* man you would have did what the boss said'.[35] Insulating ships was also perceived as a man's job, where wages were by results, bonus systems prevailed and there was no place for 'slackers'.[36] In some cases, the possibility of higher wages clearly took precedence over workers' health, as with a Glasgow heating engineer who recounted working in 'bad conditions' putting 'bonus before good standards'.[37] For some men, the money was everything, and one insulator recalled how on one job, stripping asbestos down a coal mine, he earned more in daily expenses than the miners were earning in a week.[38] Another respondent commented that working overtime was the only way workers using their 'muscles' with no education could earn extra cash.[39] Insulators continued to work in the trade in Glasgow shipyards and building sites, despite full knowledge that their fathers and sometimes other kin had died of asbestos-related diseases.[40] Some even *relished* the dirtiest work if it brought a wage premium, while others took overtime and worked 12-hour shifts, seven days a week, to augment take-home-pay. A heating engineer commented on the dangers of working with a toxic paint in the confined space inside a boiler and how the job attracted a higher 'abnormal conditions' wage rate, recalling: 'And everybody was squealing to get inside the tank, you know for the dough ….'[41]

On at least one occasion, when a union intervened to warn asbestos insulators of the dangers they were facing from the dust on a building contract in Glasgow (the Red Road Flats), the men told the union official to 'get to fuck' and not interfere as they were making good money.[42] This extended in some cases to continuing to work when ill or disabled.[43] While the esteem derived from high earnings fuelled such self-exploitation, this behaviour also has to be contextualized within the insecure and volatile labour market in Glasgow shipbuilding and metal working. In their oral

---

34 Interview, Neil Rafeek with Stewart McIntosh, 9 June 2003 (SOHC).

35 SOHOHP, Interview C1.

36 SOHOHP, Interview A14.

37 SOHOHP, Interview A6.

38 SOHOHP, Interview A16.

39 SOHOHP, Interview A9.

40 SOHOHP, Interview A10; A14.

41 SOHOHP, Interview A6.

42 SOHOHP, Interview A23.

43 SOHOHP, Interview A9.

testimonies, men could justify their actions by reference to the traditional masculine role as provider and breadwinner. As one labourer noted about working in Turner's Asbestos Cement factory in the 1960s: 'I knew it was dangerous before I went in there 'cause there was people complaining but when you have two of a family to bring up it was better than walking the streets. I never was idle in my life'.[44]

Another area illuminated by oral testimony is the way in which the dominant 'hard man' mode of masculinity was constructed and perpetuated across inter-connected spaces and domains within the city, and elsewhere. Before entering employment, boys were 'toughened up' by fighting games, emulating film heroes like John Wayne, and, in some cases, by running with gangs. Gangs were prolific in Glasgow (with kids participating from as young as 13) and a number of our respondents were involved with them.[45] Workmates often drank in the pub together and went to football matches, watching a physical contact sport which epitomized competitive manhood. Working-class men shared a common upbringing on the streets and in the tenements, then progressed to the pub and the dancing, to football and to the bookmakers for a flutter. To fund such diversionary recreation, wages would invariably be 'top-sliced', and commonly wives would not know exactly how much their husbands earned. As one study (based on oral evidence) of a Glasgow shipbuilding community found: 'Earnings are regarded as belonging mainly to the earner, and overtime earnings exclusively so'.[46] Entering employment and earning a wage marked the transition to manhood, denoting certain privileges within the home. Indeed, for blue collar workers in Glasgow the hard work, the risk and the 'sacrifice' was empowering within the home, entitling the 'provider' to diversionary recreation and to limited involvement in domestic duties, including fatherhood. Moreover, for a generation through the 1940s and 1950s, military service contributed to the construction of masculinity. Again, the oral testimonies suggest that military service for many was a formative experience, matching, to some degree, the tough, brutal and dangerous day-to-day world to which many Glasgow workers were accustomed in the heavy industries.

Respondents whose work experience stretched back to the war recalled the penetration of women into jobs previously restricted to men, and there clearly

---

44 SOHOHP, Interview A26.

45 T. Brennan, *Reshaping a City* (London 1959), 138–40. For examples, see the interviews, Neil Rafeek with Hugh Cairney and with Jim O'Donnell, 26 March 2005 (SOHC).

46 Brennan, *Reshaping a City*, 142.

was some erosion of the gendering of dangerous work during wartime.[47] However, what is evident is that even during the wartime emergency, it remained the case that the male workforce dominated the more dangerous jobs, including coal-mining, iron and steel manufacture and shipbuilding. Wartime state policies legitimized this, including the Reserved Occupation Schedule.[48] This, in turn of course, was closely associated with the prevailing masculine work culture in the UK, which one wartime commentator politely termed 'the chivalry of men'.[49] Such deeply embedded male chauvinism was especially strong in industrial regions like Glasgow, which were dominated by heavy industries. Inman noted how Clydeside shipbuilding trade unions opposed female dilution and how they ignored the adverse health effects and welcomed the long wartime working hours, including Sunday working, to get extra pay.[50] Only about 7 per cent of the shipbuilding workforce was female at peak during the Second World War.[51] Most of the women who did penetrate the heavy industries during wartime were quickly pushed out in the aftermath of war. For example, in the Rutherglen Chemical Works near Glasgow one male respondent recalled women being brought in during wartime. However, he went on to minimize their contribution, noting they were employed 'mostly out in the yard, you know, doing odds and ends, but never in the furnace shop, or the crystal house, or the store'. He continued: 'once the war finished the women all disappeared, you know, bar the … where you made your breakfast, the women worked in there [in the canteen]'.[52]

It can be argued, then, that oral testimony provides a vital tool enabling us to reconstruct the contribution made by upbringing, family life, the street, male-only associations and the workplace in forging and perpetuating dominant modes of urban working-class masculinity. In addition, the co-existence of competing masculinities as well as the process of mutating manly identities are revealed by oral testimonies during a critical historical period when the heavy industries collapsed and 'white collar' work came to dominate.

---

47 See R. Johnston and A. McIvor, 'Dangerous work, hard men', 143–4. SOHOHP, Interview A3; A16; D. Crooks (ed.), *Made in Govan: An Oral History of Shipbuilding on the Upper Clyde, 1930–1950* (Glasgow 1991); M. Bellamy, *The Shipbuilders: An Anthology of Scottish Shipyard Life* (Edinburgh 2001), 68–9.

48 Certain skilled jobs were classed as being too important to release men for military service and were designated Reserved Occupations.

49 Verena Holmes (Ministry of Labour), cited in H. Murphy, 'From the crinoline to the boilersuit: women workers in British shipbuilding during the Second World War', *Contemporary British History*, 13, 4, 1999, 92.

50 P. Inman, *Labour in the Munitions Industry* (London 1957), 127–8; 308.

51 Inman, *Labour in Munitions*, 140–3.

52 Interview, David Walker with Richard Fitzpatrick, 13 August 2004 (SOHC).

Hugh Cairney: an exemplar?

Profiling one respondent in some detail illuminates some of the ways that masculinity was constructed and reinforced in Glasgow, through experience in the street, the family and the workplace. Hugh Cairney is the chosen subject, a Glaswegian of Catholic background, born in 1934, and interviewed by Neil Rafeek.[53] Hugh was born in Partick, a traditional shipbuilding community on the north bank of the river Clyde. As a youngster, he lived in a 'single end' – a basement flat with no electricity – with eight siblings and his parents. In 1947, as part of the post-war re-housing initiative, the family moved to Pollok, a new housing estate about a mile or so south of the river. Despite the apparent poverty, Hugh's recollections of childhood were positive:

> I had a good happy childhood, done the usual things like ran aboot daft and done the jumps in the backs and played football and what we called rounders. And then I joined the cubs as a young boy and then from there I went to the Boy Scouts.[54]

A year after moving to Pollok, Hugh left school at 14 and, following in his father's footsteps, went into the insulation trade. He related how choices were further constrained by the discrimination practised against Catholics at that time:

> I'll tell you why there's – there's actually more Catholics than there is Protestants work at our trade. When my father was a young boy, 16 and that looking for work, if you were a Catholic in the shipyards you didnae get employed. You got employed as a labourer or something like that but you didnae get employed to learn a *trade*, and the only thing at that time that was going was the insulation, you can go to that – we werenae a trade, *we're still no' a trade*. We've got craft status, we're still not a trade but we have craft status, and so that's why the majority of Catholics, our industry have been a majority of Catholics for the simple reason, *they couldnae get trades*. But when I left school, I never noticed myself because I only ever wanted to be a pipe-coverer anyway so I never applied for any other job.

He continued, emphasizing the kinship links in the insulation trade:

> Aye my dad was, my father was and all my father's friends *all were*. *So*, I kind of grew up in that atmosphere with insulation and that was people the people that my Da' knew and through that you get tae

[53] Interview, Neil Rafeek with Hugh Cairney, 26 March 2005 (SOHC).
[54] Interview, Neil Rafeek with Hugh Cairney, 26 March 2005 (SOHC).

> know their sons and that, you know. *And it is* very family orientated our industry.[55]

Two out of three of Hugh's brothers also went into the trade, as did three of his sons. Inevitably, contact with asbestos took its toll. Hugh's father and a younger brother died of mesothelioma, and a sister has an asbestos-related disease (pleural thickening) from washing the men's overalls.

Hugh represented a 'hard man' of sorts and in his oral testimony he referred to several formative influences and experiences that contributed to the forging of his masculine identity. These included involvement in physical contact sports as a youngster such as street football, and taking risks to attract peer group admiration. On football Hugh noted:

> I mean I remember about ten in the morning on a Sunday and you were still playing when it got dark, you know. You could go away and get dinner and come back and the game was still going on, you know and football was a great part of your life.[56]

He was also involved in a local gang, and in 'running fights' with other gangs who came into their territory:

> The place I stayed, it's a shopping centre, it was called the Bundy and anybody that came from there, you were the Bundy Boys and there was the '39 gang, there was a chain gang, everywhere had their an' gangs you know ... There wasnae so much *weaponry, maybe a stick or your fist or your boot* but there wasnae so much stabbing because at that time Lord Cameron, he was a judge, you were seven years if you were caught with a weapon in your hand than and at that time, if you killed anybody, *you got hung*, you know, so that was a wee bit of a fear an' all I suppose.[57]

As for most young men of his generation, another key formative influence was military service. Hugh was conscripted at 18 in 1952 and enjoyed the experience enough to sign up for an additional year, serving in Korea and Malaya. In the end, Hugh was discharged from the army for his part in a fight when he went to the assistance of a fellow Scot being attacked.

On returning from the army in 1955, Hugh indicated that his priorities had changed: 'When I came back there it was all work, getting money, women, girls'. He recalled the tough, brutal, dehumanising environment of the shipyards in Glasgow in the post-war decade, describing conditions as 'disgraceful', and explaining this by reference to the deferential attitudes of men who lived through the Depression: 'I suppose the mentality was still the

---

55 Interview, Neil Rafeek with Hugh Cairney, 26 March 2005 (SOHC).
56 Interview, Neil Rafeek with Hugh Cairney, 26 March 2005 (SOHC).
57 Interview, Neil Rafeek with Hugh Cairney, 26 March 2005 (SOHC).

mentality before the war broke out and people just lucky to get a job and glad to get a job and they didnae mind the conditions they worked in.'[58] Hugh was among those who were determined to fight to improve these conditions and he became involved in the Transport and General Workers' Union from an early age. Clearly, in his testimony he was very proud of his 55 years of involvement in the union, including a period as branch secretary, and saw the T&G laggers' (insulation engineers) branch as crucial in standing up to the bosses and achieving pivotal improvements in occupational health and safety standards. As he recalled: 'when I first started, the bosses didnae want to know anything about us or *talk to us.*'[59] The key campaign in the mid-late fifties was getting the job of pipe coverer upgraded to insulation engineer: 'it was getting the craft status, our rates went up, our conditions of living, *everything changed.*' The emphasis in Hugh's testimony, though, was on how the men had to fight to get recognition and decent work conditions:

> We always nearly had to hit the gates to get any health and safety, not noo we dae, but then, aye.
> *Interviewer*: In the sixties ... ?
> Yes, aye, we had to hit the gates nearly all the time for health and safety.

He continued:

> I mean we werenae actually bully boys, we just wanted what we thought we were entitled to. We're entitled to be able to wash our hands, we're entitled to take *overalls that are covered with asbestos off* and go and sit doon, have something to eat without wearing these dirty boiler suits. So we brought they things in ... And I said, it wasnae a case of bullying the bosses into you wanted more than you were entitled to, you wanted [places to put] all our things in, places to take your overalls off, to be able to clean and to sit and no' have to chase the rats out the road so that you could sit doon.[60]

As a consequence of trade union pressure such as this, the insulation trade became one of the most regulated and controlled occupations with health and safety codes and procedures formalized that continue to govern work conditions on site.[61]

While Hugh's experience encapsulated much of what might be associated with the traditional and dominant 'hard man' mode of masculinity, he also broke the template in some respects. Until he was 22, he never touched alcohol and while others were frequenting the rougher dance halls, he and a

---

58 Interview, Neil Rafeek with Hugh Cairney, 26 March 2005 (SOHC).
59 Interview, Neil Rafeek with Hugh Cairney, 26 March 2005 (SOHC).
60 Interview, Neil Rafeek with Hugh Cairney, 26 March 2005 (SOHC).
61 SOHOHP, Interview 22.

group of pals preferred the ice rink. Nevertheless, Hugh's rich and evocative narrative tells us much about men's lives in Glasgow and the intersecting effects of street culture, family, military service and work experience in the construction of male identities in the mid-twentieth century. His was also a 'solidaristic' discourse, stressing the positive role of the trade union and the power of collective action by working men in reforming and humanizing the brutal and unhealthy work conditions in the heavy industries.

Conclusion

The central argument in this chapter is that oral testimonies have great potential in exploring labour processes, attitudes towards work, as well as relationships and identities. Specifically, in this chapter, oral testimony has been shown to elucidate the work culture of male Glaswegians employed in some of the traditional heavy industries. Oral history has the power to place us side by side with such workers as they toiled in what are now, in many cases, almost forgotten occupations such as asbestos lagging. What emerges is a complex and often contradictory picture – but one that aids our understanding of the ways in which masculinity was forged in the shipyard, docks, iron works and heavy engineering factories that once dominated cities like Glasgow. Such an approach repositions the body at centre stage in urban history, reminds us that the working environment and work culture intimately affected health and well-being, and privileges workers' own voices in reconstructing such experiences.

While a wide range of views are evident, there are two particularly dominant and recurrent discourses in the oral interviews of male Glasgow workers that should be highlighted for attention. One is what can be termed the 'solidaristic' discourse, where the collective responses of workers to work conditions and bodily damage is emphasized and the active role of the trade unions is stressed. The other is the 'individualistic' discourse that emphasized 'heroic' personal struggle against grim 'hellish' work conditions with little, if any, external assistance. Frequently, in the latter narratives, the worker was presented as the passive and uninformed victim and the bosses as the 'villains' who knew all about the toxicity of dust and the carcinogenic nature of asbestos but said nothing in order to maximize their profits. While there are elements of reality in such discourses, deconstructing the material suggests that some of the narrative is the product of accumulating knowledge and the popularization of the asbestos hazard through the media over the past two decades or so, that is, since the historical events under scrutiny. Contemporary discourses influence and can reconfigure the historical narratives of our subjects. Many respondents were bitterly critical of the 'system' that had taken their livelihood away and, in some cases, their health. In the retrospective search for understanding, even the trade unions were regarded by some respondents as unresponsive and ineffective on occupational health issues, and in some cases as corrupt. This in turn partly reflects the discourses of anti-trade unionism evident in 1980s and 1990s 'Thatcherite' Britain.

What is also evident from the oral testimonies is that workers were agents in their own experience, acting individually or collectively, rather than just victims of an exploitative system. Working in the Glasgow heavy industries fostered a dominant mode of 'hard man' masculinity, where peer pressure led to risk-taking and entrenched practices that were health-eroding. For many, these included not protecting oneself adequately at work and a culture of heavy drinking and smoking. Oral testimonies have the power to elucidate how such dual exploitative pressures of a capitalistic and patriarchal nature intersected and impacted adversely upon workers' bodies. In the process, such a methodology demonstrates the variety of human experience and responses to the material world, in turn shedding further doubt upon the veracity of meta-narratives and theoretical models that patently fail to encompass the kaleidoscopic diversity of working lives.

Further reading

Bellamy, M., *The Shipbuilders: An Anthology of Scottish Shipyard Life* (Edinburgh 2001).

Bourke, J., *Working Class Cultures in Britain, 1890–1960* (London 1994).

Connell, R.W., *The Men and the Boys* (Oxford 2000).

Crooks, D. (ed.), *Made in Govan: An Oral History of Shipbuilding on the Upper Clyde, 1930–1950* (Glasgow 1991).

Finlay, R., *Modern Scotland, 1914–2000* (London 2004).

Hughes, A., 'Representations and counter-representations of domestic violence on Clydeside between the two World Wars', *Labour History Review*, 69, 2, 2004, 169–85.

Johnston, R. and A. McIvor, *Lethal Work: A History of the Asbestos Tragedy in Scotland* (East Linton 2000).

Johnston, R. and A. McIvor, 'Dangerous work, hard men and broken bodies: masculinity in the Clydeside heavy industries, *c.*1930–1970s', *Labour History Review*, 69, 2, 2004, 135–53.

Knox, W.W., *Industrial Nation: Work Culture and Society in Scotland, 1800–present* (Edinburgh 1999).

Lummis, T., *Listening to History: The Authenticity of Oral Evidence* (London 1987).

Maver, I., *Glasgow* (Edinburgh 2000).

McIvor, A. and R. Johnston, *Miner's Lung: A History of Dust Disease in British Coal Mining* (Aldershot 2007).
Mullen, K., *A Healthy Balance: Glaswegian Men Talk about Health, Tobacco and Alcohol* (Aldershot 1993).
Perks R. and A. Thomson (eds), *The Oral History Reader* (London 1998).
Roper, M., *Masculinity and the British Organization Man Since 1945* (Oxford 1994).
Thompson, P., *The Voice of the Past: Oral History* (Oxford 2000).
Wight, D., *Workers not Wasters: Masculine Respectability, Consumption and Unemployment in Central Scotland* (Edinburgh 1993).

CHAPTER THREE

The cultural identity of semi-skilled women workers in Socialist Hungary[1]

Eszter Zsófia Tóth

This chapter is based on life interviews conducted with members of an unskilled women's workers brigade who received the State Prize in 1970 and their families.[2] Though a considerable amount of work has been done on specific forms of cultural identity, these tend to rely on race, gender, sexuality, and class forms, and some labour historians even reject gender as a useful analytical category because women workers played only a minor role in traditional working class politics.[3] This chapter focuses on the concept of socially constructed identities of semi-skilled women workers as this provides a better understanding of the life-histories of ordinary people who lived under socialism in Hungary.

Personal identity can be considered to be a social representation, an organizing principle of individual positioning in a field of symbolic relationships between individuals and groups.[4] Identity is interpreted here as a social construct that changes over one's life.[5] A life-course interviewee will describe several groups to which he or she relates. Recalled identities

---

[1] This study is based on the author's PhD thesis 'Egy Állami Díjas női segédmunkásbrigád mikrotörténete' (Micro-history of a State Prize-winning brigade of unskilled female workers) (Budapest: Loránd Eötvös University of Sciences, 2004). Interviews were made by the author.

[2] The State Prize was established in Hungary in 1963. It was the most prestigious award that members of a socialist brigade could receive and was given to those for exceptional service to the State.

[3] J.W. Scott, 'Language and working-class history', in J.W. Scott, *Gender and the Politics of History* (New York 1999), 55.

[4] W. Doise, 'Social representations in personal identity', S. Worchel, et al. (eds), *Social Identity* (London 1998), hereafter *Social Identity*), 23.

[5] For summaries of research into identity see G. Bindorffer, *Kettős identitás. Etnikai és nemzeti azonosságtudat Dunabogdányban* [Dual identity. Ethnic and national sense of identity in Dunabogdány] (Budapest 2001), 18–34; F. Pataki, *Élettörténet és identitás* [Life story and identity] (Budapest 2001).

can be depicted as social constructs in which groups to which the subject has related over the life course bear symbolic importance.[6] Not only identity, but the group itself is a dynamic category that alters over time.[7] There is change over time in the significance attached to specific groups during an individual's life course. This is reflected in life-course narratives by the fact that significance is attached to belonging to different groups, according to the different stages of life. The processes of distancing from some groups and approaching others may coincide, although life-course narratives are little suited to displaying such dynamic processes.[8] The one constant stable category found in the life-course narratives was gender identity.[9] Ties to the workplace and experiences to do with the prize can be discerned as identity-forming factors in the narrative structure of the life-course interviews, as can identities linked to household or consumer goods, which were emphasized less in the propaganda of that time. The various identities feature with differing emphases in their depictions of different periods, just as they do in the narratives of individual brigade members. They were tied not only to their fellow prize-winning brigade members, the workplace 'collective' or the factory (which had failed by then), but to their places of residence, or to the Trabant car bought with the premium associated with the prize. The narrative structure was interwoven with emphasis and analysis of a great many ties, which made it easier for me to understand the values by which these working women lived in the post-war decades. What is primarily analyzed here in the narratives, where respondents repeatedly reinterpreted their relations to objects, is how they obtained such a special consumer good or dwelling. Complexity could be a useful category to reveal important aspects of women workers' identity.

The most important sources were qualitative oral history interviews carried out with skilled workers and semi-skilled women workers. The principal aim was to recall and recount the life-story narratives of retired women workers, which provided important clues to understanding the nature and meaning of everyday life in the socialist period in Hungary. Interviews were also conducted with the women's husbands and, on occasions, with their work colleagues. Some family members who had had occasional work in Budapest were interviewed, as were nine persons in Túrkeve, Mezőtúr and

---

6 W. Doise, 'Social representations in personal identity', in S. Worchel, et al., *Social Identity*, 23.

7 S. Worchel, 'A developmental view of the search for group identity', in *Social Identity*, 73.

8 On contrasts between individualism and collectivism, see D. Páez, et al., 'Constructing social identity: the role of status, collective values, collective self-esteem, perception and social behaviour', in *Social Identity*, 213.

9 See E.H. Erikson, *Identity and the Life Cycle. Selected Papers* (New York 1959).

3.1 Semi-skilled stocking factory workers, Óbuda (Old Buda) 1968

Note: This was the hottest, most humid part of the factory. Manci, who is mentioned later in the text is on the right.

3.2 Brigade meeting with the author

Zalaszentgrót, who had spent most of their lives in their native towns and still lived there.

The interviewing techniques employed resembled partly those devized by Gabriel Rosenthal.[10] Respondents asked for a chance to tell their life story, stressing the part in it played by their former factory and the state award they received. The methodology varied depending on the character of the respondent as some women did not wish nor were expected to tell their life stories from start to finish. Some instances were discussed with them more than once to enable different versions of their accounts to be analysed. The life-course interviews were interpreted as narrative constructions referring to the past.

Interviewees were obtained by snowballing, that is, by word of mouth,one respondent suggesting potential subjects from her own knowledge. Such a method was used mainly for stigmatized groups who admit 'strangers' (interviewers) only with some reluctance, if at all. Indeed, the respondents commonly viewed their previous work and the State Award associated with it as a stigma, a reflection of involvement with the former socialist regime in Hungary. To overcome their reluctance in the context of this stigma, the pretext given to them for the interview questions was that I wished to write a history of their factory and was interested mainly in factory-related memories.

At the start of the research, a brigade reunion was arranged in a restaurant that the members had often been to after work. As the conversation warmed up, some members became progressively freer in their stories. Interviewing them as a group gave additonal opportunities to hear the same stories told by several people and conduct multi-viewpoint analysis. Group interviews were also made with married couples and sibling pairs, and the desired effect was to assist recall. This was, on occasions, so successful that the 'conversation partners' helped each other's recall with one story continuing almost seamlessly into the next, with one partner sometimes snatching words out of the other's mouth. This form of interviewing did not end with the respondent bringing the narrative up to the present day. Stories from different periods would be revisited by interviewees repeatedly in narrative form. Interviews were made with and without a tape recorder. The choice of the two methods was prompted originally because several respondents refused to give a recorded interview but said they would gladly talk to me about their lives. On the other hand, it was often found that those allowing the use of a tape recorder were embarrassed by it and could not re-tell their account freely. As soon as the tape recorder was switched off, they were off, even happily relating their childhood experiences. The tape recorder

---

10 On how this applies to Hungary, see É. Kovács and J. Vajda, 'Mutatkozás. Zsidó Identitás Történetek' [Appearance. Jewish identity stories], *Múlt és Jövő*, 2002.

symbolized the expectations of a public history: they were happiest to record into the microphone what they thought was historically 'important', while feeling it was superfluous to record what was inessential.

3.3 Brigade reunion, 2 June 2000

The snowball method has several advantages, as Herbert makes clear in her chapter in this volume.[11] Most importantly, points of common contact enabled the respondents to open up, and the system of referral to a person whom a potential interviewee trusted meant winning respondents' confidence was easier – a fundamental issue in oral history. A respondent is not a file in an archive, available to any who opens it. It was easier to gain access to further conversation partners if I could relate by way of introduction to how other group members lived and what had happened in their families since the decades they had spent together. Initial anxiety was dispelled by retelling stories I had heard from others. Such re-told tales allowed a respondent to confirm that I had visited former workmates, and if these workmates had talked, then they could too. Respondents who were not former members of the brigade were chosen from articles in the factory newspaper, a necessary approach because it was important to know how the brigade's system of connections worked

[11] See J. Herbert, 'Negotiating boundaries and the cross-cultural oral history interview', chapter 12 in this volume.

within the shop and factory. Respondents themselves drew attention to other people by talking of a typical episode in their lives or role in the workplace (for example, an amateur photographer or a young unmarried mother).

Intriguingly, subjects considered taboo in relation to one's own family were often not so regarded in relation to others. Several others told versions of incidents that were to be kept secret, but did not disguize the individual who was the subject of the story. One narrator, when telling taboo stories about others, would preface her words with: 'It's not nice to say this, but ...' or, 'This is going to be nasty story ...'. Someone more closely associated with such a taboo story would blurt it out, and having once begun it, continue in an unstoppable way. The intention in the interviews was to minimize the extent to which the situation had an 'official' tone. An interview, in the classic sense, is a dialogue between interviewer and respondent, whereas the aim here was to turn the occasion into a real conversation. This was important as a way of extricating the interviewer from an 'omniscient' role and avoiding the trap that the respondent eventually says what the interview wants to hear, as can easily happen if the interviewer puts the question as something to be assessed or the respondent feels some role is being imposed and seeks to narrate accordingly.[12]

Life histories and workplace relations

Lacking qualifications, the women normally sought work immediately on arrival in the city. They could also expect help from kin and from former fellow villagers. Most of them entered domestic service, but seized the first chance to work in a factory in the early 1950s.[13] Some were married before starting factory work, but others did not marry until later, mostly to skilled workers. Many women said the greatest struggle in that early period had been finding a good workplace, not finding a husband. The workplace where

---

[12] See E. Barát, 'A nők érdekében folytatott kutatás és korlátai' [Research in the interests of women and constraints on it], *Replika*, 37, 1999, 163–8.

[13] The proportion of women entering industry began to rise only in 1951 with the first five-year plan. Before the war, unskilled female hands from the country had usually done seasonal urban work to earn money for their marriage portion and returned home in the summer for the harvest. For a detailed history of female migrant employment, see G. Gyáni, *Család, háztartás és a városi cselédség* [Family, household and urban domestics] (Budapest 1983). It became possible for rural women to gain a foothold in the city with factory labour during and especially after the Second World War. The associated migration burgeoned in the 1950s, but 'a radical change ensued in 1963: Budapest's industrial workforce began to decline and growth to give way to contraction'. G. Benda, 'Budapest társadalma 1945–1970' [Budapest society 1945–70] in N. Fokasz, and A. Örkény (eds), *Magyarország társadalomtörténete. 1945–1989* (History of Hungarian society 1945–89), Vol. III (Budapest 1999), 14.

they had then spent decades, often with a skilled-worker husband too, was the Budapest Hosiery Factory, founded in 1951.[14] Most women workers had one or two children by the end of the 1950s. As a result, and according to the propaganda, they were doubly privileged – as workers and as women – yet several had not been allocated state housing and had to solve their own housing problems or live in sub-tenancies in dank, unheated accommodation. Several had simply occupied an empty flat after the 1956 Revolution.

The women experienced state intervention in their daily lives mainly at work, where they had to take part in work competitions and form a socialist brigade. It was advisable to join the Communist Party and have a husband in the Workers' Militia if they wanted to be in a favourable position to assert their interests. Unhealthy working conditions meant that, as middle-aged women, they faced more frequent illness and accelerated ageing compared to their immediate non-manual working superiors. By the time of the State award in 1970, some of them were divorced or widowed. The oldest among them were sent into retirement not long after receiving the State Prize.

3.4 The Liberation Brigade with their immediate superiors, March 1970

[14] I. Czeglédi, *A Gyulai Harisnyagyár 75 éve. 1900–1975* [75 years of the Gyula Hosiery Factory] (Gyula: A Budapesti Harisnyagyár Gyulai Gyára, 1975), 121; Resolution of the People's Economic Council, June 22, 1951 (Népgazdasági Tanács 243/11/1951).

According to the official parlance of the time, the brigade was simultaneously a uniform social group (manual workers) and a community founded on political norms (a socialist brigade). They received a collective award, the State Prize, in 1970 because they took part in the labour competition as a socialist brigade (their name was 'Liberation Brigade'). The State Prize was established in Hungary, copying Soviet practice, in 1963, as the most prestigious award that members of a socialist brigade could receive. Among those who had received the State Prize were those who: conducted research, or engaged in research and development, those who made a substantial contribution to the construction of socialism, or innovators, those who introduced new methods of working, those who were recognized for their role in directing production, or those who achieved exceptional individual performance in production, or in the curing of patients, or in the development of public health, childcare and education.[15]

Yet brigade members, in re-telling their lives and events important to them, often emphasized the ways in which they differed, rather than resembled, their peers. Only by ignoring specific features of their stories can a single, common, overall history be assembled. They each attributed in their life stories special importance to different stages and factors in their lives and underlined different identity-forming factors.

In the narratives of these women, the significance of labour competition was not so simple, as Padraic Kenney noted about Polish workers in the very early years of socialism:

> ... labour competition was nothing less than a wager on the enthusiasm of new workers because it offered them a chance to earn more money, gain advance in the factory, and see their names in the newspaper.[16]

For the leader of brigade, taking part in the labour competition was one way to represent herself as an independent, successful woman. As a leader of socialist brigade, she could meet politicians, among them János Kádár, the first secretary of the Communist Party (MSZMP); as a leader of a prize-winning brigade she could give lectures at congresses. For another member, the socialist brigade was the group where she could help old people to do washing and ironing, for example. This shows that the narratives of interviewees were highly influenced by the state propaganda. Another woman depicted the brigade as a group, where she had to do a lot of compulsory work after she

---

[15] The State Prize was awarded to socialist brigades for the first time in 1965. By 1985, 44 brigades had received the award, accounting for 4.7 per cent of all awards made. MOL XIX-A-92. 13. d. Állami Díj bizottság. Jelölőlapok. 1970., P. Darvas-dr. T. Klement-dr J. Terjék (eds), *Kossuth-díjasok és Állami Díjasok almanachja. 1948–1985* (Budapest 1988), 449, TVRGY. 1963/36. számú törvényerejű rendelet.

[16] P. Kenney, *Rebuilding Poland: Workers and Communists, 1945–1950* (Ithaca 1997), 238.

had completed her normal day in the factory. Erzsébet[17] recounted a story about helping an old lady in the labour competition:

> Once Marika (the leader of brigade)[18] came and she told us, we have a new exercise in the labour competition: we have to help old women who live alone. Every week I had to wash her hair, to clean up her flat. I had to go to her after I finished my work in the factory. Once, I went, I heard noises behind me. I glanced back ... I thought that somebody was following me. I saw, that a man went to this old woman, too. I started to clean up, but I watched him too. I listened to the noises. I think, he was the lover of this old woman. After that, I told this story to my colleagues in the factory. I told them that a woman who is able to have a lover, should clean up herself. I didn't go anymore ...[19]

---

[17] First names of interviewees are used. At that time, the name of Hungarian married woman meant: the name of husband and the 'né'-sign. This sign means Mrs.

[18] Marika, Mária (S. Vilmosné) Mária (1931, Dévaványa–2003, Budapest). Her father worked for a bridge-building company as a labourer. She had ten siblings. After six years of elementary school, she took a job as a domestic in Mezőtúr, and then moved to Budapest in the Second World War. She worked initially as a sign writer and then as a domestic again. She married Vilmos S., a bricklayer, in 1950 and found a job in the same year at the Goldberger Factory as a semi-skilled machinist. Her son was born in 1954 and in 1957–59 she worked as a caretaker. She divorced in 1968. In 1971, she completed the eight years of primary education while working. From 1959 until she was awarded a disability pension in 1989, she worked as a boarder in the Budapest Hosiery Factory. She joined the Liberation Socialist Brigade in 1963 and became its leader in 1964. As a pensioner she continued to work in a theatre serving in the buffet and cloakroom.

[19] Interview with K. Györgyné and her husband, K. György, 16 March 2000, 8. György was born in Budapest in 1936 and brought up by his maternal grandparents in Óbuda and from 1946 in Tápiószele. His father managed the Fischer timber yard. He began work as an apprentice to a self-employed tradesman in 1950 and then worked as a turner at the Goldberger Factory. During the 1950s, he worked at the Small-Engine and Machine Factory, the Special Small-Engine Factory and the Washing-Machine Factory. He married in 1954 and they had a daughter in 1955. He worked as a mechanic at the Budapest Hosiery Factory from 1961 to 1995. He took an evening course at the Jenő Landler Machinery and Telecommunications Technical College in 1963–67. The parents of Erzsébet married in 1919. She was born in Tápiószele in 1932 as the eighth of 13 children. Her father was a carter and her mother took in sewing. She spent her childhood in Tapolca and then Kisgörbő in Zala County. In 1945, she went to work at the brickworks in Zalaszentgrót. She moved to Budapest in 1950 and worked initially as a domestic before becoming a semi-skilled worker in an arms factory in 1953. After marrying in 1954 and having a daughter in 1955, she was a semi-skilled operative in the boarding shop at the Budapest Hosiery Factory from 1957 to 1977. She was a member of the Liberation Socialist Brigade from its establishment in 1960. In 1977, she became a cleaner at the Budapest auxiliary workshop of the Zemplénagárd Fair Tisza Agricultural Cooperative. At the time of the interview, she was still doing night work for its successor company.

On the one hand, she explains in her story that she had to help to this old woman because this activity was compulsory in the labour competition. On the other hand, she emphasizes her independence in the brigade, because she had the opportunity to give up this exercise. In her story, she could decide this for herself, and the leader of brigade could not change her decision.

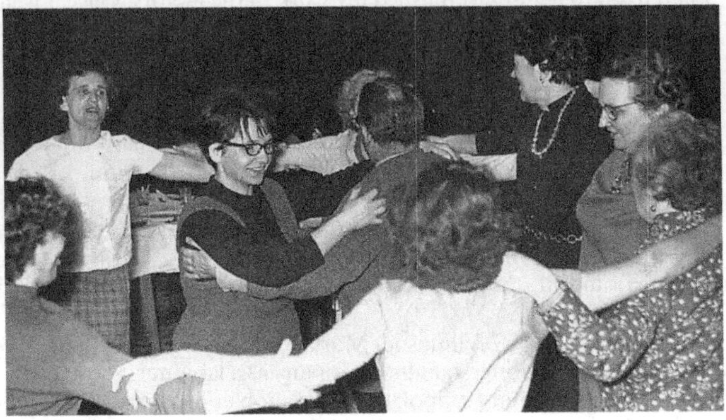

3.5 Brigade party in the factory, February 1969

These women were born and grew up in small towns and villages in extended peasant-families. They migrated to Budapest after the Second World War as young girls. In their life stories, there is an emphasis on the process of migration. The decision to migrate was not a simple process for them associated with economic circumstances. One of the interviewees mentioned further aspects of her migration process. First, she depicted herself as an obedient girl as her mother had advised her to go to the city and earn more money than in the village. Second, she emphasized the role of her migrant female relatives who depicted the city as attractive and a place of entertainment.[20] However, neither woman emphasized in their stories that one factor in their decision to migrate to the city was to escape from the patriarchy of village life and their dependence on male relatives. This interviewee's brother argued strongly for traditional notions of gender roles and used the well-known myth of the decline of the traditional family under socialism. In the construction of his argument, he emphasized that the main reason for the decline of the family was that many women had to work in industry.[21]

[20] Interview with K. Györgyné and K. György. 16 March 2000, 15; 7 July 2001, 44.

[21] Interview with F. József. Túrkeve. (Brother of Teréz), 10 October 2002, 6.

3.6 Erzsébet and György, 8 February 1959

Note: Erzsébet and György: Kiss Györgyné (Mrs Kiss György born as Gál Erzsébet) and Kiss György (Mr Kiss György). In Hungarian, Mrs = né plus the whole name of the husband.

These women used individualistic and group-oriented strategies in the process of migration. Their adaptive strategies had to be individualistic, in that migrants depended primarily upon their own resources and initiatives, and they had to be group-oriented too, despite the fact that marginal migrants from rural areas are usually mentioned in the anthropological literature as reliant upon others, usually kinfolk or fellow villagers.[22]

After they migrated to and lived in the city, these women never returned to the countryside for anything more than brief visits. At first they worked as domestic servants, and then from the early 1950s to the mid-1970s as semi-skilled industrial workers in the same textile factory – the Hungarian Hosiery Factory. Some of them left the factory in the mid-1970s and worked subsequently as laundresses; two continued to work there until the mid-1990s. As retired women workers, they lived in Budapest. Generally, the women recounted many stories about the factory, which occupied an important place in their life histories, about having a good job, and about how most of their husbands also worked in the same hosiery factory as skilled workers. In some narratives, the factory symbolized their integration into urban life, depicted often as a difficult process for them in contrast to their narratives of marriage and starting a family.

The power of consumption

Consumption had a meaningful use in the official discourse of socialist Hungary after the revolution of 1956. This phenomenon appeared in the official language of both Party and state as the guarantor of a higher standard of living. In contemporary propaganda, it was linked to the year 1959 when the Seventh Congress of the ruling Hungarian Socialist Workers' Party launched a new living standards policy.[23] Equally, the apparent dichotomy of the 'socialist man' and 'petty-bourgeois mentalities' was an important theme in official discourse, underlined by considerable debate in the press surrounding 'ways of life'. Commentators used normative categories to ask how 'socialist men and women' should regard certain symbolic possessions, like the car, the weekend house, the plot of land, the sewing machine or the fridge.[24]

The most important symbolic consumer good for one woman was a car. Teréz[25] was 42 years old when she bought a car in 1970. She worked at that

---

[22] G. Gmelch: 'Migration and adaption to city life', G. Gmelch and W.P. Zenner. (eds), *Urban Life. Readings in Urban Anthropology* (Illinois 1996), 191.

[23] T. Valuch, 'A "gulyáskommunizmus"', in I. Romsics (ed.), *Mítoszok, legendák és tévhitek a XX. századi magyar történelemről* (Budapest 2002), 361–90.

[24] Á. Tyekvicska, 'Frizsiderszocializmus', in *Beszélő évek. 1957–1968. A Kádár-korszak története I. rész* (Budapest 2000), 260–63.

[25] Teréz (T. Károlyné) was born in 1927 in Túrkeve and had seven siblings. Her father was a labourer and later a messenger at the council. She migrated to Budapest in 1945, working at first as a labourer on reconstruction and then returning to Túrkeve for a while to work in a sewing shop. She married in 1949 and had sons in 1949 and 1951. Her husband, who worked for Hungarian State Railways, died

3.7 Teréz with her first Trabant, 1971

time as a quality checker in the hosiery factory. Her husband had died in 1968 and she had to bring up her two sons alone. After her purchase of the new car, an article was published about it in the factory-newspaper under the banner: 'Workers who own a car'.[26] She was the first woman in her workplace to take her driving test and she was the first woman without a husband to buy a car. As a woman decorated in a labour competition, she was described by the journalist as a sad widow whose only joy in life was to be a member of a socialist brigade.

Male responses to this event were varied. In some interviews, men considered the purchase as an another example of the good and capable

in 1968. She worked from 1953 to 1997 for the Budapest Hosiery Factory and its successor, from 1953–57 in the boarding shop and from 1957–82 as a production controller. After her retirement in 1982, she worked as a pensioner on production control in the dyeing shop. She became a founder member of the Liberation Socialist Brigade in 1960.

[26] Munkás kocsitulajdonosok. I. Harisnyagyári Dolgozó. (the newspaper of the hosiery factory) 23 December 1971, 2.

worker rewarded by an item of consumption and this also contributed to Teréz's privileged self-representation. Men also told many stories about humour and practical jokes in the factory, many of which revolved around the attributes of a smart man. Some were overtly sexist in the way male workplace stories often are: an ideal man is one who is strong, and not only has a wife but also a lover. A smart man was seen as one who could use his imagination to make his workmates laugh. One of the men's stories was about the woman who bought a car, but told by Teréz. She recounted how her new car disappeared in the factory:

> One day I went out into the yard and the Trabant was nowhere to be seen, it had vanished. I asked the gatekeeper where my car had gone, I came in with it the morning, and parked it. He replied that he didn't know, as he hadn't seen it. I asked Attila, one of the electricians, whether he had seen it. He hadn't seen it either. Then I went into the dining hall, and there was the car, they had taken it inside. I became very angry, because there was barely enough space to drive the Trabant out. It later became clear, and by that time I was laughing, that the electricians had taken the car, and brought it inside.[27]

This story could be interpreted in a symbolic way. Alone among the womenfolk in the factory, this was the only woman who could have understood this masculine joke; she was proud of the story because it placed her in a different light to other women workers. But she was proud of her car, too. It was a major topic in her narrative. She had many opportunities to use the car. She travelled by car to her relatives, and so used the car given by the socialist state to strengthen contacts with her relatives in the village. Teréz also made excursions with her sons, a new form of consumption in Hungary in the 1970s. This woman depicted these years as interesting ones, and this car had a symbolic function in her life and always afterwards she bought this type of car – a Trabant. Today one of the last cars in this series is used by one of her grandsons. For Teréz, the Trabant symbolizes the period in her life when she was fully fit, was successful in her workplace, and was an independent, self-sufficient woman. The car not only played a role in forming her personal identity – it allowed her as the owner of a Trabant to identify with car drivers generally – but it also allowed her to take on roles that were defined as masculine. When she acquired her first car, she used the connections that she established by winning the award, and was thus able to navigate around the pitfalls of living in a shortage economy by avoiding the long wait for a car.

In her interview with the journalist in 1970, Teréz stressed two elements of her life. Firstly, she represented herself as a successful working-class woman

---

[27] Interview with T. Károlyné, 12 March 2001, 39.

when she stressed that as a decorated working woman she had been able to buy a car in a shorter time than others. Secondly, she argued that she needed the car, as the daughter of a sick, elderly father, so that she could go often to her home town of Túrkeve to visit her parents.

> I didn't even dream of winning a State Prize. I was delighted with the large amount of money, because I knew I could buy a car with it.[28] I wrote a letter to the Light Industry Minister[29] to ask her to help me get the car early, and I had the permit within three weeks. The whole thing only took two months, I passed my driving test, and now I often visit my sick father.[30]

When interviewed, Teréz stressed her initiative and determination: it was her idea to write a letter so that she could get the car more quickly. Furthermore, she revealed what had been left out of the newspaper article at the time. The car arrived more quickly than she expected and that she could not pay for it all instantly. She did not ask her colleagues for a loan, but went to one of her relatives. An upcoming family wedding provided the solution:

> The Trabant arrived so quickly that I didn't have the last 10,000 Forints for it. At that time the father of my son's fiancée leant me the money. I paid him back, I worked day and night, I worked as a cleaner.[31]

The leaders of the factory invited some Soviet soldiers every year to take part in the official feasts, for example, on the seventh of November.[32] Mrs T. took the Soviet soldiers by car from the barracks to the factory. She told many stories about how well these soldiers danced and she depicted the Soviet soldiers as very handsome.[33] In the life story narratives of many women, these Soviet soldiers were not represented as oppressors. For example, the dancing of the Soviet soldier was depicted in a symbolic way. On the one hand, the dance shows that the soldier came from another culture. On the other hand, the women describe the soldiers as 'poor people' who had a

---

[28] In 1970, as a result of winning the State Prize, every member of the brigade won 20,000 Forints. At that time, Teréz's monthly salary was 1,800 Forints. The down-payment on the Trabant was 9,900 Forints.

[29] This was Mrs József Nagy.

[30] Munkás kocsitulajdonosok, I., Harisnyagyári Dolgozó, 23 December 1971, p. 2.

[31] Interview with T. Károlyné, 12 March 2001, 39.

[32] The seventh of 7 November was a national public holiday in Hungary that commemorated the 'Great October Socialist Revolution' and was celebrated in every school and workplace.

[33] Interview with T. Károlyné. 9 November 1999, 8.

hard life in the barracks, separated from Hungarian everyday life, and living far from home.

3.8 Soviet soldier dancing at a Brigade party, 1967

However, Soviet soldiers were not only good dancers, but good businessmen, too. Mrs T. explained that she could buy cheap petrol from these Soviet soldiers. Her account shows another dimension of consumption in the socialist period, and so, after listening to this story, other interviewees were encouraged to explain their transactions with Soviet soldiers. As their stories show, it was very common for them to trade with Soviet soldiers; they could buy petrol, bedclothes, and television from them.

According to these oral testimonies, Teréz was the only interviewee to be allocated a new flat directly by the housing department. Her account shows signs that she had to use her connections to ensure that she got an acceptable flat. In general, interviewees confirmed that membership of the Communist Party was an advantage in the housing market in reducing the waiting times for re-housing to improved flats. As György and Erzsébet explained, Party members seemed to find it easier to get a flat:

György:	When I … married her and we were living in a sub-tenancy, we didn't have a flat of our own, right? Then I phoned up and registered, I phoned up Rákosis office.
Interviewer:	About a flat?
György:	About a flat.
Erzsébet:	They said we'd get a flat if we joined the Party.
Interviewer:	They actually said that?
Erzsébet:	Certainly did. Wasn't that what they said? Asked us if we were Party members.
György:	I told them we weren't Party members.
Erzsébet:	Neither of us. They said, join the Party.
György:	Then we'd get a flat.
Erzsébet:	There's a chance.[34]

By contrast, Manci remembered it was fruitless for Party members to plead for better housing, even with three children: 'I often complained to the Party, but I couldn't claim anything, because I was a Party member and that meant I couldn't speak out.'[35]

Teréz underlined several times in her life-course narratives that her position as a quality controller gave her a fund of contacts in the Party and trade union, so that she once even managed to obtain a flat for a colleague.[36] When discussing how her family got housing, she presented things differently,

[34] Interview with Mr and Mrs György K., 30 November 2002, 63–4. For personal details see note 19.

[35] Interview with T. Jánosné, 3 November 1999, 17. Manci was born in Tiszaszentimre in 1929 and had 12 siblings. Her father worked as a dairy herdsman receiving payment in kind. After six years of elementary school, she went to work on the family farm and migrated to Budapest in 1947. She worked as a domestic until 1951, when she got married, giving birth to sons in 1952, 1954 and 1956. Her husband worked as a fire officer at the Klement Gottwald Electrical Factory until 1957, when he was dismissed for having been a Workers' Council member after the 1956 Revolution. He then worked at the Óbuda Textile Dyeing Factory, again as a fire officer. Manci worked in the boarding shop of the Budapest Hosiery Factory from 1953 until her retirement in 1976. She became a member of the Liberation Socialist Brigade in 1963. As a pensioner, she continued to work until 1994, as a caretaker, canteen server and cleaner.

[36] Interviews with T. Károlyné, 9 November 1999, 7; 13 November 2000, 14; 12 March 2001, 37.

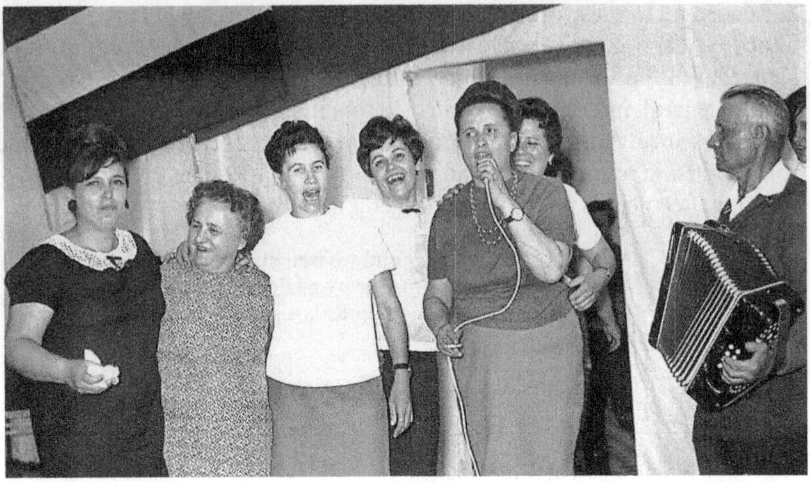

3.9 Teréz sings at a Brigade party, late 1960s

portraying herself as someone who was willing even to go against an absent husband's wishes to obtain the family a flat:

> Interviewer: You lived in a sub-tenancy to start with. How did you get a flat?
>
> Teréz: How can I tell you? My father … was a Party secretary. And they came out once for a key or something and saw what sort of flat we lived in. Because my husband said that while people were still living in wooden huts – and there were still wooden huts in those days – he wasn't going to apply for a flat, because we had a roof over us and it didn't rain in. They saw the place and said, 'We didn't think, T., you lived in such a state.' So I say, 'Look,' and pulled the shoes out from under the bed and the wall was covered in green mould. And then we got a flat in F. utca. I got well told off by my husband.[37]

Teréz told the story several times with a mixture of pride and embarrassment. It seems from her narrative that her strong position for asserting her interests came from two factors. First, her husband did not work in the factory and was a Party secretary; and, second, she was bold enough to parade her impossible housing situation in front of others who had the power to obtain a flat for her. The embarrassment may have been

[37] Interview with T. Károlyné, 9 November 1999, 9. She used the formal second person pronoun in the first interview, but turned to the familiar form after the brigade reunion. The same story occurs in the interviews on 13 April 2000, 33, and September 2002, 53.

at having gone against her husband's wishes, as he seems from the narrative not to have wanted to use his Party contacts to obtain housing and argued to his wife that others were in huts, in much worse conditions than they were. Nonetheless, as her testimony makes plain, his wife was proud to act as an independent, ingenious woman who used her husband's connections to get a better flat. They moved into it in 1957. However, when with two teenage sons this seemed small, they applied for a new three-roomed flat from the council housing department, but had no luck with Teréz's contacts and they did not get one. They then looked to the co-operative housing sector which was expanding at the time. They had to make an initial payment of 20,000 Forints to the housing cooperative and moved into a new flat in 1963. In her narratives, Teréz described the co-operative flats as elite housing: apart from her family, only factory directors and managers moved there.[38] Her husband held a managerial position at the Hungarian State Railways by that time and she was in production control at the Budapest Hosiery Factory. Often in her narratives, Teréz described how hard it was to repay the housing loan after her husband died in 1968 and that she felt she had to deny herself many things to become owner of that co-operative flat with one large and one small room. Her older son continued to live there after his marriage in 1971, and when the children became independent, Teréz's partner moved in. By 1997, she was alone again in one of the first co-operative flats, having lived there for 40 years.

Meet the neighbours

In cities, neighbourly relations, intimacy and friendship are often considered as casualties when people move from older areas to new housing estates. Relocated, they find themselves in an alien environment. Urban anthropologists present people in poorer neighbourhoods especially as showing solidarity, lending each other support and security, and making friends close by. Negative sides of such neighbourly relations are interference in each other's lives, inquisitiveness, intrusive questioning and impatience.[39] György Konrád and Iván Szelényi established from research in new Hungarian housing estates at the end of the 1960s that an extremely high proportion of friends of working-class families lived on the same estate.[40]

---

[38] Interview with T.Károlyné, 20 April 2000, 22.

[39] E. Roberts, *Women and Families. An Oral History, 1940–1970* (Oxford 1995), 232.

[40] I. Szelényi and G. Konrád, *Az új lakótelepek szociológiai problémái* [Sociological problems of new housing estates] (Budapest 1969), 22–7. 'Families arriving on new housing estates preserve to no small extent their earlier social relations; in other words, they do not enter a "social vacuum"', 97.

However, a contrasting stereotype became dominant as the status of housing estates changed. The Békásmegyer estate is presented as a hotbed of deviancy and alienation in a 1989 funding application submitted by a teacher at a local school, entitled 'School experiment in handling deviancy'.[41] A sense of the hostility and tension on the estate can be grasped from one account:

> Fear flows around the concrete blocks of Békásmegyer. Night falls early in these parts and streets soon empty. By day, there is dirt and rubbish everywhere, and in the evening – especially at weekends – hubbub, disco din and the accompanying air of violence that smothers the town.[42]

For young migrants to Budapest, the new and immediate environment consisted of relatives and colleagues, and of neighbours to whom they felt they had to adjust. Neighbours appeared in many narratives both as helpful, supportive figures and as ill-natured, scheming people. After 1956, Malvin[43] and Erzsébet and their families lived in the same house in flats they had seized and Manci[44] lived nearby, all within ten minutes of the factory. Manci and her family moved from there to Kelenföld in the mid-1970s. Erzsébet and family lived in Bogdáni út until the mid-1990s, when her mother died

---

41 Z. Lakner, 'A deviancia kezelésének iskolai kísérlete' (ms. 1989), 29. Fővárosi Szabó Ervin Könyvtár (Capital City Ervin Szabo Library), Budapest Collection.

42 Z. Lakner, 'A deviancia kezelésének iskolai kísérlete' (ms. 1989), 29.

43 Malvin (S. Józsefné) was born in Mezőhegyes in 1931 and was the oldest of six children. Her father was a stockbreeder and then worked on the co-operative farm. After the Second World War, she worked initially on the family farm and then went as an unskilled hand to the local sawmill. She moved to Budapest in 1953, working first in the carpentry shop at the Óbuda Shipyard and then from 1954–79 as a boarder at the Budapest Hosiery Factory. From 1979 until her retirement in 1986, she worked as a cleaner and kitchen server at Élépszer, a subsidiary of the Óbuda Agricultural Co-operative. She was married in 1955 to József S., who worked as a carpenter at the Óbuda Shipyard, then at the Budapest Hosiery Factory and then at Élépszer. He died in 1999. They had a daughter in 1959 and she was still living with her, her son-in-law and her grandchildren in Békásmegyer and doing clerical work as a pensioner.

44 Manci (T. Jánosné) was born in Tiszaszentimre in 1929 and had 12 siblings. Her father worked as a dairy herdsman receiving payment in kind. After six years of elementary school, she went to work on the family farm and migrated to Budapest in 1947. She worked as a domestic until 1951, when she got married, giving birth to sons in 1952, 1954 and 1956. Her husband worked as a fire officer at the Klement Gottwald Electrical Factory until 1957, when he was dismissed for having been a Workers' Council member after the 1956 Revolution. He then worked at the Óbuda Textile Dyeing Factory, again as a fire officer. Manci worked in the boarding shop of the Budapest Hosiery Factory from 1953 until her retirement in 1976. She became a member of the Liberation Socialist Brigade in 1963. As a pensioner, she continued to work until 1994, as a caretaker, canteen server and cleaner.

and they moved into her flat on the József Attila utca estate, leaving the flat in Bogdáni utca for their daughter.[45] At first sight, the neighbourly relations in the four-storey Bogdáni utca estate seem in keeping with those in a traditional neighbourhood where the fields are visible and everyone knows everyone else.

Members of these three families often told stories of their neighbours. In the interview situation, these emerged typically spontaneously and no direct questions were posed about what the neighbours were like. The neighbourly relations of immigrant women are given special attention by anthropologists, as neighbours are often the one social milieu that housewives encounter day after day. According to that anthropological approach, neighbours have an exceptional social function for women and children as the one social field to which they are tied by friendships.[46]

On the other hand, the respondents in my survey worked in a factory. How did they portray their neighbours, what significance did they attached to them, and what type of relationships did they have with them? Neighbour functions form a favourite topic in anthropological literature and research suggests that neighbours take part in every important life-time event, from birth to child-minding to looking after the sick and old and laying out the dead.[47] However, it is not my intention here to compile a catalogue of these functions, but to consider the narratives as a basis for comparing neighbourly relations in the old neighbourhoods and on the new housing estates.

The narratives of György and Erzsébet gave a lively description of neighbourly ties in the Bogdáni utca house. All the residents knew each other, watched what happened to the others, and made no secret of their opinions of their behaviour. Erzsébet jokingly related how she was at home one day and looked out through the keyhole to see a resident deceiving his wife by kissing another woman.[48] Their narratives suggest that they thought the opinion of female neighbours important in their lives. They said that 'public opinion in the house' was satisfied if a wife dressed attractively, but only in moderation, not in a provocative way.[49] The women would make remarks to those they thought had gone beyond being a 'lovely wife' and who dressed

---

[45] Altogether 8,840 dwellings were built on the József Attila utca housing estate – 285 in the 1950s, 6,826 in the 1960s, and 1,329 in the 1970s using prefabricated techniques. G. Preisich, op. cit., 79. György's mother got a flat there in 1962, having lived previously in Óbuda. Interview with K. Györgyné and K. György, 25 November 2000, 40.

[46] E. Roberts, *Women and Families*, 202.

[47] J. Ruland, *Nachbarschaft und Gemeinschaft in Dorf und Stadt* (Düsseldorf 1963). The book compares rural and urban contacts and functions, showing how they depend on local social structure, not type of settlement.

[48] Interview with K. Györgyné and K.György, 16 March 2000, 4.

[49] Interview with K. Györgyné and K.György, 29 April 2000, 17.

like an 'easy woman'. So neighbours also performed a control function in private family life. However, neighbours would speak both for and against phenomena seen as valuable in the official parlance of the socialist state. For instance, according to Erzsébet, after a time people did not look kindly on residents who walked about in the uniform of a worker's militiaman.[50]

Among the 'bad neighbours' was one who felt, as a 'true socialist', that she had to intervene to defend the laws of the socialist state, although she would probably not have told the story in those terms. According to György, a resident reported him to the district council for undertaking private television repairs alongside his job as a 'charge-hand mechanic' at the Budapest Hosiery Factory. György's version was as follows:

> After I'd done the Landler Technical Secondary School course, I always took on television repairs after work. I took a big bag. There was one neighbour whose wife was a big red-haired woman. She'd ask where I was going, was I off to repair a telly? No, I'd say. What was the big bag for, then? She carried on until one day she reported me to the district council. She was envious that things were going well for us at the time. I was called in, but luckily, the man the complaint went to had been at the technical college with me. He's there in the picture.[51] So I go and say, 'Remember me?' 'Of course,' he says. And we managed to smooth the matter over.[52]

In official parlance, those who moonlighted in that way were materialistic and not truly socialist. The state did not support the idea of people taking second jobs, which could be held officially only from 1971 onwards, and then only with permission from the main employer. The second job was also recorded in a person's work record.[53] György interpreted his ability to repair televisions after completing the technical-college course, and in addition to his work on three shifts as ensuring a higher standard of living for the family. He stressed that the neighbours had reported him out of envy for his extra income, but his acquaintance with the council official had thwarted the 'malicious neighbour', so that György was not punished for repairing televisions on the side.

Erzsébet often mentioned that living close to them at the Bogdáni utca housing estate was not only Malvin but another brigade member, Manci, and her family. They all worked in the same shop. Malvin and Erzsébet were on

---

[50] The context of the story would place it in the early 1970s. Interview with K. Györgyné and K.György, 16 March 2000, 9.

[51] He pointed out the photograph on the wall of the evening class of 1967 at the Jenő Landler Technical College, with György and the council official.

[52] Interview with K. Györgyné and K.György, 30 November 2002, 100.

[53] Labour Ministry Regulation No. 17/1971. (VII. 22.) on second jobs, side work and work performed in other work-related legal frameworks.

the same machine but did not usually meet outside work. Manci mentioned two instances of neighbourly relations that affected her.[54] Manci had taken on the job of caretaker of the old Óbuda house, so she knew the six resident families well. This is how she presented the close neighbourly relations:

> We'd go across to each other; the key was under mat. It was there when we went to work and there when we got back. If a brother or sister of mine came by they'd find the key. There was no reason to be fearful. We lent things to each other. My best friend lived there as well, who was godmother to my middle son. We were like sisters ... When she died, poor thing, she was still worrying about me, look after Manci, she said, because I'd just had a heart attack. Now her younger brother's died. My daughter-in-law was very fond of him. We were on good terms with the whole street, not just the people in the house. There was the baker's, M's ... If I go over to Óbuda, I meet them sometimes, they were very sweet. If I have to order a cake, I go over to the pastry cook there ... Russian creams, he does, very tasty.[55]

Manci talked of her old Óbuda neighbours as if they were relatives, especially when she chose a godmother for her middle son from among the house tenants. Although the story took place in the city, it is as if it had occurred in the village where she had spent her childhood. Her provincial brothers and sisters were frequent visitors there too, and felt at home, finding the key under the mat. Everyone knew everyone else, like neighbours in a village, and the neighbours were helpful, as well as playing a helping function in all the events of life. The narrator in this story is seen as a young woman, choosing a godparent for a baby.

Eventually, the old house was scheduled for demolition and, in 1976, the occupants had to move to the new housing estates that were being built. Neither Malvin nor Manci did so happily. Malvin complained that it was very difficult to integrate into the Kelenföld estate to start with. There were shopping and transport difficulties on the estate, and general complaints from new Kelenföld residents appeared frequently in the factory reports. Initially, there was no state greengrocer, just a private shop that was too dear. They called for more shops, and would also have liked a more frequent service on the 86 bus that brought them from Kosztolányi Dezső tér to the factory without having to change.[56] This counted as especially important for people used to strolling in to work from their old homes in five or ten minutes.

---

[54] Interview with T. Jánosné, 3 November 1999, 17.

[55] Interview with T. Jánosné, 3 November 1999, 18.

[56] BFL BB Fond 8 XXXV (8) C, Budapesti Harisnyagyár iratai. Mood reports to the Third District MSZMP committee, 9 May 1969; 8 August 1971.

One by one, all the old neighbours moved to houses in Etele út on the same estate, and then Manci began to feel more at home. She was soon on similar terms with the new neighbours on the estate as she had been in the old house. One person, a neighbour in the old house as well as on the new estate, was Mrs B., and she was presented in the narratives as if she had almost superhuman powers:

> Mrs B. was envious. I always asked her and the two children if we were off for a coffee or a soft drink, but she never asked me. She was even envious in the end of my husband. I even wondered if she wasn't the one who did my husband in, as she died in February and my husband in July the same year. When she was very ill and just laying there – liver disease – I went up to visit her, she lived here on the fifth floor. And she always asked how my husband was. Fine, I'd say, but then he went soon after Mrs B., poor thing, him as well.[57]

According to the narrative, the dying neighbour, whom Manci visited and helped just as she had her best friend in the old house, had irrational powers, for if she asked after anyone's health they died soon after. Perhaps these were stories like the ones she had heard as a child, in a village environment. Mrs T. also tried to present the neighbours on the Kelenföld estate as people she would confide in. She related more than once how she had first confided before her husband's death to a neighbour, not to a member of the family, that she would like a 'scattering funeral' – cremation and her ashes scattered at the cemetery.[58] When she spoke of the present, she often complained, like Malvin, that the occupants had changed since the housing privatization and that she could not establish such close relations with the new neighbours as with the old. She missed having real neighbours that she could always chat with.

Members of the Liberation Brigade and their workmates were able to assert their interests on the housing market only to a moderate extent. Some who had extensive connections within the factory found it much easier to get a flat than others who were in a weaker position, even if they joined the Communist Party. The latter worked out tactics and strategies so that they would not have to wait for years for a council flat or an exchange for a better flat. They occupied a flat, joined a housing co-operative or concluded a maintenance contract. When the old dwellings were being demolished in Óbuda, they were reluctant to move to the new housing estates even if they were healthier and more comfortable than their old flats, as the propaganda stated. Initially, they often remained surrounded by their old workmates and neighbours in their new flats as well, though this ceased to be true with the change of system when, under free market conditions, the turnover of

57 Interview with T. Jánosné , 1 May 2002, 46–47.

58 Interview with T. Jánosné, 1 May 2002, 50.

occupants became faster. The respondents then felt that their everyday living environment was degenerating into a slum.

The micro-environment of the neighbourhood of some respondents acted as the kind of reference group their provincial neighbours had in childhood. They depicted neighbours in the old Óbuda houses and on the new estates as people they had to relate to and form a community with, and who would say or at least try to say how they should behave. Although the norms the neighbours wanted to impose on them might be rejected (over moonlighting, for example), they were never a matter of indifference. Interviewees repeated the stereotypical judgements of housing estates in their life-course narratives, yet seem to have adapted many elements of their way of life to the housing-estate environment (above all, a high level of sociability), so that it gave them, by and large, a feeling of being at home.

Multiple identities

For these women, as young girls it had been natural for them to work in the family or as domestic servants. These conditions helped to define their attitude towards work which was regarded as a necessary expenditure of time and energy for the purpose of making a living and, if possible, for increasing the pleasure of life outside the job.[59] For these semi-skilled women, it was an unquestionable part of their duties to work after their migration to Budapest.

Teréz emphasized that as a young girl she was expected to work within her extended peasant family. She did not like it because she was the eldest girl in the family. She depicted her duties as traditional female work: she was required to do the housework and her duty was to look after the children. In her life history narrative, this traditional female work was the most important push factor from the village. After migration to Budapest, Teréz did not want to work as a domestic servant. She worked as a semi-skilled worker in the building trade. She lost her job, and returned to her village for a short time, working as a needlewoman. After her marriage, she again migrated again to Budapest and had two sons in the early 1950s. In her life history, she emphasized that her husband did not want her to work. She recounted this situation in her story:

> I told my husband, I want to work in a factory because we had no money to buy a coat. He let me to work, but he advised me to work only for a short time. We bought the coat. After that I told my husband we ought to buy coats for the children too.[60]

---

[59] H.J. Gans: *The Urban Villagers* (New York 1962), 122.

[60] Interview with T. Károlyné. 13 April 2000, 33.

She depicted this situation as a hard one. She had to persuade her husband. In other stories, she recalled her workplace as a symbol of her independence. She was a trade unionist and a keen member of the Communist Party. In her stories, she described herself as a woman, who knew the director of the factory very well, and who spoke her mind in front of everybody at work. In her narratives, we can analyse the influence of state propaganda.

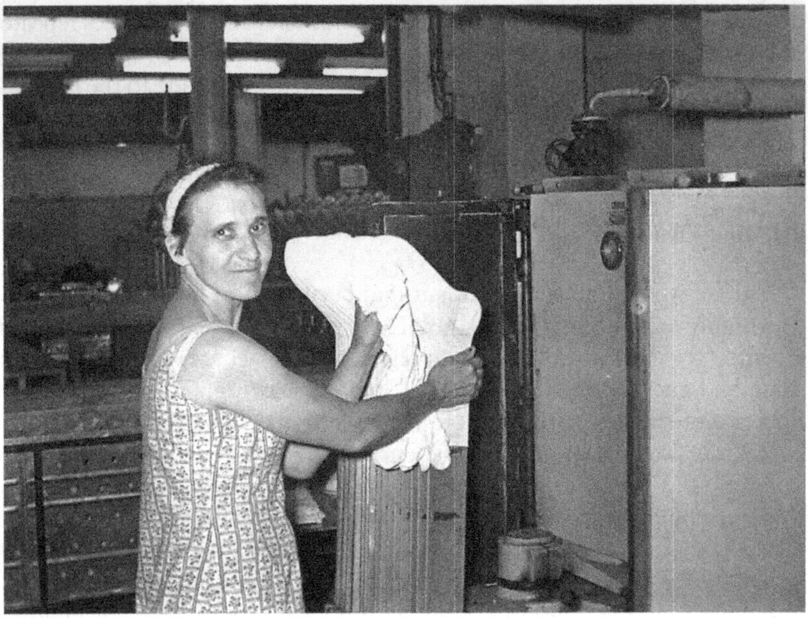

3.10 Manci at the stocking factory works, Óbuda (Old Buda), 1968

Manci emphasized in the interviews the pressure of the double burden. She represented her married life as a struggle on two fronts: the first front was at work; the second was in the family.

> For me it was always work, work, so that I could earn. I was often so tired when my sons were small, and I took them around with one in the push-chair, one on top of the push-chair, the third in my tummy and my hands froze, because I didn't have anything for gloves, didn't have anything for anything.[61]

Manci described herself as a good cook, and she considered it was responsibility to wash and iron all the clothes, not only for her husband

---

[61] Interview with T. Jánosné 3, November 1999, 14.

and her sons, but for her brother also. She now washes and irons the clothes of her lodger.

There is another type of narrative. Mária, for example, emphasized as ideal the traditional lifestyle of women. Such stories also bring into the open already existing areas of the particularly traditional social lifestyle of women involving the transmission of experiences and stories from mother to daughter. It can be claimed that these stereotypes in their stories appear both as a self-image and as a tradition received from previous generations.

Men's narratives commonly emphasized the importance of work in their life. The male workers interviewed very often used expressions like 'I'm a skilled worker'. Paradoxically, the women workers interviewed never used expressions like 'I'm a semi-skilled woman worker'. The idea of being a good worker appears repeatedly in women's life stories, but in more complicated and contradictory ways. Women's narratives often began with an emphasis on the importance of work, but was not always indicative of the dominant identity constructed in the interview overall.

These men and women spoke at length about work, materialism, and their flats. The women rarely depicted themselves as 'working women'. In their life stories, there are complex and multiple identities and a few have been shown in some detail. The narratives of these Budapest women offer a sense of having belonged to more than one group in their life – as consumers, workers and neighbours – and accordingly the varied identities overlapped one another and at different stages of their life stories. Also, major differences in the narrations of these women materialized. Understanding how working people came to be storytellers in interview situations is only the first step towards a better understanding of how and why they structured their life accounts the way they did, and how they understood, and ultimately structured, their lives.

Further reading

Brettel, C.B. 'Women are migrants too', in G. Gmelch and W.P. Zenner (eds), *Urban Life. Readings in Urban Anthropology* (Illinois 1996).

Cosslett, T., C. Lury, and P. Summerfield (eds), *Feminism and Autobiography: Texts, Theories, Methods* (London 2000).

Davis, M.P., *Mexican Voices–American Dreams: An Oral History of Mexican Immigrants to the United States* (New York 1990).

Gluck, S. and D. Patai (eds), *Women's Words: The Feminist Practice of Oral History* (New York 1991).

Lampland M., *The Object of Labour: Commodification in Socialist Hungary* (Chicago 1995).

Oakley, A., *Housewife* (London 1987).

Portelli, A., 'Oral history as a genre', in M. Chamberlain and P. Thompson (eds), *Narrative and Genre* (London 1998), 23–46.

Páez, P., et al., 'Constructing social identity: the role of status, collective values, collective self-esteem, perception and social behaviour', in S. Worchel, et al. (eds), *Social Identity* (London 1998).

Personal Narrative Group (eds), *Interpreting Women's Lives: Feminist Theory and Personal Narratives* (Bloomington 1989).

Roberts, E., *Women and Families: An Oral History, 1940–1970*. (Oxford 1995).

Scott, J.W., *Gender and the Politics of History* (New York 1999).

Swan, J., 'Ways of speaking', in F. Bonner, et al. (eds), *Imagining Women: Cultural Representations and Gender* (Cambridge 1992) 56–67.

Thompson, P., *The Voice of the Past: Oral History* (Oxford 1978).

Wolf, N., *Misconceptions. Truth, Lies and the Unexpected Journey of Motherhood* (London 2002).

Zaborowska, M.J., *How We Found America. Reading Gender through East European Immigrant Narratives* (Chapel Hill 1995).

CHAPTER FOUR

Myths of the Great Tree Gang: constructing urban spaces and youth culture in the 'socialist' Budapest

Sándor Horváth

'If you work in a factory, you've got no time to sleep till mid-day.' So Peregrin Orsós, the muscular, dusky-skinned lad, a manual worker, remembered his father's words from long ago as he looked round at the yawning, sleepily indifferent people around him in the factory. 'Still, that would be good, dozing till noon, stuffing in a good lunch, then beer with the boys. Towards evening and at night would be time for the gang.' The words are from the beginning of a 1975 documentary crime story, ostensibly a 'true tale' of a 'notorious gang in the capital', with the names changed. The story belonged to the construction of urban legends and of the best-known Hungarian youth gang in the 1960s and 1970s.[1]

The boys' gang on which the story is modelled was called the Indiáns. Indián was considered the strongest by the others in the gang: they did what he told them. The Indiáns began in 1968 to frequent the Great Tree (*nagyfa*), along with members of several other gangs. The tree was at the foot of the wall of Buda Castle above the Youth Park run by the Communist Youth League (KISZ).[2] People would congregate there to hear the music if they were denied admission to the Youth Park because of their dress, or if they had no money for a ticket. The opening of the 'Youth Cultural Park' on 20 August 1961 had been the idea of the Budapest KISZ Committee.

---

1 Kálmán Tolnai, *A Mohikán-galeri* (Táncsics 1975), 9.

2 Communist Youth League (Kommunista Ifjúsági Szövetség – KISZ) was founded in 1957 as a successor of the Association of the Working Youth (Dolgozó Ifjúság Szövetsége – DISZ) following the pattern of the Komsomol (Комсомол), which was the official Soviet communist youth organization. The KISZ served as an organization of the ruling Communist Party, the youngest members being 14 years old, the oldest about 25, while the functionaries could be older. Younger children could join the allied Pioneers (Úttörő) organization. The main task of the KISZ was to teach the values of 'communism' and to create a new generation of party functionaries.

Entrance was five forints, and from the outset there was a dress code. As a result, numbers frequenting the Great Tree increased because to get into the park you were supposed to have short hair, a jacket, a white shirt and a tie, while girls were required to wear a skirt.[3] László Rajnák, a former first-class wrestler and the manager of the park, used to walk up and down with his bouncers, dangling rubber truncheons, encouraging the youth to make civilized, 'culturally motivated' use of their spare time.[4] The Great Tree began to be seen as a place where scruffy, long-haired, badly dressed youths hung about all day cadging off passers-by, and holding orgies with the girls associated with the bands.

'The impression we give with our feverish idling is that we're busy working. Actually we have to take very good care it doesn't degenerate into work.' That note by a 19-year-old manual labourer entered in a page of squared notebook paper was found by the police in 1968 after 14 youths had been taken in for walking up Rákóczi út (one of the busiest streets in Budapest) one May evening in unconventional clothing – fleece jackets turned inside out.[5] The youths were eventually released, partly because of the view taken by police lieutenant colonel Ferenc Györök, who reported that 'The hippy phenomenon in the capital in the month of May could not essentially broaden any further.'[6]

One of the most important factors that highlighted the social visibility of the young, giving youngsters definition as a distinct cultural entity as never before, was the mass media, which had a basic role in the formation of moral panics. Discussion about moral panic began with Stanley Cohen's *Folk Devils and Moral Panics* (1972), a classic sociological study of the Mods and Rockers phenomenon in mid-1960s Britain.[7] In this context, moral panic implied a periodic tendency towards the identification and scapegoating of folk devils whose activities were regarded by hegemonic groups as indicative of imminent social breakdown. Panics served as ideological safety valves whose effect was to restore social equilibrium.[8]

---

3 Mária Hegedűs, 'Az Ifjúsági Parkban' (In the Youth Park), *Magyar Ifjúság* (= *MI*), 6 September 1968, 9; Magdolna Balázs, 'Az Ifipark' (Youth Park), *Budapesti Negyed* 1994, 1.

4 István Ivanics, 'Rajnák, a góré' [Rajnák, boss man]. *MI*, 20 June 1969, 7.

5 Budapest Főváros Levéltára [Budapest Capital City Archives = BFL] XXV. 60. b. Capital City Prosecution Service. TÜK (Titkos ügyekezelésű iratok – Secret Documents) District Prosecution administrative papers. TÜK Ig. 00223/1968. Note on occurrences of the beat-hippy phenomenon in May, 8.

6 Ibid. 9.

7 S. Cohen, *Folk Devils and Moral Panics* (New York 1972), 9.

8 For a comprehensive survey of the use of the term 'moral panic' from 1972 until the present day, see A. Hunt, '"Moral panic" and moral language in the media', *British Journal of Sociology*, 48, 1997, 4, 629–47.

4.1 Youngsters arrested for walking in unconventional clothing, May 1968

Source: Budapest Police, Budapest City Archives, Hungary.

Anti-modernism discourses: constructing the first hooligans

The first phase of the moral panic on hooliganism can be explored at the depictions of the *jampec* (spivs) in Hungary at the beginning of the 1950s. The combination of the term 'Jam-pec', Yiddish in origin, means 'great prick' in both senses. The analogous Hungarian combination probably originates from earlier than the 1950s, and the lexical development to 'very stupid' and then 'fashion-mad' would have occurred in Hungarian.[9] The figure of the *jampec* in common parlance also meant a worldly, independent, extravagant lifestyle, so that it was a term attractive to young skilled workers earning high wages after the Second World War.

The narrative of the *jampec* centred mainly on the flamboyant look of the mostly working class boys, who were similar to the Teddy boys in England (that is why the teds were called 'English jampecok' in the Hungarian newspapers). The articles that surrounded the *jampec* invasions of mainly

[9] L. Benkő (ed.), *A magyar nyelv történeti-etimológiai szótára* (Akadémiai 1970), vol. 2, 258–9.

cultural buildings[10] were exaggerated. The narrative of the *jampec* needed a place where the 'bamboozled youth' could meet the socialist narrative. The *jampec* invasions occurred in the newspapers not as news stories or police reports, but in the style of feuilleton or sketch. The *jampec* was characterized not by a membership of a gang, or by his fights against police, but by his/her individualism, hairstyle, and clothes. No police reports were created on *jampec*-gangs or on special *jampec*-criminals, and newspapers gave a free hand to the ideologically driven journalists to sketch the portrait of the *jampec*.

The image of the *jampec* in the 1950s originated from depictions of Western popular culture, based on imported newspaper articles in the Western press and the products of moral panics centred around westerns, gangster films, dime novels and comic books.[11] The construction of the *jampec* in Hungarian films and newspapers was a product of the mixture and the adaptation of Western moral panics. According to Uta G. Poiger (who compared the influence of American culture in East and West Germany), contemporary West German experts and East German functionaries claimed 'that after consuming westerns and gangster films, young male workers tried to re-live 'Wild West', 'gangster' and 'desperado' feelings for such an extended time and so intensely that they became their 'basic outlook on life'.[12] Hungarian functionaries and journalists consequently created an anthropomorphic figure, the *jampec*, in order to explain the dangers of films, comics, and all that was associated with Western popular culture. Westerns, gangster films and comic books use a special visual language, which is why the *jampec* was described mainly by visual signs. A *jampec* would wear a black or brightly coloured shirt, a patterned tie or red spotted scarf, a baggy-shouldered jacket, drainpipe trousers, striped socks, coloured, rubber-soled shoes and a cowboy-style hat. A girl would wear a tight skirt and floppy jacket, with plaited or permed hair tied in a ponytail.

The official discourse and moral panic on the 'jampec-fashion' between 1950–56 gave these clothes a special meaning, and so created a social identity. *Jampec* clothing was normally obtained on the black market as a status symbol, which lent an urban character to working-class youth, along with the excitement of group affiliation and an association with Western values. 'They looked suspiciously on us. When we walked in, and not as show-offs.

[10] Especially 'houses of culture', which were special institutions mainly for leisure run by the local administration or the Communist Party.

[11] For more on these panics, see, J. Springhall, *Youth, Popular Culture and Moral Panics. Penny Gaffs to Gangsta-Rap, 1830–1996* (New York 1998)

[12] U. G. Poiger, *Jazz, Rock, and Rebels. Cold War Politics and American Culture in a Divided Germany* (Berkeley 2000), 67.

But we had our *jampi [jampec]* shoes, thick soles, rubber welts', a man who was a skilled-worker in the 1950s explained.[13]

The spread of mass-media helped to popularize notions of youth as an exciting new social force. The 'bad boys and girls' were among the favourite figures of popular culture. A new type of hooligan had been constructed at the beginning of the 1960s, and the police and the media developed a new style campaign against the youth gangs, called 'galerik'. This narrative had its roots in the official story of the revolution of 1956. As the police reports stated, the armed groups of the 'counter-revolution' gave a bad example to the youth, who with their long-hair and jeans and tuned in to Radio Luxembourg, had formed aggressive gangs. This new form of hooliganism invaded the front pages of the newspapers, and the *jampec* became an old-fashioned story. The journalists could now fill the papers with much more interesting stories about the new hooligans. To write about youth gangs (*galerik*) was to discuss rock music, street corners and street subways, sexual violence, blood and later drugs, and newspapers and magazines dealing with such topics sold well. Sensationalist journals, such as the *Esti Hírlap* and *Ifjúsági Magazin*, which appeared after 1956, and the television programmes, such as the 'Kék fény' – 'Blue Light', a popular police TV show after 1965, also fed off this new form of hooliganism because it was much more interesting for their consumers. These stories could play a metaphorical and ideological role. The mass media built up a strong connection with the police because they needed each other to demonstrate their importance. Hall and his co-authors agreed that the media were 'among the most powerful forces in the shaping of public consciousness about topical and controversial issues.'[14] But they went on to argue that moral panics about law and order typically originated in statements by members of the police and the judiciary, which were then amplified by the media. The media does not 'create' the news so much as 'reproduce and sustain' the dominant interpretations of it, and can thus be said to function, consciously or not, as an instrument of state control.

On the other hand, when, in September 1956 the West Berlin parliament discussed the youth riots that had erupted in various West German cities the previous year, it was not only a German phenomenon. Commentators in the East and West came to agree that the American 'young rebel' movies served as models for German juvenile fashions, dances, and even for the riots. 'The arrival of movies such as "The Wild One" with Marlon Brando, and "Rock Around the Clock", exacerbated parents' and officials' worries

---

[13] Recollection by János B., 26 March 2001.

[14] S. Hall, et al., *Policing the Crisis: Mugging, The State, and Law and Order* (Basingstoke 1978), 220–22.

4.2 'Fair-haired Lord', a member of the Great Tree Gang – 'ÉSZ' (brains) tattooed on his forehead

Source: *Hungarian Policeman* – Magazine, 11 December 1969.

about American culture influences.'[15] The main distinctive feature of the folk devils associated with youth culture in the official discourse became the violence, not the fashion. This phenomenon was so widespread that the topic of the 'Second United Nation Congress on the Prevention of Crime' was 'New Forms of Juvenile Delinquency: Their Origin, Prevention and Treatment'.[16]

The Hungarian press and the experts on youth gangs could explain the *galeri* (youth gang) phenomenon not only by the so-called 'counter-revolutionary' forces, but by international trends, too. The panic on youth violence also had its roots in the moral panic about comic books and films, but the most important force behind this panic was not the media, but the police. The 'Rowdytum' phenomenon in the GDR was very similar to the Hungarian *galeri*. According to Thomas Lindenberger, 'Rowdytum' in the GDR was a product of 'a military mode of perception, interpretation and reaction'. Because of the Hungarian Revolution 1956, the GDR Politburo, in December 1956 and January 1957, developed new schemes to prevent domestic uprisings in which the regular police was to play an important part. Lindenberger discerns a duplicity of discourses interpreting 'Rowdytum': a military one, focused on state security, and an ideological one, in which 'all products of the commercial entertainment industry, in particular pulp fiction, movies, and pop music, were perceived as part of a deliberate strategy to lure East German youths away from socialism. The categories used to characterize and to analyse these artifacts were derived from the long standing German tradition of anti Schund und Schmutz campaigns, youth protection – Jugendschutz – and antimodernism discourses.'[17]

In Hungary, we can identify much more clearly the military and the ideological discourses on hooliganism: the discourse on *jampec* in the 1950s, and the discourse on hippies at the end of the 1960s were driven by anti-modernism discourses and ideological moral panics. The creation of the *galeri* phenomenon gave a scope and space for military and criminological discourses on youth, focused also on state security. According to Katherine Lebow, it seems to be clear that a similar anti-modernist discourse was created in Poland, especially in Warsaw and Nowa Huta, by inventing a

---

[15] Poiger, 'Jazz, Rock, and Rebels', 71.

[16] *Report: New Forms of Juvenile Delinquency: Their Origin, Prevention and Treatment* (United Nations, Dept. of Economic and Social Affairs 1960)

[17] T. Lindenberger, *Aufklären, zersetzen, liquidieren: Policing Juvenile Rowdytum in East Germany, 1956–1968*, Paper presented to the annual GSA conference, 4–7 October. Arlington/V.A. T. Lindenberger, *Volkspolizei. Herrschaftspraxis und öffentliche Ordnung im SED-Staat 1952–1968* (Vienna 2003)

new term, *bikiniarze* – loosely 'bikini boys' – in the late 1940s and early 1950s.[18]

Military discourses and girls in the gang

The first major campaign against the *galeri* was launched by Budapest Police Headquarters in 1960–61, when several dozen gangs said to be organized on a territorial basis were broken up. The campaign provided an opportunity for associating the *galeri* in the public mind with the concept of hooliganism. The detailed reports on the elimination of particular gangs came to resemble each other, with a template account of how each had come into being. The police headquarters in every Budapest district was ordered in 1960 to eliminate a few gangs. The most assiduous police forces seem to have been in working-class districts. The types of juvenile gangs depicted by the media and by the police were different according to the official reports. For example, the 'Inner-city gang' ('Belvárosi galeri') was depicted as a gang of affluent youths who were consumer-oriented. By contrast, the gangs located in the outskirts were depicted in police reports as the remnants of a former lifestyle of the so-called 'lumpenproletariat', such as beggars, prostitutes, and the homeless. The construction of the story of the 'Great Tree Gang' in 1969 consists of many of the stereotypes about this new type of hooliganism.[19]

The police would deploy in the busy squares and places of entertainment, where young people were likely to congregate in their spare time. The eventual reports tended to state that the gang came into being in 1959, and that its members were immoral and unsupervised by parents, schools or KISZ.[20] The mass emergence of the *galeri* was ascribed throughout to the unsettled conditions that followed the 1956 Revolution. József Molnár, for instance, wrote in 1971 on *galeri* crime, 'The mass emergence of the *galeri* can be dated to the counter-revolution and immediately ensuing years … The gang-type activity manifest in many mass acts around the time of the counter-revolution has been ceasing recently,' so that hardly any *galeri* were formed in 1965, for instance.[21] The main reason, of course, was that the police, after the campaign of 1961, then placed emphasis on the importance

---

[18] K. Lebow, 'Socialist leisure in time and space. Hooliganism and Bikiniarstwo in Nowa Huta 1949–1956', in C. Brenner and P. Heumos (eds), *Sozialgeschichtliche Kommunismusforschung. Tschechoslowakei, Polen, Ungarn und DDR 1948–1968* (R. Oldenbourg 2005), 527–40.

[19] BFL XXV. 60. b. Tük. 0017/61. 409–10.

[20] Ibid., 414–621. Summary reports of accounts of the origin of the *galeri*.

[21] József Molnár, *Galeribűnözés* (*Galeri* Crime) (KJK 1971), 335–6.

of eliminating gangs in 1969. The *galeri* emerged out of the police actions and the stories they invented or instigated about them.

The main crime ascribed to the *galeri* was generally to have 'entertained themselves utterly freely, without restraint, according to their own tastes and ideas'.[22] This argument was also advanced to confirm the influence that the police exerted on youth. The police themselves brought the *galeri* into public discussion, intent on presenting these occasional groups as stable gangs and so criminalizing members for activity not connected with an officially supported institution. Apart from their alcohol consumption and rowdy behaviour, they were accused of immorality, and *galeri* members were described as enjoying a 'perverted' sexual life. One of the main crimes of this type found in the police minutes was 'fornication' by the female gang members with 'various men', consistent with the common practice of making uncleanness and unnatural sexual behaviour a primary characteristic of whatever persons or groups were being stigmatized.[23] The central events included in most of the police and press narratives on specific gangs were sexual: private parties that degenerated into orgies, rape-related events, frequent changes of partners, and provocative dresses worn by the girls.[24] The parties organized in private apartments (*házibuli*) became the symbols of immorality because the police could not control them.

Although the police paid less heed to the young women seen as *galeri* members than the male gang members did, they used similar narrative structures to depict the sex roles in the gang. Female gang members form a relatively neglected field of research into juvenile peer groups. They tend to be mentioned only in relation to some activity by male members. Noting the occasional press descriptions of female gang members as 'street feminists', Campbell asserted that the gang offered liberation where some female members could find solidarity and self-fulfilment outside the family.[25] Most literature on the subject concludes that male gang members were at least as, if not more, sexist in their language and outlook as society in general with girls were often treated as sexual property.[26]

---

[22] BFL. XXV. 60. f. Tük. 0017/61, 415.

[23] Howard M. Solomon, 'Stigma and western culture: a historical approach' in S.C. Ainlay, G. Becker and L.M. Coleman (eds), *The Dilemma of Difference. A Multidisciplinary View of Stigma* (New York 1985), 59–76. Stereotyping as 'dirty' and 'holding orgies' appeared even with the early 'heretic sects', and with several twentieth-century ethnic groups.

[24] BFL. XXV. 60. f. Tük. 205. 006/61, 228.

[25] A. Campbell, *The Girls in the Gang* (Oxford 1984).

[26] See P. Willis, *Learning to Labor: How Working Class Kids Get Working Class Jobs* (New York 1977); J. Moore, *Going Down to the Barrios. Homeboys and Homegirls in Change* (Philadelphia 1991).

This relatively schematic interpretation is apparent in an extract from a television interview with a member of the Indiáns or Great Tree Gang. The interviewer of the police TV show, László Szabó, one of the great popular 'educators' of the period, narrowed down the interviewee's views of women to the girls in the gang:

> Well as far as I'm concerned, I strongly disapprove of the girls I've met with generally. I tell you that honestly and I meant to talk about it. It's one reason why I asked for the interview. Their morals are so low they're not worth talking about. I have to say it's really so, you might change your coat or your jacket as easily as when you pick up a woman in company like that, really you just have to say come here or sit down and she'll sleep with you.[27]

The main distinction between gang girls was their sexuality: either moral or immoral. Gang girls, because of the depiction of their promiscuity, had more confrontations with the vice squad than with ordinary police on the streets, the latter being more inclined to stop and identify the youths (male) with a penchant for acts of violence.

Reports of police investigating juvenile Hungarian peer groups also tell of far fewer confrontations with female gang members than with male. During the entire campaign against the *galeri* (1960–75), the proportion of girls interviewed did not exceed 20 per cent in any police investigation, and there were some *galeri* where no female members were confronted at all. Just a single all-female *galeri* is mentioned, and this simply because the police thought they discerned the criteria of *galeri*-type organization among a group in a girls' reformatory. The explanation in the literature is that '*galeri* formation was primarily a boys' occupation.[28]

Nonetheless, girl members may well have played a decisive part in the acts of some juvenile gangs, even if the gangs' main activity was loafing. This, of course, did not mean that any gang member aspired to the kind of role played by a KISZ secretary, whose main task was to organize constructive leisure-time activities among the youth. Certainly not Mariann K., who began to frequent the Emke coffee bar, at first with a female friend and then because of a boy, but became disillusioned with him after he threatened her with his flick knife when he was drunk. She explained:

---

[27] László Szabó, *Kék fény. A hippikirály* (Blue Light. The hippy king) (Táncsics 1981), 156.

[28] József Kó, Iván Münnich and Zsolt Németh, 'A magyarországi galeribűnözés néhány jellemzője', 162 [Attributes of gang crime in Hungary], in *Kriminológiai és Kriminalisztikai évkönyv. Kriminológiai és Kriminalisztikai Tanulmányok* [Yearbook of Criminological and Criminal Studies], vol. 32 (IKVA 1995), 156–72.

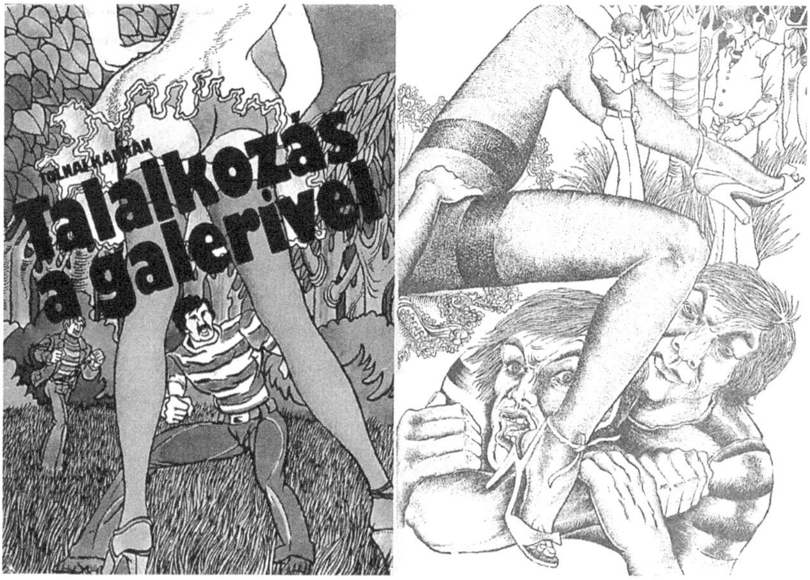

4.3 Depiction of gender in the Great Tree Gang

Source: From the socialist 'pulp-fiction' Kálmán Tolnai: Találkozás a galerival [Meeting the galeri], 1975 (1984).

> Doktor appealed to me. I'm not nobody, but I was the only girl in the gang and took care of myself. Doktor was different from the others ... Meanwhile Doktor got mean ... Then Tigris ['Tiger'] had the authority. At first I was just his bird [*csaj*], then junior [*öcsi*], then pal [*havér*]. He never touched me, because he doesn't touch his pals. He liked reformatory girls from Villám utca ... The ones that kept escaping.[29]

So the top of the ladder for a girl member was to become a pal instead of a sex object and to feel that she had the status of an equal in the gang.

Ancsa started going round with the Béla tér and Vidámpark *galeri* in 1967, aged 14.[30] She lived with her mother, a chief bookkeeper, her father, a draughtsman, and her six-year-old brother, in a three-room flat. She was introduced to the Emke *galeri* in 1968 by Lord of Óbuda, as his girlfriend. She soon became a junior rather than a 'bird', known as Black Ancsa or Hippy Ancsa to the others. After Lord, she became Oszkár's girlfriend, and

[29] Recollection by Mariann K, Ferenc Komornik, 'Csavargók voltunk' [We were tramps]. *MI*, 23 February 1968, 9.

[30] *Állambiztosnsági Szolgálatok Történeti Szaklevéltára* [Archive of Security Services = ÁSZTL] O–13708. 71. Report. By 'Mrs Tamási'. 1970. március 16. Papers on Hippy Ancsa. 79–80, 93, 136–7 and 144. Recollection by Ancsa.

in December 1969, she met Doxa, a muscular loader with a criminal record, who stood high in the gang hierarchy and, like Tigris, was fond of girls from Villám utca. According to a report by an agent of the secret police, Ancsa had been wandering and 'drain-piping' since the age of 14. 'Sometimes the Children's Protection took her home, sometimes another police organization. Sometimes she went home of her own accord.'[31] In August 1969, Ancsa was placed by her parents in the Villám utca reformatory where she made friends with another girl, Erzsi, with whom she would often escape.[32]

Ancsa told Doxa on 4 March 1970 that she and Erzsi were due to be transferred to the Rákospalota reformatory, a much stricter institution from which it was harder to escape. So Ancsa did not return to the reformatory. According to Doxa, they went together and according to 'Kék Fény' (a police TV show), they were led by Ancsa to the girls' reformatory next day to spring Erzsi. Ancsa rang the bell, and when the door opened, Doxa, Jimi, Georg and others burst into the reformatory. Ancsa later described what each had done. She had watched out for the police; Georg ripped out the telephone wires and threw vases at the heads of the wardens; Jimi dashed about the reformatory looking for Erzsi. Doxa used his fist with a mermaid signet ring to knock down the doctor, who rushed to assist reformatory staff. Once the staff found out who the intruders were after, Erzsi was locked into a changing room in the cellar of the building. Jimi failed to break in the door by charging it with his shoulder, as Erzsi kicked from inside, shouting, 'Let me out, or I'll die if you don't take me with you.' Meanwhile, other reformatory girls started fighting, as some of them were for the abduction and some against. When they heard the police-car siren, they all ran off except Doxa, who still tried to prise open the bars on the window, but without success.

They returned to the Emke and then went to the Kisluxor [Little Luxor] pub, one of their haunts, where they said they had done well, and some others were indignant at being left out of the fray. Nine of them set out for the reformatory again, to free Erzsi at all costs. They went on foot, looking in at several bars on the way, so that it was about 11pm before they reached the reformatory. Nobody opened up when they rang, and so Georg attacked the door, which gave way immediately. But Erzsi could not be found as she had been taken to another institution. They then tried to break into the office for the money Ancsa had deposited in the safe, but the police arrived. Doxa and Ancsa managed to flee, but were picked up later.

According to Ancsa's account, she had played a leading part throughout. Others also described her not just as an assistant, but as a liberator of equal

---

[31] ÁSZTL. O – 13708. 79–80.

[32] L. Szabó, 'Huligánok, szélhámosok, körözöttek' [Hooligans, swindlers, the wanted], in L. Szabó, 'Kék fény', 142.

rank. It was believed in the gang world that she could act like a boy, being given a knife, a weapon, and thereby a feeling of power temporarily.

When the hippy movement became known in Hungary at the end of the 1960s, *galeri* members often identified themselves with the hippies. According to the official discourse, hippy-gang members were against society, work and war.[33] If opposition to war was considered to be positive while the war still meant the war in Vietnam, after the invasion of Czechoslovakia (1968), protests were tolerated less in police circles. Police tolerance declined further after agents of the secret police planted among hippies reported the gossip under the Great Tree that János Kádár, first secretary of the Communist Party, had been taken prisoner, and that Hungarians had also entered Czechoslovakia. László Szabó, the television front man of the period, reported that members of the hippy *galeri* 'usually did not work, or hardly at all, but drank a lot nonetheless'.[34] Asked how they spent their time, they replied, 'We loaf about' or 'We stand about, tongues wag, we take off and stand a bit further over.' A hippy girl added, 'Yeah, and of course our dress is so hip the other guys just whirl around us like demented apes.'[35] They viewed time and urban space in a way that differed from official expectations. However, because journalists made their interviews during police raids, these testimonies were given during a police prosecution.[36]

The Great Tree Gang: constructing violence in urban space

As in other years, several issues of the youth weekly *Magyar Ifjúság* in the summer of 1969 pictured slim girls in bikinis on the cover under the slogan, 'Workers of all lands, unite!' and invited young people to attend KISZ work camps.[37] But many from working-class districts went not to a work camp but to the Great Tree to loaf. On 7 July 1969, during a heat wave, ambulances were called 120 times in Budapest to assist people who had collapsed in the heat.[38] The Great Tree crowd were looking forward to a concert in the Youth Park the following evening by a subsequently legendary guitarist,

---

[33] It was not rare that the 'hippies' in communist countries became associated with elements of national and regional resistance also. See W.J. Risch, 'Soviet "flower children". Hippies and the youth counter-culture in 1970s L'viv', *Journal of Contemporary History*, 40, 2005, 3, 565–84.

[34] Szabó, 'Kék fény', 146.

[35] Éva Bedecs, 'Hippik' [Hippies], *MI*, 12 December 1969, 4–5.

[36] Recollection by Éva Bedecs, 4 February 2005. Her article about the Great Tree Gang appeared in the most popular Hungarian youth magazine (*Magyar Ifjúság*).

[37] For example, *MI*, 11 July, 25 July and 1 August 1969.

[38] *Népszabadság*, 8 July 1969, 9.

Béla Radics, and his first band, Sakk-Matt, playing progressive and blues music including numbers by Jimi Hendrix and Cream. Although Sakk-Matt were still persecuted in that period, they had drawn a crowd of 5,000–6,000 in June and had their photo in *Magyar Ifjúság* in July.[39]

4.4 The Great Tree in 1969

Source: *Hungarian Policeman* magazine, 11 December 1969.

The *galeri* members had probably not read their *Népszabadság* (Communist Party newspaper) regularly, or they would have learned of János Kádár's fascinating visit to Bulgaria and seen that a cold front was forecast. The concert on 8 July had to be postponed because of bad weather. Kacsa, a seminal figure at the Great Tree, persuaded the others to take a trip into the city. An argument broke out about whether to go to Hűvösvölgy or to Margaret Island (a 'middle-class' public park). To give them time to decide, they set out in twos on a hippy walk across the Elizabeth Bridge, a symbol of

[39] *MI*, 18 July 1969, 10. On Béla Radics, see Miklós Ómolnár, *R. B. kapitány avagy pengék és halak* [Captain BR, or blades and fish] (Ifjúsági Rendező Iroda 1986). Tamás Béla Tóth, *Csodálatos utazás: könyv Radics Béláról* (Zoltán és Zoltán Bt. 2002) Memorial website by BR Society: see www.radicsrb.hu/index.php?p=eletrajz&l=en

1960s modernization. They had first heard of hippy walks, they stated later, from a 15-year-old Swedish girl who 'seemed much more developed than her years'.[40] Some 80–100 strangely dressed, long-haired young people in jeans sang the songs '*Lánc, lánc eszterlánc*' (Chain, chain [nonsense word]) and '*Sétálunk, sétálunk*' (Walking and walking – both are children's songs). The police, not too familiar with the words, later recounted in their reports how the hippies had repeatedly 'squatted on reaching the part in the song that goes "*egy kis dombra lecsücsülni, csüccs*"'[sit down on a little hill, sit].[41]

They went on along Váci street, the symbol of the 1960s consumption where one of them bought half a kilo of bread. The others surrounded him, shouting, 'Work, bread!' According to Lekvár (Jam), who later described himself as a robber, it was fashionable among the Great Tree people to choose a job that had relatively few duties and plenty of time out in the open.[42] The group in Váci street began chanting 'Work without bread!' which the police later interpreted as a demand for dole payments.

Kacsa led the people out of Váci utca towards St Stephen's Basilica (the landmark of the Hungarian Catholic Church) to hold a beat mass in memory of Brian Jones, the blond Rolling Stones guitarist who had been discovered drowned in his swimming pool a few days earlier with high levels of alcohol and drugs in his blood. His fans had immediately begun to suspect murder and requiem masses were organized all over the world, as in the ancient church of St Mary in Cheltenham, England, which was overrun by girls in miniskirts at his funeral on 10 July.[43] News of beat masses spread around Budapest in 1968 as the church, like KISZ, discovered that a light version of rock music was a good way of winning over young people. In May 1968, the communist daily *Népszabadság* reported indignantly how 'girls wearing Coca-Cola badges swayed to the blues tunes' in the Matthias Church.[44] When the 'hippies' of the Great Tree reached St Stephen's Basilica the doors were shut. The Great Tree people sat down on the steps for a time and engaged some passing older women in conversation.

They then set off towards Szabadság tér [Place of Freedom, with the largest monument to the 'Soviet soldiers who died in the liberation of Hungary']. Encouraged by the fact that nothing had happened to them so far, they intended to go to the American Embassy as a tribute to Brian Jones who,

---

40 Recollection of Sz. Gyula, ÁSZTL V-158094.

41 ÁSZTL V–158094/1, 6. Report by the Youth and Child Protection Examination Sub-department of Budapest Police Headquarters, 1 August 1969. Where not otherwise specified, the sources on the march are ÁSZTL V–158094/1–3; O–13575; O–13708.

42 Recollection by Lekvár in the film *Passengers in a Water-driven Moskvich* (2000, director: Gábor Kresalek).

43 See http://www.beatzenith.com/the_rolling_stones/bjones.htm

44 F. Sz, 'Beatmise' (Beat mass). *Népszabadság*, 28 May 1968.

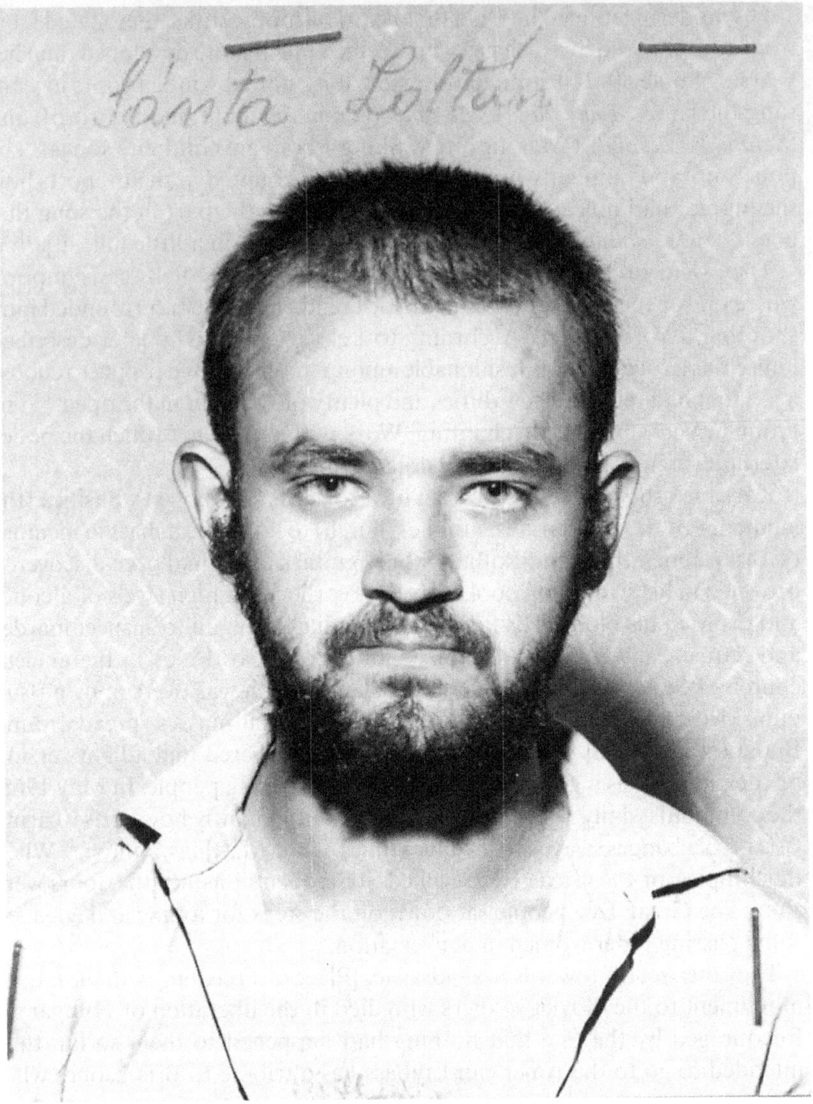

4.5 Kacsa ('Duck') on the day of the 'hippy walk'

Source: Photograph taken by Budapest Police, Budapest City Archives, Hungary.

in their eyes represented American hippies, although he was British. On the way, some of them sang an SS march which they had learned from an American war film (Battle of the Bulge).[45] Szöszi ['Blondie'], Goebbels Röfi ['Goebbels Pup'] and their group excelled in this. They were in the habit of greeting each other at the Great Tree with 'Heil Hitler' and, according to one hippy agent, expected Germany to defeat the Soviet Union quite soon after which Hungary would become like America.

That evening, Péter B. and his girlfriend, a shorthand typist, went off to a concert. They came down from his girlfriend's flat near the Basilica about half past seven and noticed the German march being sung. B. told the police, 'When I heard the march, I thought they might be German tourists,' but soon realized they were not. He then telephoned the duty officers at Budapest police headquarters and followed the group. B. then went into the Workers' Militia headquarters there to ask for help.[46]

The police car arrived as Kacsa and his group entered Szabadság tér.[47] The young people scattered. The police only managed to arrest four of them and although the Workers' Militia hurried to the scene, there was nothing for them to do by the time they arrived.[48] Proceedings were taken by Budapest Police Headquarters against those detained, and the case then passed to Group III/b of the Political Department which set itself the task of breaking up the 'Great Tree *galeri*'. During the mopping-up operation, almost a hundred ostensible members were recorded and over a dozen informers recruited. Eventually on 16 February 1970, ten members were convicted of agitation against the state by Pest Central District Court and given jail sentences of eight months to two years.[49] After their release, several of those who served sentences were kept under observation by the agents who infiltrated or were recruited from the gang.[50] Articles appeared in the press about them and how 'loafing' had turned into 'agitating against the

45 Directed by Ken Annakin, 1965. The film was shown in Hungary in 1968–1969 ['A halál ötven órája'], some of the Great Tree people have seen it many times. This was the first film that was actually advertised in the trailers as being shown in the so-called 'Super-Cinerama' format.

46 ÁSZTL V–158094/1, 33–4 and 37–8.

47 Only one or two police cars went on patrol in every Budapest district at the end of the 1960s, that is why only one police car arrived to arrest some members of the group. On numbers of the so called prowl police cars see (URH-járművek): Magyar Országos Levéltár. [Hungarian National Archive = MOL] XIX–B–1–Z. BM Kollégium. 39. d. 11 June 1970. MOL. ORFK. (National Police Headquarter) 164. d. 50–362–1970.

48 ÁSZTL V–158094/1. 35. Gyula B., workers' militiaman.

49 ÁSZTL V–158094/3. 237–8. Pest Central District Court. 9.B.23598/1969, No. 14.

50 For example, ÁSZTL O–14729.

state'. László L. Lőrinc and Kálmán Tolnai wrote books about the Great Tree people that met the official expectations.[51]

In the summer of 1970, when several of the Great Tree people were already in jail, Indián appeared on the *Kék fény* television programme saying he would like to speak plainly and reveal the 'bare truth' about the hippy movement. He admitted to being the leader, to the delight of both other gang members and the police. The police were pleased because of Indián's criminal record of multiple rape, so that the gang was criminalized by association. The Great Tree people themselves were pleased because it meant he had taken some of the odium on to himself. Indián said on the programme that although the poor conditions meant that hippies showed their age, he had no age and never would have. He said they had made an amateur film for showing on *Kék fény* one day, and then it would emerge what a hippy party and free love really were.[52]

Conclusion

The 'moral outrage' or 'moral panic' in the press showed the Great Tree people as young people with a perception of time diametrically opposed to that of the dominant culture. More specifically, the time concept of gang members and that of the police were on several occasions contradictory. The police tried to show the activity of the peer groups as linear, pointing in time and sequence towards some concrete goal, and not just to occasional meetings. This also explains why official discourse devised the concept of *galeri*, drawing on public utterances about Soviet hooliganism. Prompted only by the various police procedures against them, these informants identified themselves as '*galeri* members' and 'loafers' and portrayed their activities, as recorded in edited responses to constructed questions, as purposeful and sequential. The institution with which the ostensibly deviant gang members dealt with most intensively was not KISZ but the police. Their constant games of cat and mouse with the police were what gave shape to their narrative about their groups. The police, in a story that can also be interpreted as a cultural conflict, appear as the basic agency of social control, their prime purpose being to eradicate the groups, which also meant criminalizing the groups' use of space and time.

The urban spaces used by the Great Tree Gang belonged to the most controlled and representative spaces of the 'socialist capital of the socialist Hungary'. However, it seems clear, that the mental maps of the *galeri*

---

[51] Tolnai, '*A Mohikán-galeri*'; L.L. Lőrinc, *A nagy fa árnyékában* [In the shade of the Great Tree] (Kozmosz 1979)

[52] Szabó, *Kék fény*, 142–65.

members were different from those of the police. The construction of hooliganism belonged to a new interpretation of urban space because the places and streets described in reports and articles on hooligans became the 'dark side' of the city. The expression 'otherness' also denoted the development of a self-identity and personal autonomy among young people opposed to the officially supported processes of socialization in a society that generally tried on an everyday level to deny this to young people. The process included the view that spare time was a resource that could be used for society's good if it was spent well. However the media and the police did not simply react to youth's perception of time, but by opposing and criminalizing it as a deviant sub-culture, they became the forces creating it.

Description of the concepts of the youth subcultures may symbolize cultural conflict, as people try to hold on to their freedom and autonomy under a system of rule that invokes a normative system. Since official discourse in the socialist period prescribed officially supported, institutionalized forms of leisure activity for young people, this placed in a prescriptive frame the sub-cultures of those who used their spare time freely. So the sub-cultures of the autonomy-seeking young emerged as decisive identity-forming factors in juvenile socialization.

Depiction of the *jampec* and *galeri* in the press and the appearance of 'moral panic' in relation to them was not just a consequence of the operation of the press. After a time, it became one of the objectives of the press. *Magyar Ifjúság*, the official paper of KISZ, regularly published articles about hooliganism, not simply to meet and reflect official expectations, but to prove the necessity for the press to exist. Police-prepared strictly confidential reports in the Interior Ministry strove for the same reason to identify extreme right-wing actions among the Great Tree people. To that extent, KISZ and the media (from *Magyar Ifjúság* to *Kék Fény*) were writing a novel about the Great Tree people. Alternatively, the police can be seen as 'moral entrepreneurs', representing 'hooligans' as a force menacing the interests and values of society and thereby acquiring a justification for acting in that role, as society's redeemers. Even in Indián's television interview, he, too, appears in his story as a moral entrepreneur, a social redeemer, a warrior 'hippy' tilting against 'productive work' and 'consumption'.[53]

An important role is usually ascribed to the middle level of power in an outbreak of moral panic.[54] With the Great Tree people, KISZ and the district police headquarters can be seen as a kind of starting point, for in this case too, the first condemnations did not come from above but from the middle, the level of everyday ID checks. The press found a suitable subject in the

---

[53] Szabó, *Kék fény*, 155.

[54] A. McRobbie, *Postmodernism and popular culture* (London 1994).

Great Tree affair to arouse a moral panic and so distract the public from everyday problems. Instead, a kind of 'chaos narrative' presented young people as being infected by rock music and negative elements of 'Western' lifestyle so that they gather into gangs and display violence towards other members of society. It was not by chance that the *galeri* were traced back to the 1956 groups, which had also appeared primarily as constructs of post-1956 counter-revolutionary propaganda, well-organized and continuous rather than as *ad hoc* groupings.

One important aim of the state was to control the socialization of the young and their urban space. Full control over society could not be exercised, of course, and it was much less costly and more spectacular to single out a few youth groups and punish them. It was more conspicuous for the authorities to punish young people in jeans than to reconcile the 1960s 'materialism' (in popular jargon) with socialist principles. It seemed more practical to restore a semblance of social unity by exploring the subject of decadence – juvenile crime, violence, sexual permissiveness, mass cultural products, and the decline of the family – which gradually became subjects of press campaigns.

Further reading

Cohen, S., *Folk Devils and Moral Panics* (New York 1972).

Hall, S., et al., *Policing the Crisis: Mugging, the State, and Law and Order* (London 1978).

Lebow, K., 'Socialist leisure in time and space: hooliganism and Bikiniarstwo in Nowa Huta 1949–1956', in C. Brenner and P. Heumos (eds), *Sozialgeschichtliche Kommunismusforschung. Tschechoslowakei, Polen, Ungarn und DDR 1948–1968* (München 2005), 527–40.

McRobbie, A., *Feminism and Youth Culture: from 'Jackie' to 'Just Seventeen'* (Boston 1991).

McRobbie, A., *Postmodernism and Popular Culture* (London 1994).

Mungham, G. and Geoff Pearson, eds., *Working Class Youth Culture* (London – Boston 1976).

Neuberger, J., *Hooliganism: Crime, Culture, and Power in St. Petersburg, 1900–1914* (Berkeley 1993).

Pearson, G., *Hooligan: A History of Respectable Fears* (London 1983).

Pilkington, H., *Russia's Youth and Its Culture: a Nation's Constructors and Constructed* (London 1994).

Poiger, U.G., *Jazz, Rock, and Rebels: Cold War Politics and American Culture in a Divided Germany* (Berkeley – Los Angeles 2000).

Risch, W.J., 'Soviet "Flower Children", hippies and the youth counter-culture in 1970s L'viv', *Journal of Contemporary History*, 40, 2005, 3, 565–84.

Schildt, A. and D. Siegfried (eds), *European Cities, Youth and the Public Sphere in the Twentieth Century* (Aldershot 2005).

Siegfried, D., '"Don't trust anyone older than 30?" Voices of conflict and consensus between generations in 1960s West Germany', *Journal of Contemporary History*, 40, 2005, 4, 727–44.

Springhall, J., *Youth, Popular Culture and Moral Panics. Penny Gaffs to Gangsta-Rap, 1830–1996* (New York 1998).

Willis, P.E., *Learning to Labour: How Working Class Kids Get Working Class Jobs* (Farnborough 1977).

PART 2

COMMUNITY, NEIGHBOURHOOD AND DAILY LIFE

CHAPTER FIVE

Meanings of the city: Zagreb's new housing communities since the 1950s

Valentina Gulin Zrnić[1]

During the second half of the twentieth century, the city of Zagreb expanded on a grand scale by building new housing estates or housing communities (neighbourhoods), each planned for approximately 10,000 people living in large, high-rise buildings constructed over an area of 30–40 hectares. Each housing estate was supplied with all the amenities for everyday living including shops, service outlets, a primary school, social hall, health care, and sports and recreation facilities. Such housing communities are viewed as a functional and tangible expression of rational urban order, and of a discourse concerning the standardization and uniformity of human needs. Housing estates are the embodiment of modernist city planning and architectural design, as defined by the manifestos of the Congrès Internationaux d'Architecture Moderne (CIAM), whose modernist and functionalist principles have been implemented in many post-war cities throughout the world, including Zagreb.[2]

Some ten new housing communities were built from the end of the 1950s until the mid-1980s on what had been large tracts of agricultural land in the southern part of Zagreb. They make up an urban entity that is called *Novi Zagreb* [New Zagreb]. This name bears numerous, interwoven meanings. It implies a new organization of physical space, time, relationships, and a new social landscape for the newly settled inhabitants of the city. New Zagreb was a new city for the new people of the new society.

However, it was not long before criticism was directed at the new housing estates, largely expressed in terms of the 'dormitory' and 'socialist city' metaphors. As early as the 1960s, architects criticized the social, cultural and political consequences of the town-planning practice being implemented.

---

1 Translated by Nina H. Antoljak.

2 'Atenska povelja: CIAM 1933', in U. Conrads (ed.), *Programi i manifesti arhitekture XX stoljeća* [Programmes and Manifestos of Architecture in the 20th Century] (Zagreb 1997), 244–270; *Atlas arhitekture* [The Atlas of Architecture] vol. 2 (Zagreb 1999), 527–564.

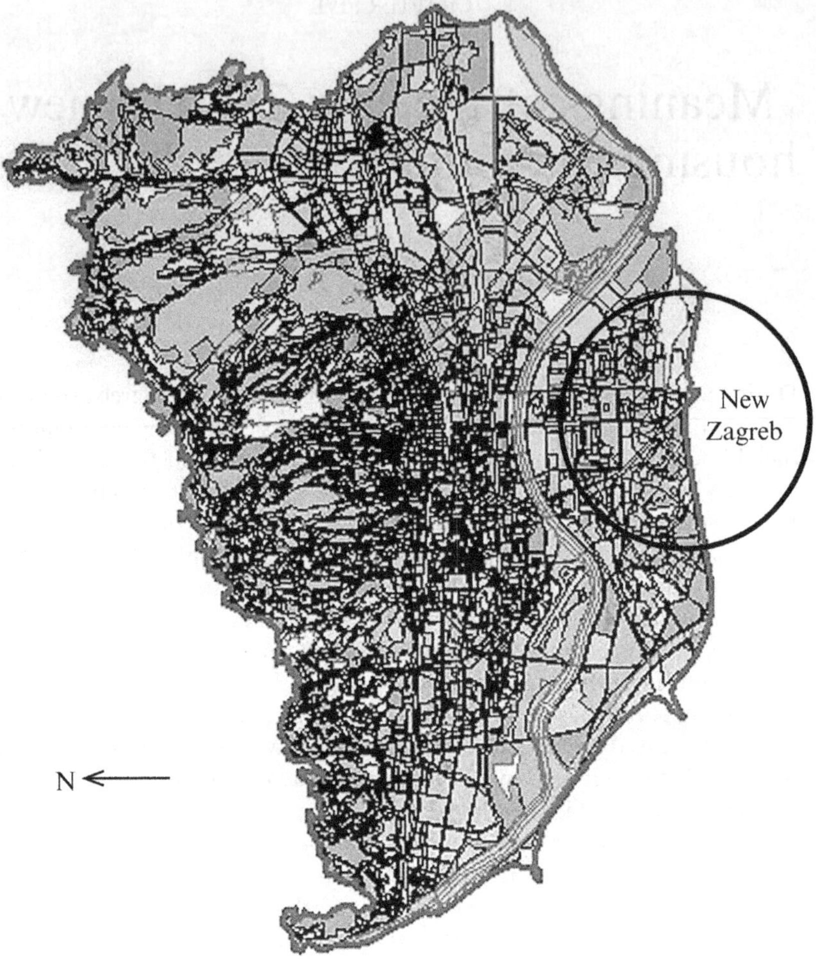

5.1 New Zagreb located south of the Sava river

Source: Master plan of Zagreb, 2003.

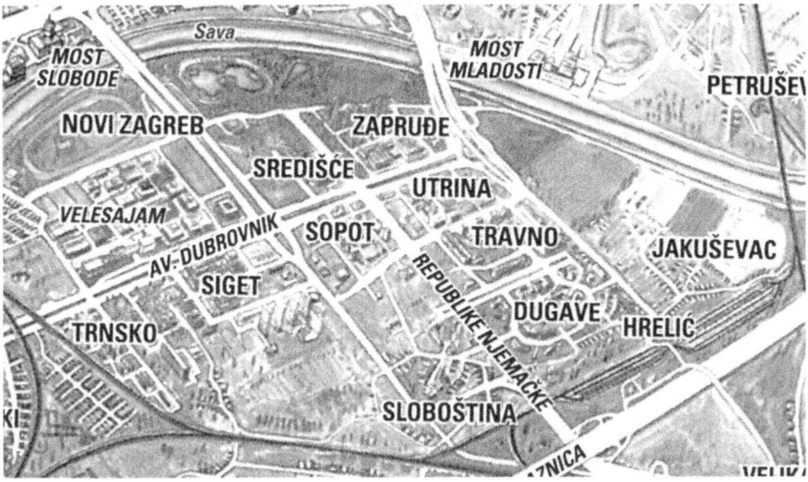

5.2 New Zagreb housing communities (neighbourhoods): Trnsko, Siget, Središće, Zapruđe, Sopot, Utrina, Travno, Dugave, Sloboština

Source: Zagreb tourist map, 2005.

5.3 Dugave: community housing scheme built mid- to late 1970s

Source: http://www.dugave.org/step.jsp?page=1051.

These were neighbourhoods, they claimed, 'lacking a heart of their own' in which the experience of the community was quantitative; one's neighbour was an amorphic and hostile stranger, and no social cohesion was being achieved.[3] One architect called New Zagreb a 'non-city', stripping it of all the qualities of urban life.[4] Sociological criticism during the 1970s and 1980s described the new estates as being 'nameless' and 'expressionless' places ruled by the 'drabness and anonymity, [and] social and moral nothingness' that was ascribed to the effects of modern housing communities.[5] Finally, art historians concluded during the 1990s that socialism did not create the 'symbolic accents that people could emphasize with pride'; there was a lack of public squares and public buildings that would have shaped New Zagreb, and 'symbolically built up the city'.[6]

Conventional discourses in the disciplines of architecture, sociology and art history on the relationship between people and the city tend to focus on symbolic identification from above. This means that certain buildings, structures, parks, and monuments, though planned and produced as representative forms in urban landscapes, permit an individual only to appropriate them as material symbols. Conversely, cultural-anthropological interpretation focuses on symbolic identification from below, that is, in terms of relationships that an individual creates with his/her living environment, while the entire housing community becomes a symbolic place.[7] That relationship is contextualized within the interweaving of semantic structures and the creating of subjective meanings.[8] Meanings of the city, studied in this project from the perspective of the contemporary urban housing

---

3 M. Prelog, *Prostor Vrijeme* [Space Time] (Zagreb 1991), 85–6.

4 A. Pasinović, *Izazov mišljenja o prostornom jedinstvu* [A Challenge to the Notion of Spatial Unity] (S. Križić Roban, ed.) (Zagreb 2001), 375.

5 R. Supek, *Grad po mjeri čovjeka* [The City Made to Measure for Man] (Zagreb 1987), 232–3.

6 I. Maroević, *Zagreb njim samim* [Zagreb on Its Own Account] (Zagreb 1999), 150–151.

7 This text results from part of the research carried out in preparation of my dissertation 'Urban anthropology of New Zagreb neighbourhoods: the culture of everyday life in Travno housing community', University of Zagreb, 2004. The research was focused on processes of community building and place-making, social production and construction of space, residential urban identity, the culture of everyday urban life during socialism, and contemporary social and cultural transformation of the post-socialist city.

8 My cultural-anthropological interpretation of the city relies on the semantic definition of culture. Culture is constituted by 'webs of significance' that people spin and are simultaneously suspended in these meaningful threads. At the core of anthropological interpretive analysis is the search for meanings. C. Geertz, 'Thick description: toward an interpretive theory of culture', in *The Interpretation of Cultures* (New York 1973), 3–30.

areas and communities in my own society, derive from lived experience, which becomes the basis for the creation of cultural meaning. On the one hand, it has its source in the negotiation of ideological, architectural, and sociological meanings already inscribed in producing and shaping space. On the other hand, cultural meanings are also constructed from personal and shared meanings. In this chapter, the focus is on the latter, emphasizing the phenomenological and symbolic experience of the city. This interpretation is based on the corpus of urban experience collected by means of a qualitative methodology, particularly through open-type interviews testifying to life in the socialist and post-socialist city.

There are two main strands to the chapter. Firstly, there is a reflective consideration of the methodological and epistemological framework of conducting research when the researcher almost entirely – practically, contextually and cognitively – participates in the researched community. Secondly, based on a body of narrative testimony, there is an analysis of the processes by which newly built housing estates grew to symbolize the communities as perceived by the inhabitants. Thus, the dominant discourses of the city – the functionalism of modernist architecture, the socialist vision of the city, and the statistics of urban sociology – are opposed by the voices of personal, individual narrative on experience and everyday life, which become the basis for a different interpretation of the city in the second half of the twentieth century.

Methodological perspectives: auto-cultural de-familiarization

This research is based on long-term fieldwork carried out in one of the new housing estates.[9] Although the research derives from the field of urban anthropology, there are significant methodological convergences with oral history in the aspect of the interview method.[10] Some 40 individuals of different age, gender, origins, social status and education, who live in this particular housing community were interviewed. The interviews were also conducted with 15 primary school children in three age groups (9-, 11- and 14-year-olds). All these interviews were pre-arranged and tape-recorded.

[9] The backbone of the research material is provided from one housing community in New Zagreb. It is a case study of the housing community Travno, built in the mid-1970s. Research was also undertaken in other housing communities but was of limited scope.

[10] Beside interviews, the research was based on the participant observation fieldwork method, thus including prolonged living within the researched community and participating in different social interactions and community networks. Town-planning archival material was also used, as well as local newspapers from the researched period. Moreover, virtual local housing community networks on the Internet also became a significant source for the research.

In addition, as a resident of the area, it was inevitable that in a number of informal meetings in cafes, shops, in the street and the park, at meetings of various kinds, people expressed their attitudes and opinions. Such informal conversations were not tape-recorded, but the data was noted down immediately later on in fieldwork notes.

Because I have lived in different New Zagreb housing communities all my life, my urban research was 'situated between autobiography and anthropology'.[11] I have found that much of my initial thinking about my research has been deeply affected by my life in New Zagreb. Therefore, my personal life became 'the very ground' on which knowledge was produced,[12] and in a number of aspects that fact enhanced my research. On the other hand, I have been aware that my involvement could also impair scholarly sensitivity. Unlike empathy with the people and community under research – a widely discussed concept in anthropology – my research position has demanded a contrary procedure of estrangement or de-familiarization.[13] A step back from entrenched and taken-for-granted thought and practice was needed to rationalize internalized knowledge, and to distance oneself from the personal and experiential. Clifford Geertz wrote about 'transcultural identification' as a necessary basis for carrying out fieldwork in foreign cultures.[14] By contrast, one could designate the key field characteristic of research in one's own culture and community as auto-cultural de-familiarization.

In a situation in which my personal life overlaps with my professional research, I was considering the possibility to use 'myself as an informant about my own society'.[15] I decided to appear as an informant and tape-recorded my story following the themes and questions I had used for interviewing others in my research. But then, I was not sure about the status of my personal story in becoming part of the corpus of overall collected narratives about urban life. Should I set it apart as a separate

[11] K. Hastrup, 'Writing ethnography: state of the art', in J. Okely and H. Callaway (eds), *Anthropology and Autobiography* (London–New York 1992), 119.

[12] M. Povrzanović-Frykman, '"Experimental ethnicity": meetings in the Diaspora', *Narodna umjetnost* (Croatian Journal of Ethnology and Folklore Research), 41/1, 2004, 90.

[13] For a more extended discussion based on my research on the 'construction of the field' in one's own culture with regards to traditional and post-modern methodological and epistemological paradigm in anthropology, see V. Gulin Zrnić, 'Domestic, one's own, and personal: auto-cultural defamiliarisation', *Narodna umjetnost* (Croatian Journal of Ethnology and Folklore Research), 42/1, 2005, 161–81.

[14] C. Geertz, '"From the native's point of view": on the nature of anthropological understanding', in *Local Knowledge. Further Essays in Interpretive Anthropology* (New York 1983), 56.

[15] M. Gullestad, 'Cultural sharing and cultural diversity', *Ethnologia Europaea*, 21/1, 1991, 89.

autobiographical-analytical essay? But why should it be given separate status, and how would one carry out some sort of separate, autonomous analytical process on that material? Or, should it be included with all other narrative material and life stories (under a pseudonym or my own name?), from which quotations, concentrated fragments and illustrative parts would be set apart for the interpretation? Many different solutions have been offered through the post-modern scope of auto-ethnography as a hybrid genre of ethnography and autobiography.[16] The characteristic of my interview with myself was that a re-evaluation of personal experience took place at the same time. The research has stimulated my greater reflexivity towards personal experiential situations, places, and encounters, provoking some new emphases, evaluations, and richer memories in parts of my personal life story. Or, in other words, reflecting on my life in New Zagreb during socialism through the looking glass of my urban anthropological interest and analysis, 'I find that new light is shed on many of the experiences that have shaped me into the person – and professional – I am today.'[17]

When conducting interviews with New Zagreb inhabitants, my (existential) participation has considerably expanded a range of themes and experiences upon which I have been able to speak with them, adding depth to their general responses by focusing on the specificity of a particular period, or on the relations that we have been talking about. This is the 'basic insideness' that implies the sharing of certain basic knowledge, feelings of belonging, and emotions, between the researcher and people involved in the research.[18] It did not take long for the people I interviewed to recognize me as someone who has been sharing with them the experience of life in a specific living environment. Thus, their initial formal attitude towards me grew into a freer and more relaxed one. The interviews thus became akin to dialogues and often developed from more formal interviews into a conversation that was more like an exchange of experiences, opinions, comments, agreements or disagreements. In the first interviews, I tried to reduce my voice to a minimum of involvement, forcing myself to maintain objective distance. With time, I succumbed to the pleasure of conversation and the interviews themselves became richer. Furthermore, on the basis of current conversations, I developed some theses during the interviews and rejected others, leaving them open for my interlocutors to react immediately and to comment on them directly. Therefore, these conversations were permanently

[16] See D. Reed-Danahy (ed.), *Auto/Ethnography. Rewriting the Self and the Social* (Oxford 1997); J. Okely and H. Callaway (eds), *Anthropology and Autobiography* (London 1992).

[17] K. Narayan, 'How native is a "native" anthropologist?', *American Anthropologist* , 95/3, 1993, 678.

[18] Povrzanović-Frykman, '"Experimental" ethnicity', 87–90.

open processes in creation of the research undertaking, according to the post-modern idea of co-operative production of ethnography that annuls the researcher's monopoly in creating knowledge.[19]

Talking about life on a housing estate is a testimony to 'lived experience'.[20] These stories are not simply information on society and culture in general; they are testimonies of particular lives lived inside them. Although individual and personal, they also make up a 'social' in urban history conveying what is in common in the events, situations and lives described, and in the senses or feelings expressed.[21] Moreover, those testimonies reveal the meaningful structures within which people conceptualize their urban experience, assess their situation and conceive and contemplate about the city. Those structures are usually internalized and taken for granted, or in phenomenological terms, they are tools people 'think with' while creating meanings in the reality of an individual 'life-world', that is, of 'material and human environment' in which one lives.[22] To a certain extent, those meaningful structures were expressed in personal stories as 'cultural themes and narrative conventions',[23] which are internalized, cognitive and value-based categories used to think generally about the city, and particularly about one's own urban life. Some of the most frequent narrative conventions in my research on New Zagreb spaces and communities have been formed by symbolic tensions between rural:urban, natural:built environment, and closeness:alienation. The alienation in the city and the deterioration of urban communities, as well as the dormitory metaphor, have been some of the knowledge inscribed into space by dominant sociological discourse, and people have taken this over in order to situate their own experiences. In my research, people would usually start our conversation with such general comments. However, during the same interview, some narrative conventions were reflectively questioned by

---

19 G. Marcus and M. Fisher, *Anthropology as Cultural Critique. An Experimental Moment in the Human Sciences* (Chicago 1986), 71. The snare of post-modern thought should also be considered: 'At the autobiographical level ethnographers and informants are equals; but at the level of anthropological discourse their relationship is hierarchical. It is *our* choice to encompass their stories in a narrative of a different order. *We* select the quotations and edit the statements. We must not blur this major responsibility of ours by rhetorics of "many voices" and "multiple authorship" in ethnographic writing.' (Narayan, 'How native is', 122).

20 Lived experience is the basis of the phenomenological perspective that has recently inspired some new approaches in anthropological cultural analysis. See J. Frykman and N. Gilje (eds), *Being There. New Perspectives on Phenomenology and the Analysis of Culture* (Lund 2003).

21 S. Schrager, 'What is social in oral history?', in R. Perks and A. Thompson (eds), *The Oral History Reader* (London 1998), 288.

22 Frykman and Gilje, *Being There*, 36–7.

23 R. Finnegan, *Tales of the City. A Study of Narrative and Urban Life* (Cambridge 1998), 2.

the interviewees themselves as stereotypical concepts adopted for example, through the media – like the dormitory metaphor[24] – and disregarded as not quite suitable for their urban experience. Other cultural themes were used very ambivalently, for example, in the case of positive and negative valorization of the rural in personal stories. On the one hand, uncultured behaviour such as throwing garbage on the street was often assigned to the supposed rural origins of the people who were doing this; on the other hand, rural life was a rhetorical constant of idyllic life between nice, helpful people often mentioned as a contrast to the alienated character of urban life. Through the interviews, many similar internalized narrative conventions were disregarded as not being appropriate for one's own particular living situation, and lived experience would spin the webs of meaning from the logic of personal situations, family life cycle, growing up or forming attachments.

To live on a housing estate, to be 'in place', means to locate certain urban physical experiences and to transform the experiences of space into a 'culturally meaningful and shared symbol'.[25] By that process, the place itself – the estate, the neighbourhood – becomes a symbol, a signifier of specific experiences, praxes, social relations and cultural attributes. The following chapter explores those meanings that are created from personal and shared experiences, through the threads of the process that transforms the 'anonymous' and 'faceless' housing estates into symbolic and identity-related communities.

Testimonies of lived experience: from planned residential community to symbolic community

After the first inhabitants moved into the newly built estate, the material space of the city was converted into the lived experience of everyday life. That experience, which was shared to a large extent, is voiced in numerous interviews. Shared experience is the dimension of the city's history between personal stories and the official discourses about the city. In this research on Zagreb, the physical proximity of living in the new housing communities is the specific context within which the shared urban experience came about.

---

[24] The general image of New Zagreb conveyed in sociological or architectural discourses, in political discourses or in the media is the one of the dormitory, implying that there are not enough amenities and that the estates are faceless. To such characterization, my interviewees were opposed, comparing New Zagreb estates to other parts of the city, praising the benefits of living in New Zagreb (green areas and parks, the pedestrian character of the estates, safety for children, peace and quiet) and expressing their attachment to the community.

[25] S.M. Low, 'Symbolic ties that bind: place attachment in the Plaza' in I. Altman and S.M. Low (eds), *Place Attachment* (New York 1992), 166.

It figures as part of the overall urban experience. In the research into community building, reliance is placed on the interpretative framework that focuses on the experience of the community and the meanings that participants attach to the community: a community is thus treated as a symbolic, subjective, mental and imagined construct.[26] Apart from objective factors that delineate the housing estate, such as boundary roads inscribed in town-planning or local government administration that formally identifies people on the basis of residential address, there are also subjective factors that create the sense of belonging to a particular neighbourhood: the subjective perception of community is revealed through the interpretation of narratives by participants.[27] Thus the planned and built estate becomes a symbolic community over the years, based on a relationship created between inhabitants and their neighbourhood through practical, emotional and cognitive experience.[28]

This, then, is the conceptual background to an analysis of the processes by which inhabitants create symbolic relationships and construct their sense of attachment to the neighbourhood. For some, this results in a very strong local residential identity. The collected narratives illustrate, therefore, how meaning has been created in shared urban experiences through which the housing estate became a symbolic community.

A characteristic of the New Zagreb estates is the fact that some 10,000 people – as new residents – settled in each newly built neighbourhood in a very few years. As soon as the first buildings were completed, the new neighbours started to move in. One of my interlocutors called it 'mass settlement' – the tenants of 160 flats in her skyscraper moved in during the autumn of 1976.[29] The other parts of the estate had still not been built. People told me that there was no school or shop or any other amenities during the first year, and public transport had still not been organized. They moved into a space that was still a building site. 'There were still branches of the Sava River here, with frogs croaking, and we were all the same', said one man in his early 60s.[30] 'We were all the same' was something remembered by many interlocutors. The sameness referred to was not only the environment in which they found themselves, but also to generational similarity, since it was mostly young families who moved to these new estates.

---

26 A. Cohen, *The Symbolic Construction of Community* (London 1995).

27 J. Čapo Žmegač, 'Objektivni i subjektivni čimbenici identifikacije sa zajednicom' [Objective and subjective factors of community identification], *Etnološka tribina*, 20, 1997, 71.

28 Low, ' Symbolic ties', 165.

29 Interview with Mrs Ana, 29 May 2003. All the names of interviewees are fictional.

30 Interview with Mr Ivan, 14 May 2003.

Settling into these new homes in the formative phase of a new neighbourhood community, where the quality of urban amenities did not meet expectations, needs to be considered in the context of personal and family circumstances. Moving home can be regarded as 'wholly successful' if it achieves an improvement in material conditions along with a 'greater sense of autonomy and self-esteem.'[31] Indeed, housing improvement is a calibrated evaluation of change based on individual perceptions, alternatives, choices, and personal expectations, as stated in the interviews. In New Zagreb, many of the tenants were moving into their own private flats for the first time, having previously lived in joint households; others came from exceptionally poor living conditions and moved into flats with excellent amenities; some relocated to flats that had been allocated to them in exchange for the low-standard cottages on the outskirts of the city that had been demolished; while there were yet others who had moved to more generous accommodation from smaller flats.[32] One 60-year-old woman, who had relocated from the centre of the city to a one-roomed flat on the 16th floor of a New Zagreb high-rise, described her feeling: 'Well, the first impressions were all right, because I was overjoyed to get a flat at all (...) it was a bit strange, but the main thing to me was that it was *mine*, now I had something of my own.'[33] Many people stated that their positive evaluation of their personal situation and newly achieved independence far outstripped the downside of the potentially unpleasant environment. First contacts were made in helping each other at the moving-in stage, and then among neighbours who worked together in the same companies. A significant point of communication and integration, around which neighbourliness was formed, were the pre-school and school children. Many of those interviewed stated that children were the basis of first social contacts through whom 'they established their friendship and neighbourly bonds'.[34] Some 30–40 years later, those shared experiences of the first years would become a powerful argument laying down symbolic borders of one's own community.

---

[31] S. Wallman, 'New identities and the local factor – or when is home in town a good move?', in N. Rapport and A. Dawson (eds), *Migrants of Identity. Perceptions of Home in a World of Movement* (Oxford 1998), 199.

[32] The majority of inhabitants of New Zagreb, as in other new housing estates in the city, did not buy flats directly but through the credits given by their companies and firms. Thus, the formal owner of the flat was the company, and inhabitants were 'protected tenants'. It was a specific legal regulation of ownership and use during socialism. Tenants could live in flats as if they were theirs, they could exchange them with the agreement of the company, and they could pass the flats to their children, but they could not sell them.

[33] Interview with Mrs Ana, 29 May 2003.

[34] Interview with Mrs Sofia, 15 May 2003.

There were also some organizational frameworks that fostered the sense of neighbourhood community. The Local Community Board was set up soon after the first inhabitants moved into the estate,[35] organizing, among other things, many social activities aimed at children, young people, women, pensioners, and the inhabitants of the community who were ill or poor. The key characteristic of the Local Community Board's work, in keeping with the principles of the socialist system, was mass inclusion of the inhabitants on the basis of solidarity and reciprocity at the micro-level. The Local Community Board provided the organizational framework that promoted a feeling of belonging in the housing community in urban conditions, through its social and cultural activities. A second organizational framework was the parish, set up more or less secretly in many new estates. Although churches were not foreseen in socialist urban planning, Roman Catholic parishes were established simultaneously with the construction of the new estates, and they carried out their activities in flats bought in the housing blocks by the archdiocese.[36] All religious activities, such as the celebration of mass, religious instruction, and gatherings, took place in these flats. For many people, they were also a socializing focus for the neighbourhood, although quite a number of residents spoke of an atmosphere of secrecy and concealment under which they participated in religious observances.

The public areas of the estate, such as the parks, were also an important factor in the process of symbolic community creation, as testified by respondents. Unlike the transitory and fluid character of public areas in the city centre, those in the residential communities have been quieter and more stable. Parks in these communities are aimed primarily at inhabitants

---

[35] Each new housing estate became a single Local Community unit. Under socialism, that was the unit in which people were organized on the residential principle. This produced certain common needs and interests regarding the general improvements of the estate, housing, communal services, education and culture. It had certain self-management competences and partial financial independence. In the Constitution of the Federative Socialist Republic of Yugoslavia 1974, the Local Community unit became the mainstay of the political system – as it was the smallest unit – through which self-management socialism was put into practice. See: *Enciklopedija Jugoslavije* [The Encyclopaedia of Yugoslavia] (Jugoslavenski leksikografski zavod 1978), vol. 4 (Jugoslavija).

[36] By the Constitution of Socialist Federative Republic of Yugoslavia (1974), as well as by the Constitutions of separate Republics within Yugoslavia, 'the freedom of conscience and faith' was declared as a kind of 'personal freedom of man and citizen'. All religious communities were separated from the state, but they were free in their religious activity and ceremonies. The greatest fear of the system was that religious activity could be used in subversive political aims. Parishes founded in new housing estates regularly reported that religious activities would be organized in the flats, but they were never given either permission nor a formal ban from the authorities.

5.4 Central park in Travno housing community built in early 1970s

Source: Photograph: Valentina Gulin Zrnić, 2004.

5.5 Travno: a neighbourhood playground in front of 'the Mamooth' – the largest housing block

Source: http://www.travno.hr/travno%20proljece/P7080031.jpg

of the estate: other people from the city rarely come here to enjoy the benefits of New Zagreb's green spaces. These parks are local public spaces, characterized by routine everyday use, leisure time, and an informality in dress and behaviour. The fact that the residents themselves are the main users of the parks allows a critical mass of encounters between inhabitants. When a significant number of individuals meet each other frequently, a sense of 'public familiarity' appears, which gradually turns into a sense of community.[37] The experience of community is also significantly founded on 'neighbourhood use', that is, on the amount of time an individual spends in the housing community, and the types and intensity of interactions one encounters in the residential estate.[38] Interactions, such as among parents with children, dog-walkers, or membership in the bowls-playing groups and other social networks described by interviewees and realised in the space and time of the residential estate, usually form the initial framework for more profound and active social bonding between individuals and their families. Moreover, people often took the initiative to improve parts of the park, to plant a tree, to install park benches or to construct the bowl courts, thus adopting the space of the estate as their own. People's narratives testify to the different types and levels of intensity of their involvements in the estate's life, appropriating its space, and bonding with neighbours. Each threat has constituted an aspect of the community construction based on experience and participation.

Public familiarity also enables a minimal knowledge of others living in the same housing estate that has become the basis for social evaluation of the community. All the interviewees were aware of the fact that people of diverse occupations, origins, education and ethnic and religious membership moved into the flats in the residential community. It was 'some sort of mixture' they say, and was not regarded as a negative characteristic. Of course, social heterogeneity in the new housing communities was a desirable feature of socialist urban development. Paradoxically, although residents were aware of and spoke of real social and cultural heterogeneity, they all perceived their housing communities in homogeneous terms. One 30-year-old man who had recently moved to a New Zagreb estate commented: 'I like New Zagreb, I have the feeling that we are all one community, and there are no great oscillations in the cultural, or the material sense ... I have the feeling that when you come to New Zagreb it is all levelled off somehow.'[39] Moreover, some would generalize about the character of the people living in their estate, with the use of one personality feature. Thus, some respondents

---

[37] T. Blokland, *Urban Bonds. Social Relationships in an Inner City Neighbourhood* (Cambridge 2003), 93.

[38] Ibid.

[39] Interview with Nikola, 21 May 2003.

said that good, approachable and communicative people lived on their particular housing estate. This perception of homogeneity is a significant element of the creation of an imagined community.

People who grew up in the neighbourhood developed a particularly strong relationship with it. As children, they were closely bonded to their living space. The estate was identified as 'my home', 'my shelter', 'a perfect place', 'my native place'.[40] Unlike adults, who often shape their stories by 'cultural terms and narrative conventions' for example in terms of the oppositional rural:urban, natural:man-made, inclusive:alienated, children experienced the estate in the form of an integrated landscape in which the buildings, the meadows, the cars and the trees, the parking lots and the dogs, the height of the buildings and autumn all become one and the same experience of the neighbourhood in their narratives. Many people in their thirties now remember their childhood and adolescence on the new housing estates with vivid descriptions of, for example, playing on the building sites of the still incomplete blocks of flats, hiding in the garages, rock get-togethers with guitars, and the fist-fights between youths from different housing communities. One woman who had grown up in one New Zagreb community stated: 'Travno [housing community] was a part of my life ... To me, Travno is home, despite the fact that I am no longer there, it's closer to me.'[41]

Memories create semantic relationships both with the space in which one lives and also with perceptions of community. The interviewees' memories often related to life in the community in socialist times. They recalled that 'everything was different', people were closer to each other, more intimate, 'more polite and more solicitous, they took greater care of each other', there was solidarity, 'interpersonal relations were much better'.[42] Those collective memories of socialism during the 1950s to the 1980s are defined in relation to materialism, the fast pace of current life, and the feeling of insecurity they experience in the contemporary situation. What is implicitly concealed in the accounts about socialism is the existence of a sense of togetherness, communitarianism, a certain egalitarianism and, ultimately, the existence of a neighbourhood community that rested on those fundamentals. These are stories of bygone customs, relationships and times as a type of memory, which claim that things were once better, while the experience of

[40] In addition to adults who spent their childhood in the New Zagreb communities, I spoke with children who are growing up there now. During Autumn 2003, I carried out the research with children in co-operation with one of the primary schools. More than 60 pupils were asked to write an essay on their neighbourhood, and with 15 of them I later conducted an interview.

[41] Interview with Nataša, 22 May 2003.

[42] Interviews with Sanja, 12 May 2003; Mrs Tamara and Mr Ivan, 14 May 2003; Mrs Sofia, 15 May 2003; Klara, 24 June 2003; Marko, 26 June 2003.

change is felt as a loss.[43] We could speak partly about nostalgia as 'selective recollection of the past' in the description of a pleasant and reasonable time, which is confirmed by the negative evaluation of the situation today.[44] In Croatia, radical political, economic and social changes took place during the 1990s. Inhabitants perceive those changes at the level of real everyday life in the community, for example, the change in working hours, and high unemployment among the inhabitants. But also they felt them in the spirit of the housing estate, which is difficult to define: 'some sort of sense of community' is lost, is how respondents put it.[45]

In narratives, many people express their attachment to the place they live, and a sense of belonging to the neighbourhood. It is sometimes explicitly stated as 'becoming rooted', as in the words of one older woman who came to a New Zagreb housing estate 30 years ago from the city centre: 'I think that people know me, and I know the majority of people living here, it is one of the reasons that I like to say that my roots are here … I could not leave this place.'[46] The social groups with greatest persistence and sense of belonging to the neighbourhood have been peer groups. They grew up together and often remained on the same estate. For example, in one community, there is a group of 40 to 50 males in their thirties today, who had similar interests and social standing. In the mid-1980s, when they were adolescents, 'a thread of rebelliousness' bonded the group. When in the city, the group behaved as a neighbourhood 'gang' and this, in their view, was what developed a feeling of 'neighbourhood and mutual belonging'.[47] They created an identity-based relationship: the individual has a feeling of belonging to the neighbourhood, and also feels that the neighbourhood belongs to him. 'I truly love my neighbourhood', explained one of them, 'I consider myself as the real native here.'[48]

Over the years, the housing estates became experiential communities. That became evident at times when people who did not share that experience moved into the community. These are people who have moved to the estates in recent years.[49] On the one hand, residential mobility was prompted by the

---

43 Blokland, *Urban Bonds*, 193–95.

44 Ibid., 190.

45 Interview with Nataša, 22 May 2003.

46 Interview with Mrs Lidia, 15 May 2003.

47 Interview with Luka. 3 July 2003.

48 Ibid.

49 The population of the housing estates was more or less stable during these decades. This was because of several factors: the real estate market was of limited scope during the socialist period, residential mobility was minimal once a family obtained an apartment, and it was a period when young families who moved in were growing up. Some decades later, there has been a generational shift, and significant changes have been introduced in the political, social and the economic system.

great resettlement of the Croatian population as a result of the war during the 1990s and, on the other hand, by the opening up of the real estate market, which stimulated movement of the population within the city. Many of these newly settled neighbours are criticized for a lack of refinement that, in the interviewees' opinions, reveals their (ostensibly) non-urban origins.[50] These 'new tenants', according to people interviewed, do not respect the house rules in the buildings, are noisy, lack a sense of responsibility towards their neighbours and the area generally, and even differ in character from the early tenants, since they do not share their culture of life in the housing community and do not respect the city as a collective. They are foreign to them, unfamiliar, and are, as they say, 'some other sort of people.'[51]

Compared to the newcomers of the 1990s, many of those who moved in first assumed the stance of 'early settlers', and implicitly constituted an 'Us' group that had shared experiences since moving in. As they said, this created 'a certain bond' between them, based on shared experiences and interactions in the residential community. When they moved in during the 1960s and 1970s, they were all newcomers settling into a new urban setting without people, without tradition, without life and without history. Several decades later, they make up the community whose mainstay is their shared experience. Early settler status is also stressed when 'rights' are in question. They claim that they have certain decision-making rights in managing the housing blocks or using certain areas, on the basis of primacy that 'we were among the first to come to this building', so 'we feel like early settlers', as a fifty-year-old woman proudly said.[52] By assigning negative characteristics to new inhabitants, they lay down borders by which the 'early settlers' constitute themselves as a community.[53] It is that very 'entry' of others that is the catalyst in defining relationships and recounting experiences built up in particular residential localities and channelled into perceptions of community. Defining the community and the 'Us' group is interactive and reflective, since 'the basis for creating the notion about one's own group is the relationship towards others.'[54] Therefore, in the New Zagreb housing estates,

---

[50] Although interviewees frequently assign new tenants non-urban origins from other parts of Croatia, this is often simply not so. Many of the incoming inhabitants had moved from other parts of Zagreb.

[51] Interviews with Mrs Tamara and Mr Ivan, 14 May 2003; Klara, 24 June 2003; Marko, 26 June 2003.

[52] Interview with Mrs Tamara, 15 May 2003. Many residents used the term 'native' when describing their status in the housing community.

[53] N. Elias and J.L. Scotson. *The Established and the Outsiders. A Sociological Enquiry into Community Problems* (London 1965).

[54] J. Čapo Žmegač, *Srijemski Hrvati. Etnološka studija migracije, identifikacije i interakcije* [The Croats of Srijem. An Anthropological Research into Migration, Identification, and Interaction] (Zagreb 2002), 21.

it was only by establishing relational attitudes towards those conceived as different, the new and 'others' that the symbolic community was revealed. In turn, it becomes a strong foundation for the development of a feeling of belonging.

Overview

A community is 'a phenomenon of culture' and people construct it meaningfully 'through their symbolic prowess and resources'.[55] It emerges through social interaction and subjective interpretation, leading to the appearance of a similar 'sense of things', shaping itself and reproducing as a shared 'symbolic repertoire' by which individualities and differences are aggregated.[56] In my research, briefly described here, the symbolic community and its common symbolic corpus have been constituted through several aspects. First, there is a shared experience of the first years of living on the estate, melded in the notion of (situational and generational) sameness. Second, shared living experience was proliferated through two alternative organizational frameworks: the local community and the Catholic parish. Third, local public spaces created shared experience and public familiarity through everyday life and involvement. Fourth, perception of homogeneous heterogeneity allowed for an imagined similarity. Fifth, growing up is shown to be a strong meaningful process for creating symbolic bonds with the neighbourhood. Sixth, there is a corpus of shared memories, nowadays flavoured with nostalgia. Seventh, people developed cognitive and emotional attachments to the estate, creating the sense of belonging. Eighth, the community of shared experiences began to sparkle only when 'Others' stepped on to the scene.

Perceived and conceived similarity is indeed a condition for symbolic construction of community, implied in many ways in the interviews. However, when asked directly, interviewees stated that their housing estate did not form a community of any kind. At the same time, they used the 'we' form in their narratives – '*we* built the school' or 'they took *our* meadows'.[57] This very fact proves the existence of community as a 'mental construct', contained in 'the thinking' about it, and existing 'in the minds of its members', thus becoming an imagined community.[58] The community is the referential narrative framework implied in the conversations and it becomes the symbolic construct upon which the interviewees rely rhetorically. It is

---

[55] Cohen, *Symbolic Construction*, 38.

[56] Ibid., 12–21.

[57] Interviews with Mrs Lidia, 15 May 2003; Mrs Ana, 29 May 2003.

[58] Cohen, *Symbolic Construction*, 97–8.

precisely through their oral narratives that they confirm the perception of a community on the residential estate. In terms of the phenomenological approach, it becomes something people 'think with', rather than 'think about'.

These are communities of experience, or more specifically, of shared experience and of shared meanings. By their contextual framework (the physical proximity of living in a housing community) and the semantic framework (the shared symbolic corpus) the people have constructed a specific lived experience of the city. A certain 'type of experience' exists that is recognisable only to those who live in a particular space, while 'all those experiences, the sum of them, makes up the city.'[59] Testimony to those experiences is an inescapable part of the city's history.

Concluding remarks: city builders

Historical, ideological, political, architectural and technological factors materially produce the city.[60] However, understanding urban life through the knowledge of the people who live there[61], through its social spaces emanating from everyday life and by way of the phenomenological and symbolic experience of city life[62] is all part of the social construction of the city. The construction process includes the individual who, on the basis of personal experiences, practical uses of the city's space, social interactions and memories, transforms the spaces of the city into symbolic places. It is through such transformations that an individual constructs a real and symbolic identification with the city as a whole and with its districts. To reveal these relationships, the qualitative methodology of urban anthropology and oral history is almost inescapable in such a dimension. The emphasis is on the people who creatively adopt the physical environment, adapt it, alter and transform it, who 'invest' it with culture and humanise it, who '*shape the*

---

[59] A. Rossi, *Arhitektura grada* [The Architecture of the City] (Karlovac 1999), 30–32.

[60] Setha M. Low discusses two complementary perspectives of social production and social construction of space. The first perspective consists of the above-mentioned factors, which physically produce the material setting. The second perspective focuses on the transformation of space through social praxes, negotiations of meanings, perceptions and memories. S.M. Low, 'Spatializing culture. The social production and social construction of public space in Costa Rica' in S.M. Low (ed.), *Theorizing the City. The New Urban Anthropology Reader* (New Brunswick 1999), 111–12. I introduce those perspectives when interpreting the city.

[61] R. Rotenberg, 'Introduction', in R. Rotenberg and G. McDonogh (eds), *The Cultural Meaning of Urban Space* (Connecticut 1993), xi–xix.

[62] Low, 'Spatializing culture', 112.

city through their everyday resourcefulness'.[63] Through this, people nullify all assumed spatial determinism, and place everyday and individual lived experience at the centre of their interest. The corpus of urban narratives, as it emerges from interviews, illuminates how people construct their own experience of urban life in the interplay between defined physical space, given meanings, representations, everyday life, personal expectations, and the imagining of the city.

Such an approach brings to the fore the processes of the city from below. The relationship between the individual and these city processes is active, creative, and dynamic, promoting people as city builders.[64] With reference to New Zagreb history, it is inadequate to speak predominantly through the narrative structures of inhuman buildings, the socialist city, dormitories or nameless communities that are often applied in the architectural and sociological literature, and even media discourses about that part of the city. This generalized image of New Zagreb is therefore challenged by a discourse based on personal stories, urban experience and everyday life; it presents quite a different image of the city's history. The city is a process involving the creation of symbolic communities, transformations of physical space into semantic places, and the dynamics of urban experiences forming multiple meanings. In that perspective, inhabitants also become creators and builders of the city.

Further reading

Åström, A., P. Korkiakangas and P. Olsson (eds), *Memories of My Town. The Identities of Town Dwellers and Their Places in Three Finnish Towns* (Helsinki 2004).

Bridge G. and S. Watson, 'City Publics', in G. Bridge and S. Watson (eds), *A Companion to the City* (Oxford 2003), 369–79.

de Certeau, M., *The Practice of Everyday Life* (Berkeley–Los Angeles 1988), 91–130.

Emerson, R. (ed.), *Contemporary Field Research* (Prospect Heights 2001).

---

[63] A. Cohen, 'Introduction', in A. Cohen and K. Fukui (eds), *Humanising the City* (Edinburgh 1993), 3–6,17.

[64] I paraphrase the concept of *culture builders*, which denoted a paradigmatic shift in the conceptualization of culture in the anthropological discourse of the 1980s. Culture has been defined as a process with an emphasis on people who constantly re-build it in their everyday lives, trying to handle contradictions and inconsistencies by creating new meanings and modifying old ones. J. Frykman and O. Löfgren, *Culture Builders. A Historical Anthropology of Middle-class Life* (New Brunswick 1987).

Feld, S. and K.H. Basso, 'Introduction', in S. Feld and K.H. Basso (eds), *Senses of Place* (Santa Fe, NM 1996), 3–12.

Holston, J., *The Modernist City. An Anthropological Critique of Brasília* (Chicago – London 1989).

Hummon, D.M. 'Community attachment: local sentiment and sense of place', in I. Altman and S.M. Low (eds), *Place Attachment* (New York–London 1992), 253–78.

Jackson, A. (ed.), *Anthropology at Home* (London 1987).

Lefebvre, H., *The Production of Space* (Oxford 2003), 1–67.

Richardson, M., 'Being-in-the market versus being-in-the-plaza: material culture and the construction of social reality in Spanish America', in S.M. Low and D. Lawrence-Zúñiga (eds), *The Anthropology of Space and Place. Locating Culture* (Oxford 2003), 74–91.

Rodman, M., 'Beyond built form and culture in the anthropological study of residential community spaces', in R. Rotenberg and G. McDonogh (eds), *The Cultural Meaning of Urban Space* (Westpoint, CT 1993), 123–38.

Rodman. M., 'Empowering place: multilocality and multivocality', *American Anthropologist*, 94/3, 1992, 640–56.

Vukić, F. (ed.), *Zagreb. Modernity and the City* (Zagreb 2003).

CHAPTER SIX

Unfolding urban memories and ethnic identities: narratives of ethnic diversity in Limburg, Belgium[1]

Leen Beyers

> They came for a saucepan, a plate, a spoon, a fork. I then repeated it [the word in their language], they looked up then. And eh yes, they felt directly a bit at home then. Oh I have had good times in the shop, I soon had strangers as clients and it all went very well.[2]

These are the words of Elza. From the 1940s to the 1970s, she kept a hardware store at the border of an ethnically diverse mining town in the Limburg mining region in Flanders, the Dutch-speaking northern part of Belgium. She was not a 'stranger' herself, but Flemish-born, originating from a rural village nearby. The town where her clientele lived was one of seven towns that developed from the very beginning to the decline of the coal industry in the province between 1917 and 1992. The local labour market could never supply the work force for the seven Limburg mines that employed some 30,000 miners at their peak in the 1950s, and so these mining towns grew out of a modest Belgian immigration and from three international migration waves. The first to arrive in the 1920s were East European miners and their families. Just after the Second World War, the increased demand for coal associated with the recovery of Belgian industry led to a substantial recruitment of Displaced Persons and Italians, followed by smaller influxes from Greece and Spain. Despite the decline of the coal industry after 1958, the widening of alternative employment opportunities in

---

[1] I am indebted to the editors, Valentina Gulin Zrnić and other contributors to this volume for their comments, and to the Fund for Scientific Research Flanders–Belgium for funding the research on which this chapter is based.

[2] Interview for L. Beyers, 'Iedereen Zwart? De Impact van Bedrijfshomogeniteit en Klassensegregatie op de Interetnische Burenrelaties in Zwartberg, 1930–1980', unpublished PhD thesis, Leuven, 2004, referred to as 'Iedereen Zwart?' All interview fragments quoted in this chapter are translated from the local Flemish dialect. Part of the discourse is, thus, inevitably lost in translation. All of the informants have been given fictitious names.

the province in the 1960s again created a shortage for miners. Hence Turks, and to a lesser extent Moroccans, were employed in the Limburg mines. As such, the mining towns evolved from 4,000 in the 1930s to a population of some 10,000 inhabitants in the 1980s.[3]

Elza served women and men from all these backgrounds in her store. This makes her story highly relevant to an understanding of how inter-ethnic relationships in the Limburg mining towns have evolved in the last century when ethnic boundaries have been strongly in flux in the region. As such, first generation Polish and Italian immigrants had been looked down upon by local Limburg inhabitants, but their grown-up children and especially their grandchildren were later perceived as 'integrated', a label they also use for themselves. In the words of Norbert Elias, while Polish and Italian miners were 'outsiders', their descendants have in the meantime become members of the 'established' population.[4] While historians of the region were not unaware of this distinction, little attention had been paid to how, when and why the ethnic boundaries in the neighbourhood life of the mining towns evolved. To explore this further, oral history was a crucial tool.

It was impossible to come close to the former neighbourhood interactions and the related identities without the use of oral testimonies. Press and associated records were useful, but they told little about informal social life and were from an external point of view. It was equally evident, however, that the focus on neighbourhood and ethnic identity required a specific way of reading urban memories, based on a combination of historical, ethnographical and discourse-oriented perspectives. The field of 'oral history' offers much on how to collect oral testimonies nowadays, but less on how to read and understand them.[5] Consequently, a blending with other

---

[3] After the reopening of the Suez Canal in 1958, which brought Middle Eastern gas and oil on to European market, the Limburg mines were involved in the global energy crisis. On immigration and population growth, see F. Caestecker, *Alien Policy in Belgium, 1840–1940. The Creation of Guestworkers, Refugees and Illegal Aliens* (New York 2000); A. Martens, *Les Immigrés. Flux et Réflux d'une Main-d'oeuvre d'Appoint. La Politique Belge de l'Immigration de 1945 à 1970* (Leuven 1976); National Institute for Statistics Belgium, *Population Census, 1930–1981*; Population Data Municipalities Genk, Beringen, Maasmechelen, Heusden-Zolder, Houthalen-Helchteren.

[4] N. Elias, 'Introduction: a theoretical essay on the established and the outsiders', in N. Elias and J.L. Scotson (eds), *The Established and the Outsiders: A Sociological Enquiry into Community Problems* (London 1994), 15–52.

[5] See the comments of L. Passerini, 'Work, ideology and consensus under Italian Fascism', *History Workshop Journal*, 8, 1979, 84–92; S. Leydesdorff, 'Gender and the categories of experienced history', *Gender and History*, 11, 1999, 599–600. It is remarkable how some of the main guides to oral history have dismissed the issue of analysis. See for instance V. Yow, *Recording Oral History. A Practical Guide for Social Scientists* (London 1994).

perspectives was particularly fruitful with regard to the analysis of urban memories as constructions of ethnic identities and as memories embedded in space.

By considering how these different approaches were blended, this chapter hopes to show how life-stories represent a mine of information concerning the social identities of city dwellers, not just for *what* they might reveal about the past, but even more for *how* they construct the past. First of all, this chapter argues for a double-layered reading that explicitly combines an approach to oral memories as descriptions of the past and as an analysis of the way they narrate the past. Second, the chapter points to those narrative aspects that are most relevant for an understanding of ethnic identity processes in the Limburg mining towns and, probably, in neighbourhoods in general. They have to with the representation of the self and others, the sense of place, and the division of time.

Two ways of reading

Oral testimonies are approached in at least two different ways by historians and other social scientists.[6] On the one hand, they are often read as descriptions of the past, descriptions of facts and also of former routines, beliefs and identities. In that case, the analysis consists of a content analysis, summarizing the main points of the testimony and reducing the quantity of less useful information. This was one of the stances taken when studying the evolution of neighbourhood life in the Limburg mining towns. Unmistakably, the life-stories of former inhabitants were relevant for *what* they told about the past. They revealed, for instance, that the informal work of women that had never been registered. Also, in their life-stories, Polish miners' sons who grew up in the mining towns suggested a higher degree of ethnic segregation than appeared to be the case from the ten-yearly census. This led to a reconsideration of other population data and, indeed, to refinements in the demographic map of the area.

On the other hand, life-stories have long since been considered as ways of constructing the past. From that point of view, there is no redundant information. Instead, the narrative or discursive analysis is focused on how things are emphasized, forgotten and associated. This approach was equally useful for the study of the identity processes at neighbourhood-level because paying attention to narrative aspects definitely enriched the understanding of

[6] Another important approach, but one that is less central to the argument here, is the social interactionist analysis, focusing on the interaction between interviewers and respondents or between narrators and their public. See, for example, J. Herbert, 'Negotiating boundaries and the cross-cultural oral history interview' in this volume.

social identities. Actually, in every social group, certain narrative repertoires or tropes are more legitimate than others. As socialized beings, narrators both intentionally and unconsciously tend to reproduce these repertoires. They do so in the oppositions, repetitions, selective attention to details and other rhetorical traits of their stories. Hence, narrative aspects of life-stories can be interpreted as reflecting and constructing the association of individuals to social groups, or their social identities. To be sure, people refer to repertoires in idiosyncratic ways. This individuality is an evident consequence of the fact that they are always 'nodes in a web', that is, connected to more than one social group. As such, people simultaneously nurture gender, ethnic, class, religious and other identities, both actual and historical.[7]

The example of Elza's story clarifies concretely how relevant it is to take not only the descriptive, but also the narrative dimension into account when studying (urban) identities. Elza offered two kinds of data when she recounted:

> *They* came for a saucepan, a plate, a spoon, a fork. I then repeated it [the word in their language], *they* looked up then. And eh yes, *they* felt directly a bit at home then. Oh I have had good times in the shop, I soon had strangers as clients and it all went very well.[8]

The fact that the shopkeeper had immigrants as clients and the explicit description of her attitude ('all went very well') are relevant data. At the same time, however, the repetition of 'they' and the use of 'strangers' represent interesting narrative data. The repetition of the pronouns and the anonymous label 'strangers' depersonalize the customers of immigrant background. Apparently their proper names were not relevant to the shopkeeper's construction of the past. The confrontation of the descriptive dimension of this fragment with the narrative elements and the subsequent comparison of this testimony with those of other shopkeepers, revealed the social distance between prestigious native shopkeepers and immigrants. The narrative elements helped especially to interpret this interaction pattern as 'distant friendliness' or a friendly interaction in which ethnic and class hierarchies were nevertheless confirmed, not weakened.[9]

---

[7] E. Tonkin, *Narrating Our Pasts. The Social Construction of Oral History* (Cambridge 1992). On legitimate repertoires, see also P. Antze and M. Lambek, 'Introduction. Forecasting memory', in P. Antze and M. Lambek (eds), *Tense Past. Cultural Essays in Trauma and Memory* (New York 1996), xi–xxxviii.

[8] Some words in this and other fragments have been italicized to illustrate the argument, not to indicate an original emphasis.

[9] L. Beyers, 'Everyone black? Ethnic, class and gender identities at street level in a Belgian mining town, 1930–50', in S. Berger, A. Croll and N. Laporte

For those who are less convinced that memories and their narrative features are relevant for the understanding of past identities, two points are worth stressing. First, there is only an apparent contradiction between paying attention to how the past is narrated and the assumption that oral sources reveal how the past really was, which is the general assumption behind any content analysis. In fact, narrative aspects are an element of bias when one looks for real facts, but they are revealing for the equally real phenomenon of identification. While theoretical debates in the social sciences have led to the juxtaposition of these two approaches, in empirical studies they often complement the understanding.[10] Second, there are good reasons to assume that life-stories refer to both contemporary and older identities. As noted previously, people are 'nodes in a web', connected to the present, but also to the past. The experience of 'I' is exactly based on the ability to relate to past repertoires and identities. Consequently, while life-stories are no doubt coloured by the present, including the interview context, they are as much shaped by the past.[11]

Thus, drawing attention to both the descriptive and the narrative dimension of oral sources strengthens each of the two approaches. It adds to the critical triangulation or 'cross-analysis' of data. On the one hand, a keen understanding of the way life-stories are indebted to narrative repertoires makes the researcher aware that even seemingly very accurate descriptions of facts in testimonies, as, for instance, general professional data, are narratively modelled. Narrative aspects convey in that sense the bias of factual accounts. On the other hand, narrative aspects need to be confronted with factual and other descriptive data, not to check factual truth but to find out with which particular social contexts in the present or the past they are associated.[12]

For example, without a sound knowledge of the economic and social evolutions in Limburg, it is impossible to grasp the contextual meaning of

---

(eds), *Towards a Comparative History of Coalfield Societies* (Aldershot 2005), 151 and 155.

[10] About the combination of these two dimensions, descriptive versus discursive, see, for instance, D. Silverman, *Interpreting Qualitative Data. Methods for Analyzing Talk, Text and Interaction* (London 2001), 98–101; J. Giles, *Women, Identity and Private Life in Britain, 1900–50* (New York 1995) 20–27; M. Chanfrault-Duchet, 'Narrative structures, social models and symbolic representation in the life story', in S. Berger Gluck and D. Patai (eds), *Women's Words: the Feminist Practice of Oral History* (New York 1991), 78–9; E. Morawska, *Insecure Prosperity. Small-Town Jews in Industrial America, 1890–1940* (Princeton 1996), 258 and 357–58.

[11] See also A. Portelli, 'The peculiarities of oral history', *History Workshop Journal*, 12, 1981, 102–3; Giles, *Women*, 25.

[12] See also P. Thompson, *The Voice of the Past. Oral History* (Oxford 2001), 270–72. Thompson calls this the reconstructive cross-analysis. Since a complete reconstruction is impossible, I prefer the term historical cross-analysis.

terms of abuse. Life-stories suggested that in the 1920s and 1930s 'kompel' was a term of abuse for immigrants in the province. To understand how this work-related label functioned as a xenophobic label, similar to the German 'Kumpel', it is important to know that until the second half of the 1930s only a small proportion of the Flemish locals became underground miners. Mining was considered mean and rough and so were the Poles who filled the vacancies in the mining industry. In that particular context, immigrants were strongly stigmatized for the type of work they did.[13]

After highlighting the general relevance of a context-bound narrative analysis, attention is now directed to the specific context and genre of memories of the pluri-ethnic neighbourhood to exemplify this strategy. Methods of narrative analysis are difficult to generalize about because narrative repertoires are highly context-, time- and genre-specific. As the example of the terms of abuse illustrates, words in themselves do not reflect a social identity; they only get a social meaning due to the repeated association with other words, sentences and stories in a certain context and by certain speakers. As a consequence, the procedures of analysis depend to a considerable extent on the period studied, and also on the questions asked. Not only would a linguist develop a more detailed analysis than a historian, the points of interest also differ according to whether the subject studied is urban life or work relations. They furthermore depend on the text-genre under consideration. Incidentally, to acknowledge the narrative nature of life-stories the term 'narrative analysis' is preferred here instead of the broader term 'discursive analysis'.[14]

Three types of narrative analysis offer guidelines to unfolding urban memories so that the ethnic identity processes of city dwellers come to the fore. The main source of inspiration is discourse analytic studies focused on representations of the self and the others, and in particular, those on the language of racism. Not all of them, however, apply to the setting of the neighbourhood or to the genre of the life-story. So, secondly, anthropological work on the sense of place and, thirdly, writings on representations of the past provide additional insights in ethnic identity construction, specific to narratives of ethnically diverse neighbourhoods.

---

13 See Beyers, 'Everyone black?', 156.

14 'Discourse' is often used in a very broad sense, referring to the construction of meaning in all kinds of texts, as well as in institutions and practices. On the context- and genre-specificity of discourses, see D. Maingueneau, *Nouvelles Tendances en Analyse du Discours* (Paris 1987), 97–100; D. Fairclough, *Discourse and Social Change* (Cambridge 1992), 185–190; M. Wetherell and J. Potter, *Mapping the Language of Racism. Discourse and the Legitimation of Exploitation* (New York 1992), 90–93.

The 'others' of the town

With regard to the representation of ethnic others and the language of racism, critical discourse analysis and social psychological discourse analysis offer especially valuable insights. A general observation of these discourse analysts is that, in language, social distinctions tend to come in the form of positive representations of the self and opposite representations of the others.[15] This 'othering' can happen in an explicit way, first by using words and metaphors that contain evaluations of social groups; second, by literally contrasting groups; third, by using active and passive language; and fourth, constructions that prioritize the selection of certain information and privilege specific causal explanations. Each of these elements of 'othering' is considered below.

First, when negative labels and metaphors concerning other ethnic groups are used in life-stories, often this happens with considerable hesitance, as Teun van Dijk also observed.[16] The positive self-representation projected in the presence of an interviewer who does not belong to the same social group is a tolerant and polite one. When researching ethnic distinctions, negative labels or terms of abuse pop up far more easily in anecdotes than in direct answers. It is, thus, interesting and more discrete for an interviewer to ask for stories before asking for straight opinions. Moreover, this invites narrators to give a more detailed account of the context in which the negative labels make sense.

The inhabitants of the mining towns, for instance, frequently stated that 'they were not racists, but ...' or 'that in the mine everyone was black, but ...'. It was even difficult to make native Limburgers talk directly about the terms of abuse, such as the label 'kompel', that they used sixty years ago for the first East European immigrants. These only came to the surface in detailed anecdotes of those former newcomers on their interactions in the mine. Negative labels also tended to arise in a reverse way, by representing one of the 'others' as the good exception. For instance, established inhabitants actually emphasized the exceptionality of Turkish neighbours whose children pursued higher studies or whose house was clean.[17]

The second category of 'othering' relates to contrasting groups directly. Literally contrasting 'we' and 'them' is something tellers do far more spontaneously because it is a way to define themselves. In fact, social identity, or the definition of who 'we' are, is always constructed vis-à-vis

---

[15] See T. van Dijk, *Communicating Racism. Ethnic Prejudice in Thought and Talk* (London 1987), 385–9; T. van Dijk, 'Principles of critical discourse analysis', *Discourse and Society*, 4, 1993, 263–5.

[16] van Dijk, *Communicating*, 386–8.

[17] Beyers, 'Everyone black?', 156; Interviews for Beyers, 'Iedereen Zwart?'.

others. Similarly, the 'self' is constituted simultaneously in terms of similarity with some people, some 'we', and in terms of difference with other people, with 'they'.[18] 'They' is then a group of people having opposite, and often inferior, characteristics. The explicit mentioning of pronouns as 'they', 'them' or 'those ones' reinforces the distinction, as it depersonalizes the others. Incidentally, it is very useful to encourage people to talk about the differences between themselves and others because the comparison with others is an everyday practice. In contrast, it is far less evident for people to formulate an opinion about others immediately.[19]

An opposition is, for instance, present in the following statement of a Polish miner's daughter. Her mother, living in Genk in the 1930s and 1940s, did not know Dutch, the native language. Also the post-war Italian immigrants of the first generation never really learned to speak Dutch. However, the similar histories result in her drawing only a weak comparison with the Italians:

> My father spoke Dutch very well, my mother didn't. That's just like the Italian people today. The Polish people wanted that. But the Italians, some of *them*, *they* have lived here for so many years, but *they* refuse to speak it. *They* do not want it eh!

Immediately after connecting Polish and Italian people in this way, she contrasted them and referred to the mainstream narrative of Poles about Italians. This narrative emphasizes that 'they', the Italians, adapted less quickly to Belgian society than 'we', the Poles. It was a way for Polish people to distinguish themselves from the later newcomers. In fact, a Polish association with the Italians threatened their own status because they were not yet fully established immigrants themselves. In a similar way, Italians nowadays tend to counter all possible associations with the later Turkish newcomers.[20] Interestingly the distinction between Poles and Italians, dating back to the 1940s, remains vital to the Polish second generation that grew up in the 1940s, though it is much more traceable in the narrative aspects of their life-stories than in the general content.

A third important narrative strategy of self-representation and 'othering' is the use of active and passive verbs and words indicating an active role or a victim's role. For example, the explicit and repeated mentioning of 'I', or rather the use of 'we' instead of 'I', is often significant. Passive constructions

---

[18] See the instructive work of R. Jenkins, *Social Identity* (London 1996).

[19] See van Dijk, *Communicating*, 388–9; V. Mottier, 'Narratives of national identity: sexuality, race and the Swiss dream of order', *Swiss Journal of Sociology*, 26, 2000, 538–41; Wetherell and Potter, *Mapping*, 95.

[20] On these efforts of the least 'established' who have not much more power than the real 'outsiders', see Elias, 'A Theoretical Essay'.

tend to obscure responsibility or causes while active constructions can underpin heroic stories or underline the guilt of a particular group or individual.[21] Italian miners' sons who grew up in the towns in the 1960s and 1970s had a remarkably heroic style of storytelling. Two of them, Salvatore and Claudio, told a series of heroic anecdotes about the peer group of which they were a part in their adolescence. One of their peers worked in a service station.

> Salvatore: Yes, he took the cars of the clients and then we set out.
> Claudio: And then in the evening driving through gardens and things like that …
> Salvatore: We all in the car eh. Small streets, but he could drive very well, S. He raised the handbrake. Then he often turned 3–4 pirouettes. Really spin-off. And suddenly, caramel! The car crashed against a tree! [exclamations]

Not only what Salvatore, Claudio and their peers did, but also the way they re-told it, reflects the particular challenges and pride that the peer group offered. The exclamations and their use of words also bring to the fore how those challenges did not fit with the norms of the mainstream society. The fact that Salvatore and Claudio told the story of their peer group together incited them especially to this heroic style. On another occasion, Salvatore had also recounted an episode about his youth, though on this occasion it was not only in my presence, but also that of his mother, which made him disguise far more of the petty crime. While neither of the interview settings led to an accurate factual account of their criminal past, the first interview setting was certainly more appropriate to bring the patterns of pride within the peer group to the fore.

Some background information is needed to interpret this heroic tone. Actually, the Mediterranean family culture incited Italian boys to take up active roles in the public sphere, while their sisters were expected to play a passive role with regard to the family honour. The structure of education within Limburg, which provided mining schools for working-class boys and domestic science schools for girls, fitted quite neatly with this gender pattern. The mines, however, did not offer sufficient challenges to Italian boys, since due to the coal crisis and the generalization of secondary and higher education in the 1970s, it became second class to have only a vocational training and to become a miner. Moreover, immigrants' sons suffered from ethnocentrism, especially when, active as they were, they discovered the world outside the mining towns. Consequently, Italian boys with short

---

[21] On agency in language see Fairclough, *Discourse*, 235–6; Thompson, *The Voice*, 277 and 279.

school careers tended to nest within their own peer group, which developed an oppositional culture and discouraged them from taking part in activities with a native cachet.[22]

A fourth rhetoric element of 'othering' concerns the causal frames that people deploy to order information about others. Causal explanations often entail generalizations of the other's negative qualities and inversely individualizations of one's own negative properties as well as the unilateral association of a social group with one problem.[23] For example, post-war Italian immigrants were largely labelled as unsatisfactory workers by the established population in the Limburg mining basin. Interestingly, Italian underground miners were always hired for jobs at the lowest level, such as quarrying. Miners of Flemish or Polish origin who did similar heavy and dirty work had equally high levels of absenteeism. Nevertheless, this was perceived as an Italian problem, not as a Flemish or Polish one, as Flemings and Poles were also present in the higher ranks of the mine. One former native miner for instance stated that 'it were the Italians that ruined the mines.'[24]

Another common way to explain away things is by representing them as natural, and this naturalization is an especially strong rhetorical device to construct gender differences. With regard to ethnic distinctions, it is actually deployed less. However, culturalization is almost as strong a vehicle to construct ethnic differences. In general, since the holocaust, 'culture' has become a more legitimate concept than 'race' when discussing migration. In Belgium, the discourse of 'culture' came to dominate the debate on immigration particularly in the 1980s when cultural anthropologists largely contributed to the information on immigrants. Moreover, since legal labour immigration ceased in 1974, the interest in immigrant (non)adaptation increased, while previously an economic focus on immigration was predominant. Also in the Limburg mining towns, the discourse of 'culture' strengthens the ethnic boundaries between the Turkish working class and the established inhabitants nowadays. In fact, cultural issues have replaced the work-related issues that divided insiders and outsiders at the time of the Italian immigration.[25]

---

[22] L. Beyers, 'Trajectoires et identités italiennes dans la région minière limbourgeoise (années 1940–1970)', in M. Dumoulin (ed.), *L'Italie et la Belgique en Europe depuis 1918* (Rome forthcoming).

[23] See van Dijk, 'Principles', 263–5.

[24] Interviews for Beyers, 'Iedereen zwart?'. On the absenteeism of Italians and others in the lowest ranks, see De Rijck, *De ereburgers,* 176–8 and 183–5.

[25] K. Malik, *The Meaning of Race. Race, History and Culture in Western Society* (London 1996), 140–77. V. Stolcke, 'Talking culture: new boundaries, new rhetorics of exclusion in Europe', *Current Anthropology*, 36, 1995, 1–24. On Belgium see J. Blommaert, *Debating Diversity: Analysing the Discourse of Tolerance* (London 1998), 29 and 91–101; Interviews Beyers, 'Iedereen zwart?'.

Selecting information, therefore, and thus privileging certain casual explanations is a major element in representing others as different. Selective information involves excessive description or repeatedly returning to a topic.[26] Detailed transcriptions, therefore, are absolutely essential in order to discern patterns of selective information because transcriptions in which all silences, repetitions and other, at first sight, seemingly irrelevant details are summarized, do not reflect the selectivity of the interviewee any longer.[27]

An interesting example of selective information comes from the testimony of a Belgian engineer living in one of the mining towns. It was very important for him to indicate that he was not a snob and to distinguish himself from the other, in his eyes, more elitist engineers. He started by telling about how many people with whom he and his wife were on good terms had died recently. Other interviewees who were in their eighties made similar nostalgic remarks. Surprisingly, for the engineer this was just a vehicle to start talking about his preferred subject. He proceeded with:

> Yeah oh yes. I never have ... That mentality, that mentality, I never have supported that very well. It was awful yeah. I know in those days, *I haven't told you that yet*, the post office was here yeah. And when I started working, the head of our department was Benoit ...[28]

After this a long anecdote followed on how he openly criticized the wife of Benoit in the post office for the fact she did not wait her turn, as if she did not need to as the wife of a department's head. The 'I haven't told you that yet' and the fact that he repeatedly came back to the subject contributed to my understanding of the primary importance of upper class and company identities for the engineers. The weight of these identities explains why their ethnic distinctions vis-à-vis immigrants were less pronounced than those of the native working class.

---

[26] Of course, in a broader sense, causal explanations, active-passive representations and we-them contrasts are also a matter of selective information. See D. Fairclough, *Language and Power* (London 1989), 115; van Dijk, 'Principles', 264; Wetherell and Potter, *Mapping*, 95.

[27] See Taylor, 'Locating and conducting discourse analytic research', in M. Wetherell, S. Taylor and S.J. Yates (eds), *Discourse as Data: a Guide for Analysis* (London 2001), 24–38; Fairclough, *Discourse*, 229–230.

[28] Interview for Beyers, 'Iedereen zwart?'.

'A proper house': dividing space

When analysing oral testimonies concerning the evolution of ethnic identities in neighbourhoods, not only constructions of the self and others should be problematized, but so should the ways places are delimited and described. Memories of place deserve particular attention because dividing space is one way in which city dwellers construct social boundaries between themselves and their neighbours. Actually, in urban history, places have predictably been approached in geographical terms, as fixed points on a map where some kind of economic and social activity intersect. It is, however, highly revealing to consider places and maps as always under construction and as embedded in social dynamics, as social scientists have shown in the last decades.[29]

In fact, places are always shaped by, as well as conditioning, social boundaries.[30] On the one hand, the division of space into meaningful places, into a concrete urban landscape, is the result of ever-evolving social processes of power and identity. For the Limburg mining towns, which were erected by the mining companies in the 1920s, this is strikingly obvious. For example, the monumental churches in the mining towns reflected the efforts of the companies to impress the catholic, rural province that did not welcome the new industry. Furthermore, street names in the mining towns refer to the first executive staff. The companies thus did not just built the towns, but also 'signed' them, so as to create a corporate identity.

On the other hand, the spatial order thereby produced is also instrumental with reference to social relations and identities of its dwellers. It limits not just where people go and who they meet, but also offers vehicles for social identities and boundaries. That is what happens, for example, when street names become social labels or, otherwise placed, when they become significant points on people's 'mental maps'. As such, the 'Place de Cockerill' in the mining town Zwartberg referred first of all to the parent company, the steel enterprise 'John Cockerill'. Subsequently, it became a label for the upper-middle class, which was allocated to that area by the mine. Then, immigrant children who lived opposite started to distinguish themselves from 'those of Place Cockerill'. Incidentally, the (re)production of space

---

[29] Actually, attempts to theorize globalization have heightened this awareness. See for instance D. Massey, *Space, Place and Gender* (Minneapolis 1994); A. Appadurai, 'Global ethnoscapes: Notes and queries for a transnational anthropology', in R. Fox (ed.), *Recapturing Anthropology: Working in the Present* (Santa Fe 1991), 191–210; S. Feld and K. Basso, *Senses of Place* (Santa Fe 1996); N. Lovell, *Locality and Belonging* (London 1998).

[30] This understanding of space refers, in the works of the above mentioned authors, to the definition of space given by H.Lefebvre, *La Production de l'Espace* (Paris 1974).

continues when such positive or negative labels attract specific types of building projects.[31]

When spaces turn into vehicles of social identification, memory and history are often at play. Memories help to tie people to places and in that way to tie them together, into communities in fact. As Nadia Lovell states: 'Belonging may thus be seen as remembering, instrumental in the construction of collective memory surrounding place'.[32] Two narrative aspects of testimonies of place refer specifically to mental maps. First of all, the use of places as metaphors or labels for 'we' and 'them' is indicative. Often these metaphors are part of a second notable rhetorical feature, that is, the opposition of 'here' and 'there'. When people reflect their belonging to places in their narratives, they easily imagine it in oppositional terms, as they do when they talk about 'we' and 'them'. Actually, the opposition of 'here' and 'there' parallels and reinforces the opposition between 'we' and 'them'. As stated above, asking for differences between places and people is thus a very fruitful way to encourage people to talk about their belonging to one group and one place.[33]

The social meaning of contrasting 'here' and 'there' became very clear when interviewees evaluated the different types of housing the Limburg mining companies provided. While from the 1920s until the 1940s, the seven mining companies offered rented houses to their personnel, from the 1950s onwards the governmental and company housing policies focused on home ownership by granting miners low mortgage interest.[34] One of the quarters with owner-occupied houses for the working and the middle class, built at the beginning of the 1960s, clearly evolved into a metaphor of progress, of social mobility. Conversely, the old mining town started to be perceived as just the opposite, as a place for backward people.

---

[31] For these examples, see Beyers, 'Iedereen zwart?'. For other interesting examples, see L. Taksa, 'Like a bicycle, forever teetering between individualism and collectivism. Considering community in relation to labour history', *Labour History*, 78, 2000, 14 and 21–3. On mental maps see also: K. Scherzer, *The Unbounded Community. Neighborhood Life and Social Structure in New York City, 1830–1875* (Durham NC 1992), 137–60. See also the chapter by Maria Raluca Popa in this volume.

[32] N. Lovell, 'Belonging in need of emplacement?', in N. Lovell (ed.), *Locality and Belonging* (London1998), 1. Naturally, not only memories, but also bodily practices and other cultural dynamics tie people to places. See also the chapter by Verônica Sales Periera in this volume.

[33] See T. Blokland, *Urban Bonds. Social Relationships in an Inner City Neighbourhood* (Cambridge 2003), and with regard to memory especially pp. 191–207.

[34] On the housing policies see G. Dejongh, and P. Van Windekens, *Van Kleine Landeigendom tot Vlaamse Landmaatschappij. Vijvenzestig jaar werking op het Vlaamse platteland 1935–2001* (Brussels 2002).

When asked to explain the differences between the new quarter and the old mining town, also called the 'cité', one man said:

> First of all, having a proper house and this at a reasonable price, an affordable price. And everyone took care that his children, how should I say, [everyone took] the right way ... If I compare this with my father, they wanted to move on. And in the cités it has all remained the same ...

In the end, he concluded:

> While *there*, let's say, *they* run more in the street and they are children of the street. And *those* youngsters who then [have] eighteen, nineteen or fifteen, sixteen, they'd live on the street. While *our* children, they also are in the street, but *they* also lived inside.[35]

This fragment illustrates well how memories and stories tie social groups to places, and, at the same time, tie them together. Apart from the oppositions between 'here' and 'there' and 'we' and 'them', the use of 'and' is very significant in this testimony. The 'and everyone took care' is where having a proper house becomes connected to the social identity of doing things 'the right way'. Actually, these narratives not just reproduced the spatial hierarchy conceived by the mines; they actively magnified that spatial order long after the mines had disposed of their housing stock as a response to the coal crisis in the 1960s.

'In the old days it was better': dividing time

The ways of drawing distinctions between peoples and places outlined above are present in oral testimonies as well in other textual genres. When considering them, it is relevant to keep in mind that oral testimonies have a truly narrative structure. Like stories, they tend to have a beginning, an ending, crucial turning points and one or more plots. These elements impose order on the flow of experiences of people and enable them to make sense of the past. A rigid analysis of all narrative forms, such as all minor plots, might be unprofitable, especially if other discursive elements are already taken into account.[36] It is, however, of interest to look at how people order the flow of experiences in their testimonies by dividing time, as life-stories are more than just textual genres heavily concerned with the past.

---

35 Interview for Beyers, 'Iedereen zwart?'.

36 In this I follow less the formal analysis of Caroline Kohler Riessman than the more general analysis of Ken Plummer. See P. Thompson, *The Voice*, 279–86; K. Plummer, *Telling Sexual Stories. Power, Change and Social Worlds* (London 1995).

Studies of life-stories inform us that tellers not only distinguish phases in their lives but also tend to represent their lives as consistent time flows and possibly as a linear progression or linear decay, or as a continuous struggle starting from a certain moment. In this regard, it is relevant to look at what people consider as the decisive turning points in their own life or in their environment. Interestingly, some people will perceive none or very few turning points and have difficulties when they talk about their own 'history', as Maria Minicuci observed for a southern Italian village.[37] Furthermore, contrasting now and then and idealizing the past is a very common way to divide time. For example, in the Limburg mining towns the past is strongly idealized and a linear decay since the arrival of the latest newcomers is perceived:

> You had more Turks, Italians, Greeks and Spaniards, that was a later generation then. But up until the Spanish people, all went quite well, that was *still* European, but then the Moroccans and the Turks came and that was another sphere of influence. And I say, *then* it was not so funny to live there anymore.[38]

These idealizations of the past are first of all shaped by actual circumstances. They clearly reflect actual ethnic distinctions. Until the 1960s, most inhabitants of the mining towns were indeed of European origin. At that time, however, this common ground did not assist the formation of a collective identity. Instead, established inhabitants distinguished East European and Italian immigrants from themselves on the basis of their sensuality, laziness, criminality, immorality and communism. Indeed, only when they were asked for very detailed accounts of interactions between neighbours in the past, did informants reveal those former ethnic tensions and referred less to their actual identities.[39]

In fact, idealizations of the past might be especially typical for oral testimonies on ethnically diverse neighbourhoods for two reasons. First, they are a general feature of the memories of previous migration waves. After four or five decades, when the descendants of immigrants have had opportunities to develop economic mobility and a wave of new immigrants are considered as the real 'outsiders', ethnic distinctions have often been weakened. This process incites natives and established people of immigrant descent to construct their past as common and to obscure their former ethnic

---

[37] See M. Minicuci, 'Time and memory. Two villages in Calabria' in D. Hughes and T. Trautmann (eds), *Time: Histories and Ethnologies* (Ann Arbor 1995), 71–104; A. Portelli, '"The time of my life". Functions of time in oral history'. *International Journal of Oral History*, 2, 1981, 162–80; Thompson, *The Voice*, 274–5.

[38] Interview for Beyers, 'Iedereen zwart?'.

[39] Beyers, 'Iedereen zwart?'.

tensions. The inter-ethnic interactions of the past may be idealized or just forgotten altogether. While the idealization of the 'old immigration' is typical for American national memory, the more nationally oriented historiography in Europe suffers from the latter.[40]

Secondly, past neighbourhood life is also often idealized. Local ties in former periods are easily perceived as convivial and cohesive. Moreover, the word 'community' in common usage has a strong local connotation. Probably, this narrative repertoire is rooted in the political and public impact of late-nineteenth century sociological theories on modern social life. Amongst others, Ferdinand Tönnies and Emile Durkheim predicted the decline of 'organic' solidarity on the local level and the evolution towards a rational, 'mechanical' solidarity on a higher level. Their predictions of the decline of local solidarity have especially convinced a wide audience.[41]

The 'in the old days it was better' repertoire was very much present in the testimonies of the dwellers of the mining towns. They needed nothing more than the open question of how neighbourhood life was before, and sometimes just the word 'neighbourhood life', to refer to it. For instance, one Flemish man who grew up in a mining town in the 1940s and 1950s mentioned: 'Everyone helped everyone. And in the summer when the weather was nice, the whole street was full, until eleven o'clock, half past eleven'. More important for the analysis of ethnic boundaries was that lonely, elderly native inhabitants tended to inter-mingle the two idealizing narrative repertoires on neighbourhood life in the past and on previous immigration waves, and to voice their discontent with the recent immigration. They represented the past neighbourhood as 'one family thing' or 'one bond', with 'more Catholic people' or 'only Belgians'. Interestingly, when stating this, they really seem to forget how half their neighbours had always been of immigrant background and how they interacted with Polish and Italian newcomers in the past.[42]

Concluding thoughts: imagined boundaries and their history

Even in such a relatively small area as the Limburg mining towns, the different ethnic communities and the boundaries between them existed most of all because they were imagined as such. The people of Flemish

---

40 On the different ways of perceiving and writing migration history in America and Europe see L. Lucassen, 'Old and new migrants in the twentieth century: A European perspective', *Journal of American Ethnic History*, 21, 2002, 85–101.

41 See P. Thompson, *The Voice*, 152 and 229; Blokland, *Urban Bonds*, 1–10; J. Bourke, *Working class cultures in Britain, 1890–1960. Gender, Class and Ethnicity* (London, 1994), 137–8.

42 Interviews for Beyers, 'Iedereen zwart?'.

descent, for instance, perceived themselves as a group, but far from every Fleming knew every Fleming by name. To a lesser degree, this was even the case for the 100 or so Greeks in each of the towns, who did not even know all of the other Greeks' children. As this chapter shows, an important way in which inhabitants imagined and related to their communities was through constructing their past as part of a common past and by referring to common narrative repertoires.[43] These repertoires imply metaphors of 'we' and 'them', frames of agency and causes, a preference for topics as well as common divisions of space and time. Furthermore, the chapter has pointed to how life-stories reflect both actual and past identities and how, if triangulated with other data, they help to reveal the evolution of ethnic boundaries.

While linguists and others learn how to read life-stories as discourses, historians might have the particular task to relate narrative aspects to the specific contexts and periods in which they originate. Pioneers in the field of oral history have strongly emphasized that oral testimonies were not so much windows to the facts of the past, as traditional historicists evaluated them, but 'subjective' accounts having a value precisely because of their subjectivity.[44] 'Subjective' constructions of the past however have a history. They are produced and reproduced in particular past and actual contexts. Only a cross-analysis of descriptive and narrative data and of oral testimonies with other sources can unravel these production processes. It would probably be interesting for the debate on the value of oral sources to recognize that more explicitly.[45]

Let me underscore this argument with one final example from the mining towns. A ruling narrative repertoire in Limburg nowadays is the argument that 'in the mine everyone was black'. This is a way of stating that because miners had to co-operate across ethnic boundaries, and because of the dangerous work in the pits, the people in Limburg were and are still ethnically tolerant. Interestingly, this repertoire appears much older than it is. While it seems to have originated in the blooming period of the Limburg mining

---

[43] Benedict Anderson's 'imagined communities' is another useful concept to clarify how oral testimonies are social constructions. See B. Anderson, *Imagined Communities. Reflections on the Origin and Spread of Nationalism* (London 1990); Tonkin, *Narrating 'our' pasts*.

[44] Two famous examples are A. Passerini, 'Work ideology' and A. Portelli, 'The peculiarities'.

[45] Thompson makes interesting, if short, statements on this issue: Thompson, *The Voice*, 272. Also Portelli, while comparing oral and other data in his well-known interpretation of the stories surrounding the death of Luigi Trastulli, was more interested in distinguishing memories and facts instead of explicitly relating memories to wider contexts: A. Portelli, *The Death of Luigi Trastulli and Other Stories. Form and Meaning in Oral History* (Albany 1991).

industry, it became important mostly after the pit closures in the 1980s. In the same decade, the rise of the extreme right party in Flanders, Vlaams Blok, took off in the city of Antwerp. In fact, the story that in the mine everyone was black is most of all real in its consequences. It underpins the tolerance in Limburg nowadays because it offers the region a tool to distinguish itself from the Antwerp region. Meanwhile, the cross-analysis of different types of sources indicates that miners indeed displayed solidarity in the face of danger, but that this solidarity in itself was not enough to erase ethnic distinctions. Instead, only after three generations were immigrants' descendants perceived as 'integrated', most of all because they finally had opportunities for economic mobility and because of the arrival of new 'outsiders'.[46]

Further reading

Antze, P. and M. Lambek, 'Introduction. Forecasting memory', in P. Antze and M. Lambek (eds), *Tense Past. Cultural Essays in Trauma and Memory* (New York 1996), xi–xxxviii.

Beyers, L., 'Everyone black? Ethnic, class and gender identities at street level in a Belgian mining town, 1930–50', in S. Berger, A. Croll and N. Laporte (eds), *Towards a Comparative History of Coalfield Societies* (Aldershot 2005), 146–63.

Blokland, T., *Urban Bonds. Social Relationships in an Inner City Neighbourhood* (London 2003).

Chanfrault-Duchet, M., 'Narrative structures, social models and symbolic representation in the life story', in S. Gluck and D. Patai (eds), *Women's Words: the Feminist Practice of Oral History* (London 1991) 77–92.

Elias, N., 'Introduction: a theoretical essay on the established and the outsiders', in N. Elias and J.L. Scotson (eds), *The Established and the Outsiders: A Sociological Enquiry into Community Problems* (London 1994), 15–52.

Fairclough, N., *Discourse and Social Change* (Cambridge 1992).

Lovell, N., 'Belonging in need of emplacement?', in N. Lovell (ed.), *Locality and Belonging* (London 1998), 1–24.

Maingueneau, D., *Nouvelles Tendances en Analyse du Discours* (Paris 1987).

Minicuci, M., 'Time and memory. Two villages in Calabria', in D.O. Hughes and T.R. Trautmann (eds), *Time: Histories and Ethnologies* (Ann Arbor 1995), 71–104.

[46] Beyers, 'Iedereen zwart?'.

Portelli, A., 'The peculiarities of oral history', *History Workshop Journal*, 12, 1981, 96–107.

Taksa, L., 'Like a bicycle, forever teetering between individualism and collectivism: considering community in relation to labour history', *Labour History: A Journal of Labour and Social History*, LXXVIII (2000), 7–32.

Thompson, P., *The Voice of the Past. Oral History* (Oxford 2001).

Tonkin, E., *Narrating Our Pasts: the Social Construction of Oral History* (Cambridge 1992).

van Dijk, T., *Communicating Racism. Ethnic Prejudice in Thought and Talk* (London 1987).

Wetherell, M. and J. Potter, *Mapping the Language of Racism. Discourse and the Legitimation of Exploitation* (New York 1992).

CHAPTER SEVEN

Rhythms, rituals and routines in inter-war Paris: a sensitive experience of urban history

Caroline Varlet

Constructing the memory of the city consists of recalling in the present the state of the urban past. To conserve and to trace these memories and to insert them into the contexts of the city's evolution allows us to reach the level of the individual and the ordinariness of life. As a consequence, it is possible to shed light on that which is so often eclipsed by exceptional events: to hear the testimonies of those who are rarely given a voice. These testimonies make possible the construction of the memory of ordinary places, of practices in these ordinary places, the memory of the daily rhythms, patterns and geographies that themselves were part of city living, differentiated according to occupations, familial and social status. It is such evocations of the past that convey the essence of the city. By cross-referencing sources and the discourses employed by the use of witnesses, multiple prespectives are revealed that are essential to an understanding of a social world and an urban context. It is within this framework that the evocative testimonies of Parisians and their daily existence between 1919 and 1939 are presented.

The banality of ordinary life is the principal objective in the analysis presented in this chapter, which seeks to document what comprized the daily life of ordinary people in the city at the beginning of the twentieth century. These ordinary people, sometimes described as 'little people', are those anchored in their daily existence by an occupation, and, consequently, by the income that this work procures. It is, therefore, about labourers and specialized workers, the army of employees in the private and public sectors whose employment imposed the strict observance of schedules and a regular attendance at their place of work. They were, therefore, neither the most underpaid, with their tenuous hold on life itself, and, consequently, with unstructured daily lives, nor the elite who, as self-employed professionals, managed their own work schedule, controlling and organizing it at their convenience. It is also not about mundane rhythms of bourgeois socialites, particularly the women's, with their daily visitations and dense schedule of choreographed social activities.[1]

These questions of rhythms, rituals and routines were approached using accounts given by Parisians who had lived in the capital between the two world wars as young adults or as children. These accounts were in free-form, provided by the witnesses themselves within the framework of a general call to Parisian residents of this period, launched by the city authorities in 1993.[2] Of the 700 testimonies received by the city, a majority can be classified in the *ordinary people* category, as defined above by income and occupational status. Even though memory proceeds by reconstruction, it is these retrospective accounts that are described and analysed, and which reveal how individuals constructed their lives in the 1920s and 1930s. They also serve as a sharp reminder about styles of life and behaviour that different signfiicantly from the decade in which they were related, the 1990s.

The unit of observation is the family home; the scale of analysis is of daily domestic activities. By reconstructing patterns of behaviour, each person within the simple familial unit is shown to have different profiles. By following each person from morning to night, the various activities show structured, constrained and temporal characteristics as their memories and perceptions are recovered in their accounts. However distorted by the passage of time, these commentaries by Parisians are saturated with indicators of the mundane activities of their urban everyday existence.[3] Nonetheless, they reveal patterns and attitudes that are otherwise difficult to uncover.

Two aspects are particularly evoked: firstly, the elements of the daily life of the families in the city, with particular reference to living conditions and the practical organization of the home; secondly, the elements that articulate life in the city, in particular the rhythms of existence and the perceptions of

---

[1] See, for example, A. Martin-Fugier, *La bourgeoisie* (Paris 1983).

[2] *La Mémoire de Paris, 1919–1939*, Bibliothèque Historique de la Ville de Paris (BHVP) consists of an appeal to inhabitants who lived in Paris between 1919 and 1939 for testimonies of that era and was issued in 1993 by the social services department of Paris City Council [Bureau d'Aide Sociale de la Ville de Paris]. The appeal for testimonies was made in newspapers and in radio broadcasts during the spring of 1993 and proposed an exhibition on everyday life in Paris between the two wars. During the summer of 1993, 1,078 written testimonies were collected and complemented by a series of interviews. This collection of photographs and the random memories was intended to show the Parisians of today what kind of life their parents led through unremarkable activities and situations. The exhibition lasted from 9 December 1993 until 20 April 1994 in the City Hall, and thereafter the written testimonies were deposited in the Bibliothèque Historique de la Ville where they were consulted. Subsequent references to this material are abbreviated to BHVP.

[3] M. Halbwachs, *Les Cadres Sociaux de la Mémoire* (Paris 1994, edn 1925).

the urban space. The first aspect reveals respondents' capacity to recollect the ensemble of spaces, practices and representations, and the second is significant for what it shows of urban images tied to daily practice, from the extent of urban boundaries to the sharing of public space.

Living in the city

City life imposes particular forms of organization on ways of living, and this is heavily influenced by the distance between work and home, and living at high residential densities in communal buildings. The homes evoked in the testimonies are most often small lodgings of two rooms with a kitchen, in old buildings organized around a courtyard managed by the concierges, themselves housed in even smaller quarters. The amenities, that is to say, those elements of comfort such as running water, toilets, heating and lighting, remained mostly rudimentary in quality and limited in quantity.

Everyday comfort

Besides their often limited size, the Parisian homes situated in the buildings that date at least from the nineteenth century[4] and as described by the families of modest means, had precarious services and limited comfort.[5] According to the testimonies collected, carrying water into the home and the disposal of sewage were not insignificant activities – residents often had the use of one or the other, but rarely of both amenities. In the most rudimentary cases, residents had to descend into the building courtyard to obtain water from the stand-pipe installed there. Soiled water and human waste was manually transported in pails to the shared water closet on the landing and disposed of there.[6] Waste water was also disposed of in the street gutters. In the better class of housing, on one side of the apartment a sink in the kitchen area was equipped with a tap and a waste-pipe connected to the sewer; and on the other side of the apartment was a closet situated

---

[4] A. Daumard, *Maisons de Paris et Propriétaires Parisiens au XIXe siècle* (Paris 1965); César Daly, architect and director of the *Revue Générale de l'Architecture et des Travaux Publics*, published in 1864 *L'architecture privée au XIXe siècle sous Napoléon III* (Paris 1864), three volumes on housing one of which is dedicated to single-owner apartment buildings. A classification of three hierarchical categories, based on the criteria of construction quality, decoration, and also the ease of access and the existence of service stairs.

[5] Based on M. Perrot's criteria from *Le Mode de Vie des Familles Bourgeoises, 1873–1953* (Paris 1961).

[6] A single toilet facility on the landing for approximately every four apartments, and on the mezzanine landings, sometimes only one for every eight apartments, or eight families.

inside the home, and reserved exclusively as a toilet for inhabitants of the apartment.

In this domestic context of a limited water supply, cleanliness in the form of laundry and bathing were the principal problems confronting the inhabitants.[7] According to the residents' accounts, it was never possible to have a space exclusively reserved for personal hygiene, nor to have it installed as a fixture, let alone with hot water. A daily personal wash was accomplished in a sink of cold water, and weekly by various temporary means either using systems involving gas ranges to heat up water, or in basins for a small tub or a bath. Some residents preferred to tidy basins and tubs away and converted a closet without running water, ready for use when needed.

Daily hygiene was a ritual evoked in many of the testimonies. In front of a sink or a basin of cold water, and usually in a space adjoining the kitchen or the main room, each member of the household took her (or his) turn to bathe. This daily bathing ritual normally took place in the morning before eating a communal breakfast at the family table and before each person assumed their daily tasks at school, work or in the house. Superimposed on to this daily regime was a major weekly bathing ritual, an undertaking on a different scale to daily bathing. It differed not in its objective but in its realization: the chosen moment, the place, the form. The preparations demanded considerable time and careful preparation, and took place at a point in the week when the pressure of the work schedule was alleviated; initially this was on Sundays though, as free time increased, the ritual was often performed on Saturday afternoons. Times for the parents could differ from those for children.

As to where the weekly bathing ritual took place, there were two solutions available: either at home or at the municipal or private baths. At home, the tub or bath was removed from its normal position on the wall, positioned in the middle of the warmest room and filled with water pre-heated in a large boiler or container. Because there was no direct running water supply to the boiler, a considerable amount of time was devoted to these bathing operations: filling, carrying and emptying water was very labour intensive. As an alternative to this private bathing ritual, a visit to the municipal or private bath or shower involved the use of a shower cabin (rarely a bath), and often the hire of a towel and a quantity of soap. Longer, more detailed and more complete, this 'great' cleansing was accomplished as a prelude to wearing Sunday clothes, which were put on after emerging from the water.

As for laundry, evocative Parisian testimonies recall the wash house and the wash boiler. The latter, a nineteenth-century innovation before it was eventually replaced by an electrically powered version, was still very popular in the first third of the twentieth century. The use of the wash

[7] According to the testimonies, there were still home bath porters in 1909.

boiler, eventually replaced in the twentieth century by electrically heated boilers, reveals the difficulties of manipulating a large vessel full of water, boiling for several hours on the kitchen range and requiring the burdensome labour of refilling and emptying, as well as of managing a bucket under the sink to contain the overflow. The public wash house was an indispensable complement to the wash boiler, and housekeepers returned there once a week. An entire day was needed to do the laundry for a family of four to five people and once the washing 'cycle' had been completed and laid out, it was necessary to return the following day to collect the clothes that had been left to dry.

Traditionally, laundry was done on Mondays. But which laundry was this? Different systems and patterns depended on the family situation such as the presence of a baby, children, the sick or aged, and the financial resources of the household. The 'laundry' routine could thus vary considerably. For example, families might pass their laundry to external, industrial laundromats or to professional laundresses who picked up and brought back the clothes to the house in large canvas packages tied at the corner. This simplifed matters considerably. Labour intensive laundry activities were taken out of the home, at a price.

For those families in which laundry was done by the housekeeper herself, several options were available to her, determined by the categories of the wash: large pieces for the house (sheets and towels, items of work clothes), the 'little laundry' for smaller pieces of clothing, and the special laundry for the children. Rarely did the housekeeper undertake the entire operation from the home. It was difficult and arduous work involving the transport (carrying, filling and emptying) and heating of water in a wash boiler intended mostly for small items such as children's clothes (and nappies for the very young). In such instances, the 'laundry day' extended to several days, since drying clothes in the warmest room (the kitchen) involved hanging and folding stacks of laundry alongside cooking, the odours of which saturated the laundry.

In a second category of washday activity, the housekeeper organized everything, but used the facilities of a municipal or commercial public wash house to reduce her own labour. Again, she could divide the work, either doing it herself by carrying and washing it in a public wash house and then carrrying the wet laundry back home to dry, or alternatively, by having the larger pieces washed first on the communal paddles where all the customers' laundry soaked together, separated in numbered sacks. After her sack had been soaked all night, the actual wash took place and the housekeeper arrived to rinse and to scrub the large pre-washed pieces with the ordinary laundry that washed more easily. She could, as another option, rent a place at the dryer's and collect it the next day. Under these arrangements the housekeeper had to anticipate the preparations of pre-soaking and use part of the next day for the subsequent operations.[8] Whatever the case, the principle of the weekly Monday wash must be abandoned since this one day was insufficient to complete all the laundry operations: soaking, collecting, drying, ironing, folding and putting away.

This extended laundry work had an impact on other aspects of domestic organization. For example, the memory of a pot-au-feu stewing for hours without having to be watched was strongly associated in the memories of many Parisians with the ritual soaking of the domestic wash boiler. These associations of smells and sounds within the apartment were further features of respondents' memories. They recalled that the coal stove was generally found in the main room, the most central location, and one that opened on to the small kitchen. Heating was boosted by salamanders or portable stoves, and the kitchen itself was sometimes equipped with a range (without an oven) and in certain cases, a copper double-boiler to produce hot water, which, though in short supply, was constantly present. Heat, then, was generated from various sources, supplemented and eventually replaced by coin-operated gas meters and electricity to light the principal room. Extended laundry work in the years before 1939 was associated with warmth and condensation in the minds and memories of Parisians, and the pot-au-feu, prepared on the stove and then, as wash routines took over, abandoned to the *marmite norvégienne*, a type of crock-pot filled with insulating materials (rags and wood chips or sawdust) into which the pot containing the meat was placed to stew for hours.

Getting supplies

Non-work time was largely consumed by activities central to the maintenance of life itself, specifically obtaining supplies of water, fuel, and food. A supply of running water to the sink was far from standard. Thus, considerable labour was required to carry water-buckets and to empty toilets. Heating also required frequent trips to the basement as the coal supplied to basement cellars was cheaper because a supplement had to be paid to deliver coal upstairs.[9] These round-trips for water and coal were the responsibility of husbands and young children, and were undertaken each morning and evening at fixed and regular times determined by the family.

---

[8] There were also intermediate arrangements where large pieces of laundry were entrusted to the industrial wash houses or to professional laundry boutiques or even to the wash house while the housekeeper herself handled the rest of the laundry at the wash house or at home using the wash boiler.

[9] Naturally, there was more room for coal stocks in the basements than in the flats.

Food provision was another permanent feature of daily life. In reality, the impossibility of stocking food and limited household budgets constrained the housekeeper to go shopping daily and to make food, meal by meal, day by day.[10] There was no means of keeping products cold. Ice was intended for food conservation only in the summer; at other times, a perforated metal case called a 'garde-manger' [meat-safe] protected food, and the absence of ready-made products made meal preparation a laborious and exhausting task. Packaged food products were also very rare in the 1920s and 1930s. Consequently, there was a daily round, sometimes a twice-daily round, to merchants – one for each product. A large neighbourhood square was used for markets, which sold fresh local produce from the surrounding area, and fresh milk produced by the cows or goats living on Parisian farms were sold in bulk, with the customer bringing his or her own container.

Between 1900 and 1940, working hours were reduced from 60 to 40 per week by both the shortening of the working day and increasing leisure time at the weekend.[11] Free time increased and annual holidays also changed the rhythm of life, though not everybody left Paris to go on holiday as the cost of transport was often too high.[12] These structural changes in the pattern of work were the catalyst for an important reorganization of everyday life based on increasingly fragmented time, made up of many comings and goings to work, school and the shops. In particular, Parisians remembered how this influenced women's domestic working conditions. Housework was fitted around the logic of production in other domestic activities, as for example in the frequency of stewed dishes, which enabled the housekeeper to pursue her work without too much interruption associated with meal preparation. Parisian respondents' accounts of this period emphasize the rhythms of women's work conditioned by external factors such as the opening hours of shops and the labour-intensity of laundry work.

Both in the world of work and in city life generally, it is important to emphasize certain parameters that constrained Parisians' lives in the inter-war period. Just as domestic routines and household tasks moderated the scope for independent action among women at home, for both men and women working outside the house in the world of paid employment, in a metropolis, imposed strict limits on their daily behaviour, too. Although in receipt of a wage, the journey to work whether by public transport, bicycle or on foot constrained Parisians' scope to manage their own time and as canteens were not to be found in the workplace before 1940, so many Parisians, if they did not return home, brought a midday meal with them

---

[10] Wages were still often paid on a weekly basis.

[11] A. Sauvy, *Histoire économique de la France entre les deux guerres* (Paris 1984).

[12] A. Corbin (ed.), *L'avènement des loisirs, 1850–1960* (Paris 1995).

to be reheated in cafes close to the workplace, with an occasional drink in these cafes.[13] With the physical expansion of the city and the extended lines of communication in the 1920s and 1930s came different patterns of behaviour for metroplitan French workers.

City, council and housing

In 1929, the Bour family moved into one of the new city housing buildings in the belt around Paris, built by the Parisian municipality on the site of a demolished fortress. What were the Bours' reaction in taking possession of their new apartment? This couple, with their five children, had just left a two-roomed apartment in the 18th district with its courtyard water supply and a shared toilet on the landing. They alternately marvelled and were overwhelmed by their surroundings. A spacious and light dwelling surrounded them in comfort: water in the kitchen sink, more water in the shower cabinet, central heating, electricity, and an elevator – descent, and children, prohibited! The family said goodbye to coal chores, hauled up daily from the basement; goodbye to the oil lamps and goodbye to the so-very-fragile gas mantle covers and the perilous lighting they provided; goodbye to carrying water and to the wash house; goodbye to the cage-beds that had to be unfolded and re-folded night and morning; goodbye to doing homework in a little pool of weak light from the lamp above the kitchen table; and goodbye to the neighbourhood shower baths. Here was the sweetness and healthiness of life as provided by continuous and clean heating, washing soothed by a partition, and light that shone with a simple flick of the fingers.

The war of 1914–18 aggravated the extreme shortage of housing, as much for the rich as for the poor; virtually all city folk were tenants.[14] In these post-war circumstances, the municipal institutions were inclined nonetheless to build and to manage affordable homes. Capitalizing on Parisian experiences and the competencies of Parisian philanthropic efforts at the end of the nineteenth century, they launched into their first operations in municipal housing construction after 1919. These were intended as much for middle-class tenants as for those of more modest means because general questions of hygiene were uppermost.[15] Two main types of programme were employed:

---

[13] Also mentioned are the hot creameries, offering servings of milk, coffee, chicory and chocolate with bread in the morning, and also serving eggs, omelettes, sandwiches, and dessert cheeses to employees who did not have access to a canteen.

[14] A. Hirsh, 'Le logement', in A. Sauvy, *Histoire économique de la France entre les deux guerres* (Paris 1984), vol. 2, 264–94.

[15] M.-J. Dumont, *Le logement social à Paris, 1850–1930* (Liège 1991).

affordable housing for modest families like the Bours, and larger homes for the middle class, with a more elaborate interior layout than those of affordable housing, and where 'modern comfort' went beyond a shower stall alcove in the kitchen to a separate bath room and dedicated bathtub.

Memories of moving-in, like that of the Bour family, were rarely mentioned in the testimonies in this study: only three per cent of the accounts recall, for example, the municipal housing construction programme, which, along with schools, represented the great Parisian construction projects of the period between the two wars. Nevertheless, to this three per cent can be added the people who remember the transformation of urban space bordering the slums, including abandoned areas like the dismantled old fortresses. What counts in this case for the narrator is to recall how the changing physiognomy of the city brought about transformations in the habits of the residents.

Living the city

Rhythms of life and individuals

Women and men, at the heart of the family home, articulated the rhythms of their respective activities as cog wheels. This metaphor was a strong and recurrent one. The men, for whom the rhythm of paid work figured in the foreground of family life, participated in the interstices of domestic rhythms such as fetching water and coal, collecting children from school, making and moving furniture for the house, and scrubbing the floorboards with steel wool. These practices were extended further to include doing the grocery shopping, a little cooking, and taking out the laundry when the wife also had paid employment outside the home, and during childbirth.

At the moment of retirement from work, other responsibilities and patterns were assumed. Grandparents were often mobilized for baby-sitting and childcare and, depending on the situation, grandchildren were incorporated into their lives as they themselves were incorporated into the daily lives of their children. Grandfathers were often sitters on Thursdays when children had time off from school. So, children were brought into a daily rhythm that associated pleasure with utility: strolling, fishing, and gardening in the rented plot of land or one purchased in the suburbs where produce provided fruit and vegetables for the family table. Everybody benefitted from these useful 'pleasures'. Grandmothers were brought in to manage the household for their working daughters in the 1920s and 1930s when the maintenance and the management of the daily life of four to six people was a full-time activity: meals, laundry, clothing, childcare all fell upon their shoulders. In some cases, grandparents took their grandchildren into their homes and raised them during their early childhood, in Paris as elsewhere. It was a form of familial child-rearing, when the parents' working obligations were in conflict with the education and the care of their children. This system also applied in a temporary fashion for school holidays, which were also incompatible with parents' work schedules.

These patterns, derived from oral testimonies of the period 1919–39, positioned children at the heart of all the stages and sequences of family life from a very early age as adults did not construct for them a separate life protected from their worries but rather integrated them into their own rhythms and responsibilities. The apprenticeship associated with this very strict social discipline was reinforced by the school system. Little scholars of the Republic, from their tender childhood, learned these principles. Separate but intentionally equal schools in their pedagogy between girls and boys, and between different social standings as everyone wore the same uniform, schools offset their timetables in order to prevent meetings between young girls and boys. Even to have a brother or father within the vicinity of the girls' school was unacceptable, as Mrs Devoyon recalled:

> Be waited on by a boy? It was dishonourable! A friend of mine still remembers a good telling-off from the head-teacher prompted by her father's appearance – a very attractive man – at the front door of the high school.[16]

Respect for school regulations was justified under the pretext of time-discipline: a tardiness of less than five minutes after the beginning of a class resulted in being sent home with a punishment. Discipline was central to the school regime. Mrs Hiller recalled how, in an effort to produce a rounded education, each week 'the teacher gave a half hour lesson on the school rules or on some moral issue, and to complete our education, the final lesson was given by the head teacher who talked about thte choice of a husband'.[17] At the Camille Sée school, newly established in the 15th district, and where Simone de Beauvoir taught philosophy, four girls were suspended for being two minutes late for class. Simone de Beauvoir's intervention on their behalf changed nothing. As to the acquisition of knowledge, life at school flowed between silence and the sounds of the whistle. Teachers, in schools old and new, gave much to the children, preparing them for exams, helping them to obtain scholarships, and organizing outings and treats, as when a teacher bought a small projector and offered cinema showings at school on Saturdays, open also to parents, with proceeds from ticket sales going towards the rental or the purchase of films.

---

16 BHVP file 264, Mrs Devoyon, born 1922.

17 BHVP file 369, Mrs Hiller, b.1909.

References in the Parisians' accounts to other rhythms, such as those of the seasons or annual events, were relatively rare. In effect, in the world of work where holidays were still far from universal, nothing interrupted the routine of work. As for other rhythms, there were monthly payments for rent, though sometimes made on a trimestral basis. The ritual of frequenting the café, which in some families accompanied pay day on Saturday or sometimes Friday night, involved mother and children waiting for the husband to leave work and then getting together as a family to have a drink at the café as a 'treat', celebrating another payment and an assured week of expenditure ahead of them. The seasons and yearly events appear, therefore, in the middle ground compared to daily and weekly ones and collectively they form a hierarchy as mentioned in the testimonies of Parisian residents between the wars.

For the seasons, two registers seem to reveal change: specific food products and the use of clothing. Markets were scoured for the appearance of vegetables and fruits, radishes for example, but also 'the first strawberries for Father's birthday on the 6th of June and cherries for the beginning of July'.[18] Or even the crop of straw hats at Easter: 'one would never have worn a straw hat before Easter!'[19] Across this seasonality were the registers, mainly religious ones, and the rituals associated with them. Other consequences of the changing of seasons, like the evening chats on the doorstep made possible by the light of the day and the softness of the air, were appreciated but were less eagerly anticipated and thus less frequently recounted.

Annual events, like the end of school, the holidays, and the return to school, though recurring, constituted such a distended rhythm that they occurred more as exceptional in the accounts rather than as part of a cycle. Accordingly, they were linked with the occasional events such as family holidays, births, communions, weddings, and also the mournings that modified the normal range of social activities. Annual events were also linked with the memories of Parisians: significant events such as international exhibitions, state functions and visits, for example, the death of Marshall Foch and political turmoil, in February 1934.[20]

Ceremonial occasions and turmoil made an impact on the ordinary citizenry of Paris. They were often willing and accidental spectators whose mundane world, constrained by small homes and long days at work, was enriched by occasional pomp and circumstance.

---

18 BHVP file 284, Mr M. Durand, b.1915.

19 BHVP file 291, Mrs Endrebe, b.1918.

20 BHVP file 235, Mrs D. Dahinger, b.1908.

The Sunday rupture

Sunday is a day that appears as a rupture. For the family, it was an abrupt break from work or school. The daily rhythm, packed with sequences all week, shifted. Of course, by definition, Sunday broke into the normal weekday rhythm, but substituted its own rhythms and responsibilities. However, Sundays were more about replacing daily responsibilities with fun and recreational activities as Mrs Endrebe recalled:

> Amongst the petit bourgeoisie, invitations were usually made for Sunday lunch. But the custom required that guests stayed for the dinner to finish scraps, followed by a substantial dish. The custom then was that the guests invited everyone to have an aperitif in the best local café, where I got a sweet drink, a grenadine.[21]

Sundays, as brought back to life by the testimonies, were a long crescendo of pleasures. They started, in the memory of those who were children at the time, with a more light-hearted breakfast and, probably subconsciously, in their parents' relaxation before a day of pleasure. Breakfast was followed by a thorough wash and by putting on nicer, prettier clothes and items in better condition or quality than those worn during the week. Mass was then followed by a trip to the café for an aperitif (occasionally invitations would be made to members of the family for the aperitif, though only more rarely for the meal).[22] There followed the preparation of a more special meal, with the occasional purchase of cakes. Then the day culminated with the Sunday afternoon outing, either a short tour or a long stroll. For example, it could be to the Kremlin-Bicêtre in the very south of Paris, or to Vincennes in the east, or to concerts, the funfair or zoo, or occasionally to exhibitions or other special events. Anticipation, was, of course, part of the pleasure, as Mrs Cormeau recalled:

> We walked a lot: in the summer time we went to picnic at Vincennes, parents carried the youngest children. There were many exchange visits with other families who had also emigrated, the meal was always an improvement: roasted chicken and a tart prepared by my father, and pot-au-feu for dinner with pasta in place of bread, replacing the ordinary bread, what an enjoyable time![23]

---

21 BHVP file 291, Mrs Endrebe, b.1918.

22 Invitations between friends were exceptional, if not rarities, and they were made almost always in a cafe, with a specific reason, such as a birthday, to observe. Certain café owners sometimes brought contributions, offering a packet of 'petit beurres' to accompany the drinks offered by whoever was giving the party, while friends offered cigarettes.

23 BHVP file 218, Mrs Cormeau, b.1926.

This entire series of pleasant Sunday diversions might be anticipated as early as Saturday night with the irresistible shows at the cinema that attracted such interest in this period.

Sunday was, therefore, a break from the ordinariness of daily life. It was an irregularity in the cycle of days, and the peak of all kinds of satisfactions (food, appearance, meetings, relaxation). Sundays were not really about doing everything that one wanted to do, since everyone adopted the same model of behaviour, but doing it in a personally pleasing fashion, and with an element of individual choice: a special meal but a choice of menu, a stroll but a choice of place, and so on. It was about changing ones ideas, distracting oneself, about going to discover novelties, curiosities, and also about having fun. It was a release from the humdrum: a rupture.

Geography

The notion of the village was often used by respondents to describe the ambiance of the environment in which they lived. However, the testimonies are contrasted: they sometimes highlight the limited horizons of Parisian respondents. Some comment on how rarely they left their neighbourhood, and knew little of what existed beyond their immediate environment. At the same time, the witnesses' testimonies show that people often worked far from home, using a bicycle or taking the bus. Home also seemed disconnected to the place of work. The hypothesis might be advanced that because of the impersonal nature of employment, the human environment of the home mattered most: the neighbourhood of childhood, of youth, of attachments and family ties. The limited scope of daily life also contrasted with the seasonal and/or exceptional outings that allowed some city folks to stray from their homes and to travel several kilometres on foot: seasonal picnics in the bois de Vincennes or the maintenance of kitchen gardens situated in the suburbs, or even the universal expositions repeatedly visited over the course of their displays.

The street has been described as a place of distraction, of dreams, and which offered a free and much appreciated show.[24] Only occasionally did automobiles invade the street, which thus remained a public space for recreation.[25] Children's games, such as running after the ice-delivery cart to touch the melt-water dripping from the transported ice amused the young, while brief evening chats between neighbours at the front door, each installed on a chair, enagaged the elderly. There was also the occasional spectacle of

---

[24] BHVP file 168, Mr M. Bretagne, b.1919.

[25] Passageways were protected with 'clous' (nails/studs), literally large metal studs, to limit traffic. According to the testimonies of residents, pavements were only constructed from the 1930s. BHVP file 377, Mrs Jarry, b.1918.

listening to street singers' and professional artists' renditions intended to sell tickets for their shows.

Due to the circulation of people and traffic, something was always happening in the street throughout the day. Journeys from school to home, from work to home for lunch, food shopping twice a day, and street-traders' activities all provided interest and diversions. The spectacle of the horse-drawn cart, the landaus of the wealthy and carriages of state officials, the liveries of messengers and delivery men that were so acclaimed (café Caïfa, Gervais creamery), and the presence of members of the famous Society for the Protection of Animals (SPA) who held a pair of horses ready to assist carters ascend Parisian streets[26] – all of these added to the theatre of the street. There was always the bizarre, too, as Mr Cometou recalled an episode when 'Professor L., one of the most distinguished Paris surgeons, stopped his car in front of a carter who was maltreating his horse. The surgeon gave such a hiding to this carter that he had to take him to hospital to be treated.'[27]

In the period between the two wars, the presence of animals in the city brought a hint of rural life and recollections of earlier personal geographies. In each district, at least one breeder of cows and goats produced dairy products for consumption. Until the Second World War, horses brought essential deliveries of food and fuel. As a result, specific jobs such as wheelwrights and blacksmiths, which were often associated with rural life, continued in an urban setting, as did other rural practices, such as the collection of horse manure from the street as fertilizer for flower tubs on balconies or for market gardens. The habit of gathering manure was mentioned so often in the testimonies that it highlights the importance of kitchen garden practices that were simultaneously recreational, productive, a weekly diversion from the routine of work, and as a destination for children as part of an outing with grandparents on Thursdays.

Public space contributed to the definition of social status by the appearance, attitudes and the uses expressed by the city folk. Public space allowed each person to key into the social status of others and established a social map of the neighbourhood. Urban space is defined by the different positions and situations of individuals in the social mosaic: they can appear in the simplest of ordinary gestures like the purchase of bread, between the speciality bread for the 'rich' and bread by the pound for others. These positions and situations were also translated in the use of clothing: mourning as expressed by codified attitudes but also by extremely fine gradations of clothing which acted as indicators as to the nature and the date of the mourning. The professional uniforms of postal workers, delivery men, police,

---

26 Based, for example, around Boulevard St Michel.

27 BHVP file 220, Mr Cometou.

and the armed forces defined social status as did the students' ritual berets signifying polytechnics and military schools, artisans in their wide velour trousers with rolled-up belts, white-collar workers with their tie, waistcoat, cardigan, coat and fedora. 'Notables' in their gaiters and bowler hats, workers in their caps, and 'bare-headed' women each typify a social status recalled in the testimonies of Parisian witnesses.

The invisible city, or a refuge for individuals

As initial conclusions of this work based on the memories of 700 witnesses, four observations on the rhythms, on the unfolding of the ways of domestic life of the families of these witnesses can be advanced. First, daily and weekly rhythms dominated the life histories and recollections of Parisian inhabitants. Second, within these weekly rhythms, which were primarily a series of parallel rhythms for each family member, the Sunday rhythm was a communal family experience with activities. Third, within this weekday-Sunday dichotomy, which might suggest a linearity to the week, there were certain internal irregularities such as children's Thursdays, laundry Mondays that constituted 'two speeds' with rhythms superimposed upon or within each other. In relation to food, there was the extraordinary meal of Sunday noon and the no-fuss meal of Sunday evening composed, for example, of brioche, bread, butter and café au lait, a cold meal arranged ahead of time in the form of a buffet in rich homes on Sunday nights, marking an evening of rest for the servants. Finally, there was the unequal importance accorded by individuals to the scale of time: yearly rhythms relegated to lesser importance in a hierarchy that gave primacy to daily routines.

In these testimonies can be traced ordinary rhythms that reveal the inflexibility of social customs and practices at school, at home, and at work. Employees did not have the right to sit, to be absent, to smoke, to go outside, to be late, to have short hair (for women), or long hair (for men). This homogenized way of living applied to all in the same place or in the same position in the social hierarchy, where the rhythms of activity were based on a behavioural model composed of behavioural norms and group identity. Within this behavioural matrix and its framework, there was scope for individual variation. Where the Sunday stroll took place, or the route taken for the walk to work, provided a different plane of expression for individual actions, albeit within strict limits.

These testimonies bring an impressionistic understanding of the period they evoke, giving a human dimension to the debates on city living conditions, on social housing, women's roles and the uses of modern comforts in the home. The testimonies are informed by the experiences of daily life and urban change at the individual level; that is, in stark contrast to those accounts of the inter-war period (and other periods) dominated by international finance and political manoeuvrings. Tradition and modernity clashed in 'ordinary' lives too, producing real tensions and pleasures as citizens sought to reconcile change with established customs and practices.[28] The testimonies analysed proceed by contrasting that which differentiates the city of today with urban culture and behaviour from an earlier period. These respondents' accounts are intriguing for the perceptions of the city that they reveal in a different age. They stress the binary rhythms – work during the week, relaxation at the week-end; they emphasize – familiarity with ordinary, and of constrained daily lives woven within the social and physical fabric of a very limited area of the city; they note the enduring links with the communities and regions of their forbears – the rural world and the provinces were rarely far removed. As a result, the city is never an entirely foreign place. The urban world does not appear as the place where anonymity reigns triumphant. The urban world is not imagined as frightening, but more as mysterious by its ampleness, its rich diversity, glimpsed on occasion by an exceptional outing and chance encounters with others. The city emerges as a space of infinite possibilities yet one that is constrained by custom and practice.

Further reading

Beltran, A. and P. Carré, *La fée et la servante, la société française face à l'électricité, XIXe–XXe siècle* (Paris 1991).

Cabestan, J.-F., *La conquête du plain-pied. L'immeuble à Paris au XVIIIe siècle* (Paris 2004).

Cayez, P., 'Les petits logements dans les grandes villes: Lyon 1886–1968', *Le Mouvement social*, 137, 1986, 28–54.

Charvet, M., 'La question des fortifications à Paris dans les années 1900 : esthètes, sportifs, réformateurs sociaux, élus locaux', *Genèses*, 16, 1994, 23–44.

de Certeau, M. (with L. Giard and P. Mayol), *L'invention du quotidien, arts de faire* (1), *habiter, cuisiner* (2) (Paris 1980).

Delattre, S., *Les douze heures noires : la nuit à Paris au XIXe siècle* (Paris 2000).

Eleb, M. and A. Debarre, *L'invention de l'habitation moderne, Paris 1880–1914* (Paris 1995).

Fijalkow, Y., *La construction des îlots insalubres, Paris 1850–1945* (Paris 1998).

---

[28] M. Martin, 'Femmes et société: le travail ménager 1919–1939', Université de Paris VII Jussieu, PhD thesis 1984.

Flamand, J.–P., *Loger le peuple* (Paris 1989).
Florence Bourillon, 'Un immeuble dans Paris', *Cahiers d'histoire*, 44–4, 1999, 701–15.
Lucan, J., *Eau et gaz à tous les étages, Paris, 100 ans de logement* (Paris 1992).
Magri S. and C. Topalov, 'Reconstruire: l'habitat populaire au lendemain de la première guerre mondiale: France, Grande-Bretagne, Italie, Etats-Unis', *Archives européennes de sociologie*, 29–2, 1988, 319–70.
Paravicini, U., *Habitat au féminin* (Lausanne 1990).
Roncayolo, M., *Lectures de villes* (Marseille 2002).
Salvati, M., *L'inutile salotto, l'abitazione piccolo-borghese nell'Italia fascita* (Torino 1993).

PART 3

RESPONSES TO URBAN CHANGE

CHAPTER EIGHT

Understanding the urban past: the transformation of Bucharest in the late Socialist period

Maria Raluca Popa[1]

During the 1980s, the southern part of Bucharest's urban core was radically altered. These events are known in the literature as 'the socialist destruction of Bucharest's city centre'. (See Figure 8.1.) The present study shows that, with the help of oral history, what is perceived as a traumatic recent past can be better comprehended and more easily accepted. Oral history, therefore, can be considered as a tool that helps with 'coming to terms with the past', as the process is known in post-socialist historical literature.

A series of extended oral history interviews was conducted with 15 members of different professions connected with Bucharest's restructuring during the 1980s. Most of the interviewees were architects and planners, but others were historians of the city, curators and specialists involved with the protection of monuments. The focus of the interviews was to consider the accepted interpretation that the 1980s president, Nicolae Ceauşescu, was the diabolical mind behind the project, and the 'real' author of Bucharest's restructuring. The study shows that although the political regime in Romania in the 1980s was no doubt an authoritarian one, there is much more to the history of Bucharest's restructuring than the determined drive for destruction and demolition by the socialist leader.

The study challenges the mainstream interpretation of the socialist reconstruction of the Romanian capital as the result of a single historical

[1] This study, based on M.R. Popa, 'Restructuring and envisioning Bucharest: the socialist project in the context of Romanian planning for a capital, a fast changing city, and an inherited urban space 1852–1989', PhD thesis, Central European University, 2005, was made possible through the continuous support of the History Department, CEU, Budapest, and through the help and expertise of the academic advisors Susan Zimmermann, Marsha Siefert, and Gerry Kearns.

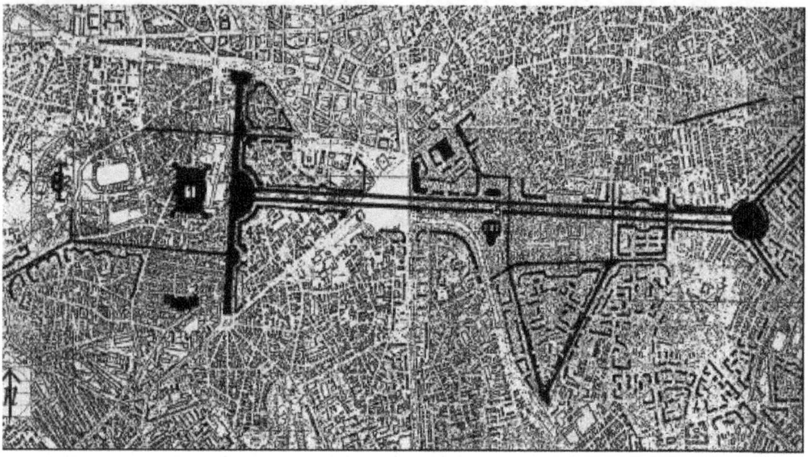

8.1 A plan of the restructured area emphasizing the linearity of the new boulevard

agent: a mad dictator.[2] Testimonies from the oral history interviews revise this interpretation in at least three dimensions. First, most of the interviews show that there has been a long history of restructuring Bucharest and that many specialists knew about these cases when they embarked upon the

[2] The need to shift the focus away from presenting urban change as the result of a single agent, the state, or the leader, and to acknowledge the plurality of groups involved is increasingly felt in the present-day literature on socialist cities. See O. Sezneva, 'Living in the Russian present with a German past: the problems of identity in the city of Kaliningrad', in D. Crowley and S.E. Read (eds), *Socialist Spaces: Sites of Everyday Life in the Eastern Bloc* (Oxford 2002), 48–9.

most recent and most disruptive attempts to restructure Bucharest in the 1980s. Second, from the story that architects and planners told, it became apparent that the restructuring of Bucharest was the result of a continuous negotiation between technical specialists and the party leadership. Even when open negotiation failed, specialists found ways of circumventing the leadership by employing cunning manoeuvres. Thus, specific historical influences, previously hidden from the accepted interpretation, could emerge. Third, several interviews with historians, art historians and curators showed that local elites often had an ambiguous relationship with the legacy inherited by the city from former times. Many historical monuments were imperfectly understood, even by the specialists, when they came under the attack of the socialist reconstruction. Moreover, the city was considered problematic, too 'Balkan', too wide, and too unusual for 'European' standards. This intellectual context of the 1980s indicates that a thorough understanding of the recent past should go beyond accusations directed at Ceauşescu and the character of the political system.

The new Bucharest civic centre built in the 1980s has often been interpreted as the result of the visceral hatred that President Nicolae Ceauşescu had for history, memory, old houses, quiet neighbourhoods and other elements of the 1990s preservationist discourse. This chapter examines the socialist project but goes beyond the post-socialist preservationist discourse and shifts the perspective towards presenting the history from the inside, as the transformations were perceived by agents of change involved in the story. The argument moves away from the common *post-factum* analysis to rescue the history behind the screen. It presents urban transformations as a process, with its hesitations, changes, intricacies and different perspectives, as revealed in oral testimony.

Several arguments move beyond the common understanding of the socialist project as the result of Ceauşescu's arbitrary will. The interplay between two interest groups, the architects and the political leadership, is explained, especially as it relates to the initial stages of the planning (1977–80). (See also Figure 8.2.) Thus, many other individual voices are rescued and the idea of the new centre emerges as the result of a negotiation between many agents, as well as a struggle between the generations.

8.2 Ceauşescu with an official delegation considering the architects' model for the new civic centre

Voices and actors: architects and political leadership

The origins of the project

It has been widely accepted that it was the earthquake on 4 March 1977 that triggered the radical urban transformation of the 1980s.[3] The conventional wisdom holds that the earthquake that shattered Bucharest revealed to Ceauşescu the fragile and transitory nature of the inherited built

---

[3] Most texts touching upon the construction of the Bucharest civic centre identify the earthquake as the triggering event. See Ş. Lungu, 'O chestiune de morală?' *Arhitectura,* 1–4, 1996, 4; C. Petcu, 'Totalitarian city, Bucharest 1980–1989, semio-clinical files' in N. Leach (ed.), *Architecture and Revolution: Contemporary Perspectives on Eastern Europe* (London 1999), 177–87. Documents of the Radio Free Europe archive show that this interpretation existed from the beginning. See for example, G. Ionescu, 'Selecţiuni din documentarul privind distrugerea unei a cincea parţi din Bucureşti în 1984 şi 1985', Radio Free Europe (RFE), 15 Aug 1985, p.3, Open Society Archives (OSA), Box 147 (812 Culture/Patrimonium, 1985). Proponents and opponents of the project alike identify 1977 as the starting point. See D.C. Giurescu, *The Razing of Romania's Past: International Preservation Report* (London 1989), 38–9, and also A. Budişteanu, 'Probleme ale dezvoltării prezente şi de perspectivă a capitalei', *Arhitectura,* 1–2, 1980, 14.

environment. As a result of this insight, Ceauşescu, it is assumed, grasped the idea that entire neighbourhoods can be pulled down and rebuilt.[4]

This interpretation seems logical when the tight timetable for the new project is considered. According to Constantin Jugurică, the Director of the Proiect-Bucureşti state-owned mega-construction firm, just a few days after the earthquake Ceauşescu invited three specialists, Octav Doicescu, Cezar Lăzărescu and Constantin Jugurică, for a closed-doors meeting at the former royal palace.[5] As explained below, the architects reacted quickly. The fact that the architects seemed predisposed to such an endeavour and that the projects evolved rapidly confirms that the origins of the project existed prior to the earthquake of 4 March 1977.

As Jugurică recalled, at this early meeting the new favourite architect, Cezar Lăzărescu, produced a previously prepared architectural sketch that proposed a plan of a civic centre located in Piaţa Eroilor [Heroes' Square], another square that had been the site of previous audacious plans for a new centre in Bucharest.[6] At a second meeting, 50 of the brightest names in the architectural and planning profession gathered. Ceauşescu proposed that the new civic centre would be built on top of Spirea Hill, again a place with a long history in visionary planning.[7] (See Figure 8.3 for these areas.)

Even if the connection was not explicit, there are clues that many architects were aware that this was the exact location of the political centre as it appeared on the 1935 masterplan, the first development plan for Bucharest conceived by trained urban planners and architects, and in many other plans

---

4 Ştefan Lungu, 'O chestiune de morală?' 4.

5 The choice of people is relevant: an old-guard, highly-respected architect (Doicescu), a new favourite architect and the new rector of the Architecture Institute (Lăzărescu), and a representative of the new type of technocratic elite, a director in an important function and a trustworthy person for the regime, who was also an architect (Jugurică). See interview with Constantin Jugurică, Arhiva de istorie orală a centrului de studii 'Memorialul Sighet' (AIOCIMS), tape 1587 I–II.

6 Piaţa Eroilor was the favoured site for the Cetatea Universitară, as it appeared in the inter-war plans. It was also the site where Constantin Argetoianu proposed that the Parliament should be built, where Octav Doicescu built the Opera in 1953, and where the Municipal Hospital was added in the early 1970s. In 1948–49, architect Duiliu Marcu took up the inter-war proposals for a University City and proposed that a new centre of Bucharest be built in this area. See D. Marcu, 'Centrul Universitar al capitalei' in A. Oprea (ed.), *Arhitectura: 50 de lucrari executate sau proiectate de la 1912 la 1960* [Architecture: 50 projects realized or planned] (Bucharest 1960), 515.

7 According to the interview with Constantin Jugurică, AIOCIMS, tapes 1587 I–II. This second meeting is confirmed by other architects. See A. Petrescu, 'How I became the designer of Ceauşescu?' interviewed by Ivan Andras Bojar, *Octogon: Architecture and Design*, 1, 2002, 63.

8.3 Perspective of the new area toward Casa Poporului

proposed in the previous half century. That architects, especially the older generation, knew in great detail about the inter-war plans for Spirea Hill, was confirmed in interviews with them.[8] According to Jugurică, not only were the pre-war educated architects aware of these, but so, too, were the technocrats of the socialist regime.[9] Out of conviction or in fear of open criticism, most of the architects present at this meeting agreed with the suggested location of the civic centre. An exception was the former rector of the Architecture Institute, Ascanio Damian, known for his independent views and daring

[8] Among the interviewees for this project, Şerban Popescu-Criveanu, Alexandu Beldiman, Ştefan Lungu and Aurelian Trişcu made the connection. Şerban Popescu-Criveanu sketched in the interview an entire history of plans for the Spirea Hill since late medieval times, AIOCIMS, tapes 1557 (Popescu-Criveanu), 1500 I–III (Beldiman), 1527 I–IIIA (Trişcu), 1528 I–II (Lungu).

[9] Constantin Jugurică narrated how in the 1970s he found in the attic of his in-law's house an old newspaper with the 1935 detailed plan for the centre of Bucharest. He talked about it with enthusiasm on some occasions and the mayor of Bucharest at that time proved to be extremely receptive to his 'discovery'. Interview with Constantin Jugurică, AIOCIMS, tapes 1587 I–II. Augustin Ioan also mentioned this story, though slightly differently and without mentioning the source. According to Ioan, Jugurică was informed by Ceauşescu that a new civic centre would be built and as a result he searched for the 1935 plan in the archives and showed it personally to Ceauşescu. See A. Ioan, *Power, Play and National Identity: Politics of Modernity in Central and Eastern European Architecture. The Romanian File* (Bucharest 1999), 258.

open criticism of the official architectural choices. He suggested Piaţa Victoriei (Victory Square) as a better location for a new centre.[10]

Some commentators considered the final product, the civic centre as it exists today, to be the work of Ceauşescu alone.[11] Nevertheless, others considered that the initial idea originated inside the circles of the architectural profession: 'I do not have any doubt that it was also an architect who conceived this project. I find it difficult now [1996] to make investigations and name that person, it was someone from among the people in power at the time.'[12] More than 20 years later, people involved in the late 1970s events are still secretive about who originally suggested to Ceauşescu the idea of a new civic centre for Bucharest.[13] During the 1980s, Radio Free Europe used the name of the chief-architect of Bucharest in the period after the earthquake, Alexandru Budişteanu, as the supposed originator of the idea of the new civic centre.[14] Regardless of the possible individuals who had a

[10] His suggestion proved more in keeping with an open market environment, since after the end of the socialist period, Piaţa Victoriei was much sought after as a prestigious location and developed into the new financial centre of Bucharest. Nevertheless, forsocialist planning logic, Victoriei Square was not an obvious choice, since the idea behind the new centre was to revive an area which was perceived as backward and not to concentrate even more resources in an already fairly developed area.

[11] Mariana Celac's article is based entirely on this assumption. See M. Celac, 'O analiză comparată a limbajului totalitar in arhitectură', in L. Boia (ed.), *Miturile comunismului românesc* [the myths of Romanian communism] (Bucharest 1998), 285–306. A similar debate evolved in the urban history literature around the question of whether Baron Haussmann or rather Napoleon III was the real initiator of the Parisian transformations 1850–70. See P. Lavedan (1952), *Histoire de l'Urbanisme*, quoted in Olsen, *The City as a Work of Art*: *London, Paris, Vienna* (New Haven 1986), 142. Other historians of Paris, like Jeanne Gaillard, blamed Haussmann for creating in Paris two different cities, separated and juxtaposed, much as Romanian public intellectuals after 1989 accused Ceauşescu of cutting Bucharest in two halves. See J. Gaillard (1977), *Paris, la ville*, quoted in Olsen, 142. By contrast, authors like David Harvey present Haussmann as a historic agent subordinated to the economic and social tendencies of his time, in no way providential or omnipotent, being overpowered in the end by the very forces he unleashed, and whose complex implications could not have possibly have been entirely foreseen. See D. Harvey, *Consciousness and the Urban Experience* (Baltimore 1985).

[12] Ştefan Lungu, 'O chestiune de morală?', 4.

[13] Constantin Jugurică professes that he knows who the mysterious person was, but was reluctant to talk about it. The same response was experienced with Ştefan Lungu, who professed in the interview that he had some 'suspicions' but was not willing to share them. Interview with Ştefan Lungu, tape 1528 I, side A, p. 10 in the transcript; interview with Constantin Jugurică, AIOCIMS, tapes 1587 I–II.

[14] Radio Free Europe, text read by V. Ierunca and A. Paruit, 'Demolările de la Bucureşti în presa franceză: Studiul despre demolările din Bucureşti apărut in *L'alternative*', radio show 'Povestea vorbii' no. 489, 6 March 1985, p. 6, OSA, Box 147 (812 Culture/Patrimonium, 1985).

direct impact on the project, the concept of a 'civic centre' for Bucharest circulated in the architectural circles long before March 1977.

During the first stages of planning (1977–79), the civic centre plan consisted of a concentration of administrative buildings on Spirea Hill, with a boulevard connecting the hill with the city centre. At this stage, the planned boulevard closely followed the trajectory of the fabled 1935 Bucharest master plan, leading to Senate Square, on the shores of the Dâmboviţa River. This initial plan, usually ignored in the literature, is of crucial importance for establishing an accurate relationship between the past and future for the project. At this early stage, the entire plan looked much like the fulfilment of an old dream. Instead of 'negating' the history of the city, as it has often been argued, on the contrary, the entire idea was perceived by the political leadership and part of the planning profession as a socialist response to pre-war dreams of a different Bucharest.

The name of the project helps illuminate this issue. The boulevard, as planned at this stage, led to Senate Square, where the traditional axis of the city, the symbol of Bucharest, Calea Victoriei, also ended (see Figure 8.4). Thus, the traditional boulevard was to meet the socialist 'magistrale' in a gesture of symbolic planning. Moreover, the name of the new axis is in itself a response to old Bucharest. Constantin Jugurică explained that while the traditional axis was called Calea Victoriei, the new axis would be called Calea Victoriei Socialismului,[15] thus situating the socialist project in a line of national 'victories', the socialist period being seen as the last and most accomplished manifestation of this historic line.[16]

---

[15] The name was retained until the early 1980s. Sometime between 1982 and 1984 the name was changed from '*Calea*' to '*Bulevardul Victoriei Socialismului*'. The word '*calea*' is the old, traditional name for the radial access roads into Bucharest (*Calea Moşilor, Calea Călăraşilor*). A geography manual from the inter-war period defines '*cale*' as a street that goes out of the city. Quoted in H. Stahl, *Bucureştii ce se duc* (Imprimeriile E. Marvan 1935), 75. The shift from '*calea*' to the more modern word 'boulevard' indicates also a shift of emphasis from the past to the future. See 'Vizita de lucru a tovarăşului Nicolae Ceauşescu', *Scânteia*, 8 August 1982, p. 2 and 'Tovarăşul Nicolae Ceauşescu a inaugurat ieri lucrările de construcţie', *România liberă*, 26 June 1984, p. 3, OSA, box 3 (Administration: National Committees). Nevertheless, the initial '*Calea Victoriei Socialismului*' creeps back in the official texts from time to time.

[16] For many people this early logic was obscured by the later developments. Later, the name of the new boulevard was mocked in the local parlance as 'the Victory of Socialism over the City'. Additionally, a story circulated in the 1990s suggested that Ceauşescu chose two inter-war buildings on the Senate Square as prototypes for the new style of the socialist boulevard. These buildings, by the famous advocate of neo-Romanian architecture, Petre Antonescu, indeed share with the new centre a sense of decorated classic monumentality. Architect Gehorghe Leahu was the first to launch the idea. Leahu, a participant in the reconstruction plans of the 1980s, turned after 1989 into one of the most ardent advocates of 'old' Bucharest and of

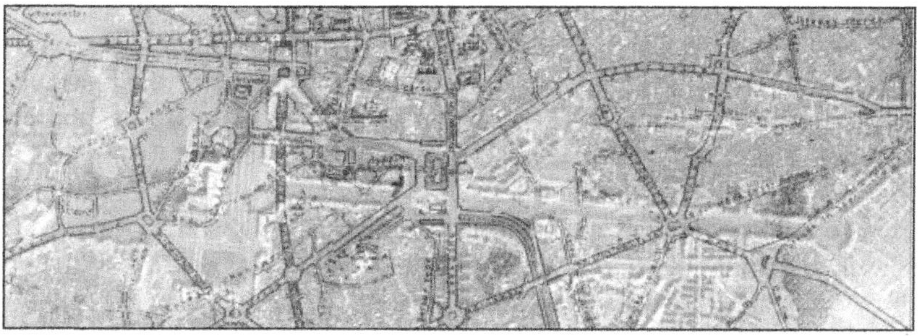

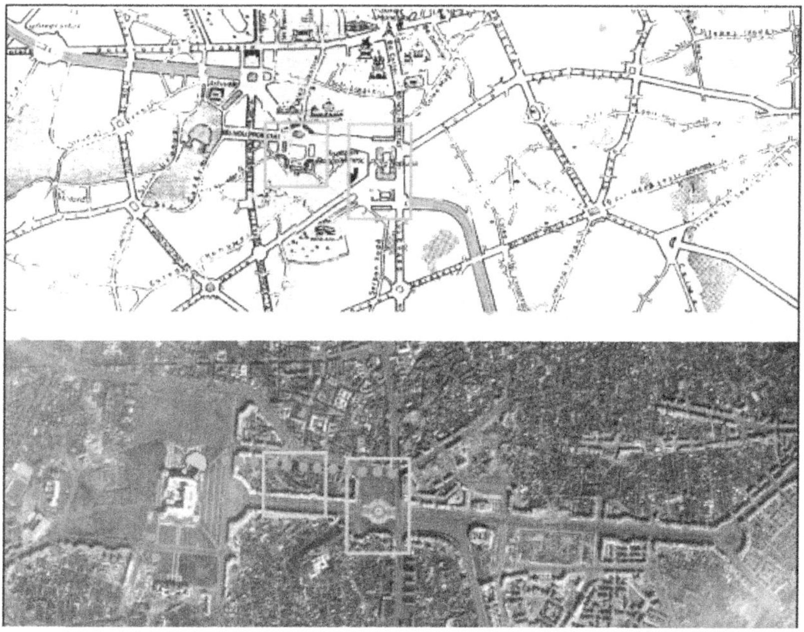

8.4 The 1935 master plan superimposed on a view of the civic centre of Bucharest

The art of deceiving: A failed negotiation

The extensive support that the plan initially received from professional circles indicates that the idea of a new civic centre for Bucharest did not run contrary to the established planning credo. In the period 1977–79, the most influential names in Romanian architecture became involved in a

the streets and districts that had disappeared. See G. Leahu, *Bucureştiul dispărut* (Bucharest 1995), and Augustin Ioan, *Power, Play and National Identity*, 258.

competition initiated by the president for the planning of a new civic centre. Initially, several teams of architects led by professors from the Institute of Architecture and a further team from the Proiect-Bucureşti construction company participated in the competition.[17] However, if the planning profession and the political leadership agreed on the need for a new civic centre with a boulevard cutting through the southern central area of the city, this does not mean that they had similar views as to how the entire project should look. On the contrary, many of the architects initially involved in the project realized that the views and tastes of the president in architectural matters could only vitiate the plans of the professionals. Nevertheless, they secretly hoped that negotiations would ensue, from which the arguments of the specialist would prevail. Many later confessed to have seen Ceauşescu merely as the motor of the project, someone that would finally provide the much-awaited opportunity of 'doing something for the city'. The political dimension was perceived as mainly the socialist wrapping, the façade behind which the architects would move freely.

> In the first phases of the project, we [the architects] honestly believed that that place [Spirea Hill] could be shaped so that its value would be emphasised. Sometimes we were commenting among ourselves, with a humour that today sounds like black humour, that only a madman [like Ceauşescu] would be able to unleash the energies required by the dimensions of the project.[18]

Inside Romanian intellectual circles, the architectural and planning profession was characterized from the beginning of the socialist period by its willingness to co-operate with the new regime. This openness is partly explained by the fact that the two spoke the same language as far as planning was concerned: a project of modernity that would bring prosperity to all through centralized planning. From the beginning until the end of the socialist period, many architects clung to the conviction that as long as the arguments were sound and the specialist convincing, party officials would listen. For example, architect Aurelian Trişcu held that even in the 1950s, a period when political matters prevailed, the Soviet experts sent to indoctrinate the local architects would give in to the wisdom of a reasonable

---

[17] Among the professors, Octav Doicescu and Cezar Lăzărescu organized their own teams. Important architects from outside Bucharest, like Nicolae Porumbescu, also participated. Other known architects were Constantin Iotzu and Romeo Belea. However, there were architects who refused to participate from the beginning. According to the subsequent testimony of architect Şerban Popescu-Criveanu, he humorously stated from the beginning: 'I am not going to make this guy [Ceauşescu] a palace' [*Io lu' ăsta nu-i fac palat*]. Pre-interview discussion with Şerban Popescu-Criveanu, 2 July 2002, not taped.

[18] Ştefan Lungu, 'O chestiune de morală?' 4.

argument.[19] Alexandru Beldiman professed the same belief about the 1980s. Even if the projects were censored on multiple levels, if one was resilient and persistent enough, Beldiman suggested, one could get a more innovative project through.

> The important thing is that there existed … such positions, one could do at least this, to stubbornly defend an idea up to the end, and they would eventually get tired, especially if one had a more tenacious nature, they would say, 'let this crazy guy go through [with his project], we ask some of our people to do a couple of more versions, we present all of them, and if his project happens to be preferred, fine.' So … they were just interested in protecting their positions, little did they care what was happening with the project.
>
> Interviewer: So, who would be 'they.' Who were they?
>
> Well … the leadership of the construction company [Proiect Bucureşti.][20]

Nevertheless, in time, negotiating the terms of the project for the new civic centre became more difficult and architects' resistance took the form of an attempt to cunningly manipulate the party leaders and especially Ceauşescu.[21] Since using reasonable arguments proved mostly ineffectual, muddling through was the next step. Alexandru Beldiman's opinions recorded this oscillation of the professionals between naïve belief in the power of argument and an awareness that deceit could also prevail. Beldiman's approach varied from dogged determination to a metaphysical or pragmatic view that, against all odds, valuable work would find a loophole in the system and come to fruition. He described how one of his designs for two buildings bordering the new boulevard was accepted and finally built:

> There were some things that went through. There was an entire conjuncture that a Westerner would probably find impossible to understand. Only if one lived it! Someone who lived in a normal world,

[19] Interview with Aurelian Trişcu, AIOCIMS, tape 1527 III, side A, p. 41 in the transcript.

[20] Interview with Alexandru Beldiman, AIOCIMS, tape 1500 II, side A, p. 24 in the transcript.

[21] Mariana Celac recalled how architects used to deceive Ceauşescu by using different scales in their projects. The buildings would be represented in a larger scale than the surroundings, so that in real terms the city would gain more open space. See interview with Mariana Celac, AIOCIMS, tape 1501 II, side A, pp. 18–19 transcript. The dominant party vision during the 1970s and 1980s was that cities should be prevented from spreading too much, in order to protect the agricultural land from urban encroachment. As a result, higher building densities were encouraged.

> would practically be at a loss to understand ... All these things that were actually possible! On one hand, the terrible restrictions that the system would impose, and one the other hand, the fact that there were ways ... due to the fact that they [officials] were clumsy, unprofessional ... and you could always find an opening, through which you could do ... something different than what they wanted. I told you about the two blocks that I built. I don't know, history of architecture will judge if they were ... if Ceauşescu chose the right project. Anyway, I made those blocks against everyone's will, with the exception of Ceauşescu. [...] Trying to extrapolate, there probably were many things that happened in this way. A book would come out, a movie, things that passed through. God knows how![22]

The second view seemed to become stronger during the 1980s struggle for the civic centre. Architects began to work on the new project with the conviction that they could handle Ceauşescu and the party leadership. In the words of Ştefan Lungu, 'One way or another, we were saying back then, if things remain under the control of the profession, in the hands of professionals, there is a chance that the city would develop as a result of this intervention.'[23] Today, there is a sense among the architects that this was a wild bet.

Cezar Lăzărescu was one of the self-appointed actors in this campaign of deceit. The rector of the Architecture Institute since 1977, the president of the Union of Architects since 1978 and well regarded by the political elite,[24] Lăzărescu was expected to lead the campaign for the new centre. He was prepared to ride the wave and balance all the interest groups involved. When it became apparent that the 'old guard' of architects was no longer supported by the political leaders, Lăzărescu dismissed the older and more respected architects, like Octav Doicescu, without much ado.[25] His project was chosen by Ceauşescu in the initial stage of the competition for the new civic centre, and, for a while, it seemed that he would provide a degree of mediation between the political and the architectural spheres. However, Cezar Lăzărescu failed to keep the project within the control of the professionals.

---

[22] Interview with Alexandru Beldiman, AIOCIMS, tape 1500 I, side B, pp. 30–31 in the transcript. The two blocks built by him on the Victoria Socialismului Boulevard (today Unirii Boulevard) have been celebrated many times since as the best examples of post-modernist design in the entire new civic centre complex. See Leahu, *Bucureştiul dispărut*, 99–100.

[23] Ştefan Lungu, 'O chestiune de morală?' *Arhitectura* 1–4 (1996): 4.

[24] He designed the prestigious summer resorts of the 1960s and 1970s, the first experiments with mass-produced architecture, made of pre-fabricated concrete blocks.

[25] In 1978, architect and theoretician Ana Maria Zahariade witnessed the rector asking Doicescu and another respected architect, Iotzu, to pull out from the contest organized for the civic centre. She recalls the event as 'saddening and shameful'. A.M. Zahariade, 'De ce avem nevoie de Octav Doicescu?', *Arhitext Design*, 3, 2000, 6–8.

An important change in the city centre project occurred at the end of the decade. Ceauşescu was in the habit of making extended visits to the construction site and reportedly enjoyed the perspective of the city from the top of Spirea Hill. Soon, a new directive was issued asking for a substantial change in the trajectory of the future Calea Victoriei Socialismului. Instead of closely following the line of the Dâmboviţa River and ending in Piaţa Senatului [Senate Square] as in the 1935 plan, the boulevard was moved some 300 metres to the south, ending in Piaţa Unirii [Unity Square].[26] It was a significant change because it meant that the area demolished was expanded much beyond the initial plan.[27] (See Figure 8.5.) It was the first sign that the established architects were no longer in control. Lăzărescu was said to have commented angrily, 'That guy [Ceauşescu] moved the axis.'[28]

A major blow to the pride of Lăzărescu as the pre-eminent architect of the day came with the rise to prominence of a previously obscure young architect, Anca Petrescu. Apparently, established architectural circles fought to exclude other architects from the competition for the new centre.[29] Anca Petrescu, nevertheless, due to boldness, persistence, connections or coincidental name[30] managed to break through the protective wall that the

---

[26] Ştefan Lungu calls this moment 'the first deviation'. Interview with Ştefan Lungu, AIOCIMS, tape 1528 I, side B, p. 12; also tape 1528 II, side A, p. 14 in the transcript.

[27] Both Ştefan Lungu and Constantin Jugurică noted in their interviews that, from 1935, a practice was established for the area around Spirea Hill of not allowing anything to be built until the project for an East–West axis was finally completed. It was a *non aedificandi* area. The decision to move the axis to a southern position meant that the boulevard was supposed to run over an area that was much more densely built than the area of the initial proposal. Consquently, the losses to the historic urban fabric were finally much higher than the architects thought. Interviews with Ştefan Lungu and Constantin Jugurică, AIOCIMS, tapes 1528 I–II and 1587 I–II.

[28] In Romanian: '*Ăla a mutat axul*'. During the last decade of the presidency of Ceauşescu, many people got into the habit of avoiding the name of the president, referring to him impersonally, in a mixture of contempt and horror. See F. Echeriu, 'Modestia nu era la ordinea zilei', *Arhitectura*, 1–4, 1996, 59.

[29] Only a few architects from the 'provinces', like the already famous Nicolae Porumbescu, took part in the competition of projects for the new centre of Bucharest. See interview with Alexandru Beldiman, AIOCIMS, tape 1500 I, side A, p. 7–8 in the transcript. Also interview with Ştefan Lungu, AIOCIMS, tape 1528 II, side A, p. 15.

[30] Ştefan Lungu stated how Anca Petrescu entered the contest. She had spoken in a public meeting and asked why young architects were left out of the competition and what were the conditions for participating in the contest (Ştefan Lungu, AIOCIMS, tape 1528 II, side A, p. 16 in the transcript). Petrescu went to Professor Octav Doicescu and asked to be part of his team, on the basis that her diploma work dealt with the same topic (an imposing building on top of Spirea Hill). Octav Doicescu could not get rid of the insistent appeals of Petrescu and suggested she organize her own team and helped her to obtain the required documents to

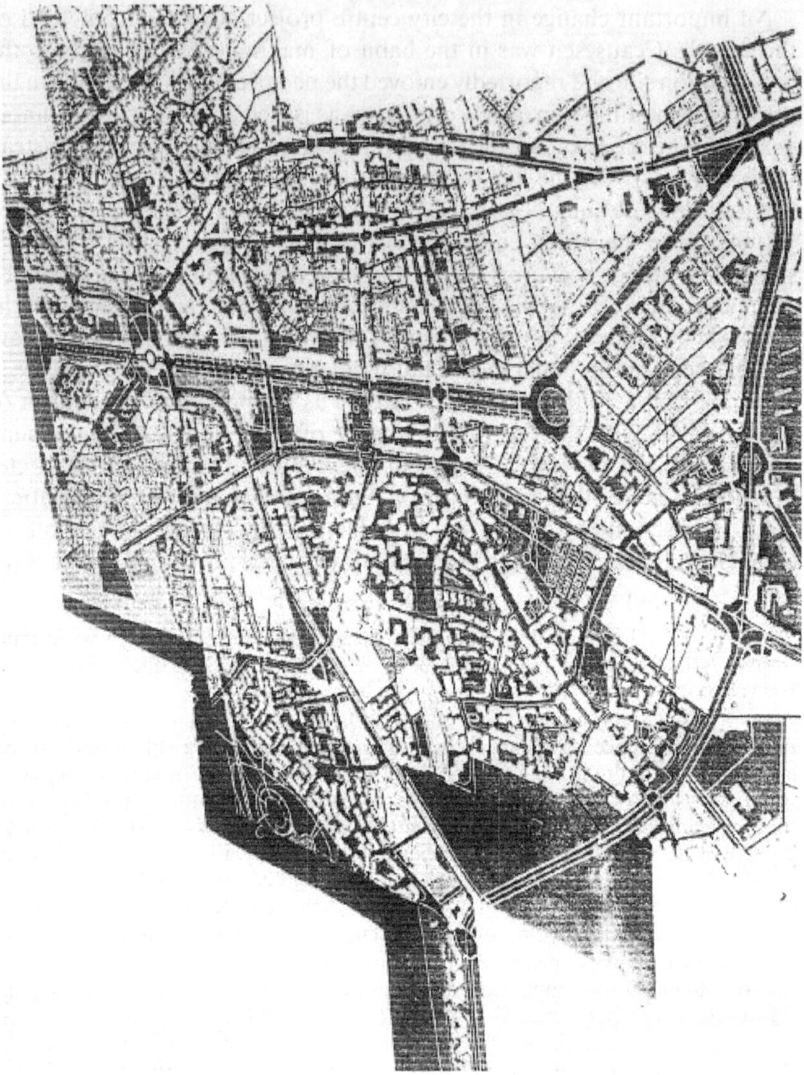

8.5 Model of the eastern extension of the civic centre, planned by the Proiect Bucureşti construction company

major names of the architectural profession built around the competition for the civic centre.[31] Although more established architects did whatever was in their power to stop Petrescu from participating in the competition, she prevailed.[32] Having done so, she won over the presidential couple with her project and was soon put on an equal footing with Lăzărescu, whose scheming to ostracize her had proved ineffective.[33] Soon, Anca Petrescu replaced Cezar Lăzărescu, just as Lăzărescu had displaced the older and more prestigious generation of architects.[34]

The fact that the architectural elite slowly lost ground in the negotiations concerning the civic centre has been customarily seen as the result of Ceauşescu's authoritarian rule, his lack of taste in architectural matters and whimsical, unstable character. Nevertheless, a contributing factor was an important generational struggle among architects that is largely overlooked. While the older generation, educated in the modernist cult of streamlined forms, was reluctant to accept the lavish decorations encouraged by Ceauşescu, the younger generation was more willing to try their hand at the drawing-board with volutes, consoles, and columns.[35]

---

enrol in the contest, but did not suspect that anyone would pay any attention to this inexperienced and supposedly not particularly gifted young architect. (See interview with Ştefan Lungu, AIOCIMS, tape 1528 II, side A, transcript, p. 15.) Beldiman recalled that although the scheming of Lăzărescu managed to keep Anca Petrescu away from the contest for a while, she showed up unexpectedly, at a general meeting at the seaside, having carried the huge and heavy model of her project on a trailer all the way from Bucharest (interview with Alexandru Beldiman, AIOCIMS, tape 1500 I, side A, transcript, p. 8.) See also A. Petrescu, 'How I became the designer of Ceauşescu' interviewed by Ivan Andras Bojar, *Octogon: Architecture and Design*, 1, 2002, 64. It has been argued that Anca Petrescu was the protégé of Nicu Ceauşescu (son of the president) and Minister of Youth, and thus took advantage of the 'new generation' ideology of the regime (Interview with Ştefan Lungu, AIOCIMS, tape 1528 II, side A, transcript pp. 16–17). Her maiden name was Elena Ceauşescu (Petrescu) and she was reportedly mistaken for a relative of the wife of the president (interview with Ştefan Lungu, AIOCIMS, tape 1528 II, side A, transcript p. 16).

[31] The over-confidence backfired on the part of the elite circles of architects.

[32] L. Duroy, 'Ubu architecte a Bucarest', *Architecture d'auhourd'hui*, February 1989, 13.

[33] Beldiman recalled that on the way to the seaside for a meeting with Ceauşescu, someone unexpectedly announced to Lăzărescu that Anca Petrescu would present her proposal as well. Lăzărescu's side turned livid. See interview with Alexandru Beldiman, AIOCIMS, tape 1500 I, side A, transcript, p. 8.

[34] Lăzărescu was born in the same year (1924) as the main propagandist of the civic centre, the writer Eugen Barbu.

[35] Aurelian Trişcu described the urge of the young generation toward different forms than those that had been taught in school. He named their attraction toward the civic centre project 'the devil's temptation'. Interview with Aurelian Trişcu, AIOCIMS, tape 1527 II, side A, transcript, p. 20.

Several factors explain the different attitude of the younger generation. First, in the real world outside the Le Corbusian temple of the Institute of Architecture, there were few commissions that required any creative use of form and space.[36] Most of the graduates of the Institute ended up building endless monotonous rows of flats in peripheral housing estates. A place in one of the professor-led teams or construction companies that were engaged with designing the new centre was the best career start for which any young architect could dream. Second, the architects that graduated in the 1960s and 1970s were increasingly attracted by the new post-modern fashion that was slowly infiltrating Bucharest from the outside world. Many architects confessed that the monumental and heavily decorated housing ensembles built by the post-modern architect Ricardo Bofill in France were admired and followed.

The muddling through continued once the building process actually began. Architect Constantin Hariton explained that Ceauşescu rejected hidden technical spaces in a building, supposedly in fear of explosions or attacks. Architects, on the other hand, could not conceive of designing an amphitheatre for hundreds of people without providing a proper ventilation system. Hariton was one of the architects in charge of the House of Science and Technology, which was secondary in importance to the House of the Republic, but still a huge building-site. During one visit, Ceauşescu noticed an empty space of two meters in depth under the main hall of the House that was designated by the architects to be the ventilation system. Taking a huge risk, Hariton came up with the wild story that they had to wait for the unstable terrain underneath to settle, before the hole could be filled with concrete. Due to this unbelievable lie, the ventilation system survived.[37]

Thus, although many architects now see the events of the 1980s as a failure of the professionals in their negotiation with the political leadership, in many small and previously unrecorded instances, the professionals did succeed in managing the situation in favour of the city. While Alexandru Beldiman now sees the entire city centre project as yet another 'lost opportunity'[38] it was never totally controlled by a single group of interests. Even if the influence of Ceauşescu was more visible, other groups successfully negotiated (or

---

[36] Alexandru Beldiman joked that architects of his generation, as well as the generation of his professors, 'were only swearing on Le Corbusier'. AIOCIMS, tape 1500 II, side A, transcript, p. 33.

[37] Interview with Constantin Hariton, AIOCIMS, tape 1529 II, side A, transcript, p. 20.

[38] 'In this case [the civic centre] I have this feeling that it was a lost opportunity. An enormous opportunity lost.' Interview with Alexandru Beldiman, AIOCIMS, tape 1500 III, side A, transcript, p. 43.

deceived) politicians and the architectural professions in the process of the design and building of the new civic centre.[39]

The intellectual context of the 1980s demolitions

During the 1980s, important demolitions of vernacular architecture and historic monuments took place in Bucharest. Several narrative histories of the demolitions have been previously attempted.[40] While the losses inflicted on Bucharest have been acknowledged and regretted many times, few attempts have been made to provide the intellectual context of these demolitions,[41] beyond blaming them on the destructive drive of Nicolae Ceauşescu.[42]

Between 1960 and 1980, most European countries experienced a change of attitude regarding the inherited urban environment.[43] While during the 1950s and 1960s, cities and towns affected by war were reconstructed along new lines that mostly ignored inherited patterns and historic buildings,[44] two decades later, the importance of continuity and preservation became much stronger in planning theory.[45] In Romania, many intellectuals were aware of this shift

---

[39] Architects' sabotage of official schemes was felt in other places as well. The rural systematization is said to have been slowed by architects who took advantage of the bureaucratic complications to postpone restructuring. See A. Barrick, 'Village destruction was slowed by architects', *Building Design*, 12 January 1990, 32.

[40] L. Anania et al., *Bisericile osandite de Ceauşescu: Bucureşti 1977–1989* (Bucharest 1995); G. Leahu, *Bucureştiul dispărut* (Bucharest 1995).

[41] D. Giurescu's book provided a sketch of some of the trends of the Romanian architectural practices that can explain the systematization policies of the 1970s and 1980s. See D.C. Giurescu, *The Razing of Romania's Past.*

[42] Especially Radio Free Europe and the exiled dissidents advanced this interpretation during the 1980s, which was taken up one decade later by Romanian intellectuals commenting on the earlier events. See D. Grigorescu, 17 April 1985, RFE document commenting on an article in *Le Matin*, in OSA, box 147 (812 Culture/ Patrimonium, 1985). See also G. Schopflin, 'Ceauşescu: The Great Destroyer', *Soviet Analyst: A fortnightly commentary*, 9 July 1986, vol. 15, no.14, in OSA, box 2 (101 Administration: National Committees: Civic Centre). After 1989, a literary version of the 'Ceauşescu – the mad destroyer' theme features in the novel of Ion Manolescu, *Alexandru* (Bucharest 1998), excerpt quoted in *Secolul XX*, 5–7, 1997, 224–5.

[43] According to François Choay, until 1980 the practice to protect monuments was extended worldwide on three accounts: 'Typological, chronological, geographical'. See F. Choay, *The Invention of the Historic Monument* (Cambridge 2001), 4.

[44] See John Betjeman, 'A preservationist's progress' in J. Fawcett (ed.), *The Future of the Past: Attitudes to Conservation 1174–1974* (London 1976), 55–63, for a list of historic monuments destroyed in Britain in the post-war period until the 1960s and described as 'major post-war crimes'.

[45] The shift of attitude was considered quite dramatic by certain commentators. Christensen wrote in 1979, 'In the 1960s, change was considered a good thing because

in attitudes.[46] Nevertheless, the predominant planning ideology continued to make use of the inter-war CIAM concept of the *tabula rasa*.[47] Only in the 1990s was a strong preservationist mentality for the inherited urban structure as a whole, as opposed to protecting selected monuments and scattered buildings, finally established in Romania.[48] Thus, the fragile preservationist mentality of the 1980s in Romania is considered here as crucial to understanding the demolition in the 1980s of the historic urban fabric of Bucharest.

To the modernist planning mentality of *tabula rasa* taught at the Institute of Architecture, a specific local tendency to disregard the 'Balkan' inheritance has to be added. Most of the buildings demolished in the 1980s were part of a nineteenth century urban vernacular architecture that was considered of little importance in the history of Romanian architecture. In 1984, the year when the works for the House of the Republic began, the senior leader of the preservationist architects, Constantin Joja, stated in an interview:

> In the university, we were told that there was no urban architecture in our country before the nineteenth century and that peasant architecture would simply be picturesque, folkloric, and impossible to revive in the modern architecture. It was believed, then, that only the churches embodied Romanian values ... Exactly this notion made the specialists believe that [urban vernacular] is architecture of Turkish origin. As a result, urbanists targeted it preponderantly for demolition, without realising that this was the purest Romanian architecture.[49]

---

it improved the city, provided new facilities, open space, new housing, all the kinds of things people wanted and then profits could be made to pay for these things. Almost overnight this became a bad thing. From insensitive development to don't touch a thing ... the whole thing went lunatic.' Quoted in P. Hall, *Cities of Tomorrow: An Intellectual History of Urban Planning and Design in the 20th Century* (Oxford 1996), 266. See also F. Choay, *The Invention of the Historic Monument*, 115.

46 As presented above, in the 1970s the review *Arhitectura* started to present alternatives to the usual clean slate approach, in articles inspired by Kevin Lynch, on the psychological impact of the built environment, on the importance of the familiar, on the need for continuity and recognisance of urban patterns. See especially the entire issue of *Arhitectura*, 4, 1973.

47 Alexandru Beldiman explained in the interview how in the 1970s, at the moment when the civic centre was being devised, the rest of Europe only started to shatter the prevailing '*tabula rasa*' ideology. Beldiman argues that the isolation of Romanian architects from outside trends delayed reconsideration of modernist planning principles inherited from the 1930s document known as *Charte d'Athène*. AIOCIMS, tape 1500 II, side A, transcript, p. 22.

48 According to Corina Popa, it was only after 1990 that the Romanian list of protected buildings consistently included other architectural categories besides very old (mainly religious architecture) monuments, AIOCIMS, tapes 1590 I–II.

49 'Arhitectul este exponent al spiritualităţii neamului sau şi apoi al lirismului personal', interview with Constantin Joja, *Flacăra*, 7 September 1984, p. 19, OSA, box 546.

This statement was aimed at the eighteenth-century 'Balkan' vernacular, but was equally valid for nineteenth-century vernacular buildings demolished in the civic centre area. The newer the building, the less likely it was to survive.[50] Official propaganda made use of these ambiguities concerning what was worth preserving, arguing that monuments of the early twentieth century were not real monuments.[51]

As for churches, monasteries and other notable historic monuments that were demolished, there is a specific context revealed through oral testimony. While a Commission for Historical Monuments had protected religious buildings since 1892,[52] certain ambiguities made them vulnerable to the radical renewal concepts of the 1980s. The lack of public knowledge about the local monuments, their improper use over the centuries, and a reluctance by conservators and curators to speak in favour of these buildings eased the way for their demolition. Three case studies illustrate this argument: Văcăreşti Monastery, the Church of the Cotroceni Monastery, and Mihai Vodă Monastery .(See Figure 8.6.)

Văcăreşti Monastery, demolished in 1984–85, had been a prison for more than a century. In the 1970s, a decision was taken to move the monastery from the jurisdiction of the Ministry of Interior to the care of the Ministry of Culture and transform it into a museum. After its partial restoration and plans for a medieval art museum were devised, Ceauşescu nevertheless decided to build a new Tribunal in its place. Despite some protests from historians, architects and art historians, the monastery and its church were eventually demolished. The building was unknown to the public, even by specialists, as a result of its century-long seclusion as a restricted prison area. Even among the handful of preservationists who knew of its existence and value, there were those who had never set eyes on the precious monastic complex.[53] Although specialized studies mention it as one of the most important eighteenth-century monastic communities in South-East Europe,

---

[50] The same happened in Britain up to the 1960s, when Georgian architecture was carefully listed for preservation while newer Victorian buildings were carelessly demolished. See N. Boulting, 'The law's delays: conservation legislation in the British Isles', in J. Fawcett (ed.), *The Future of the Past*, 26–7.

[51] The party propagandist, Corneliu Vadim Tudor, argued that the demolished Brancovenesc hospital, dating mostly from 1905, was not even listed among the protected monuments. He argued the same about the Orthodox Synod building, which was finally preserved. See C.V. Tudor, 'Minciuna are picioare scurte', *Săptămâna*, 10 January 1986, 6–7.

[52] Cezara Mucenic, 'Legislaţia privind monumentele istorice din România 1892–1992: studiu comparativ', in *Buletinul Monumentelor Istorice*, 2, 1992, 14–19.

[53] Cezara Mucenic, an art historian working across the street from the monastery in the municipal archives, never had a chance to see this important monument, although she was aware of its existence next door. Interview with Cezara Mucenic, AIOCIMS, tapes 1585, I–II.

it was inconspicuous in the public memory as a symbol of Bucharest and this certainly eased its demolition.[54]

Within the old royal summer residence, another monument, the Church of the Cotroceni Monastery, was demolished. This church was also virtually unknown to the public during its period as a royal residence from the 1880s to the end of the Second World War. With the change of regime in 1947, the palace came under attack. Some architects lobbied for its demolition, perceiving it as a 'ruin'. However, the first communist prime minister, Petru Groza, assigned the palace to the Union of Proletarian Youth. In 1950, it was open to the public as the Pioneers' Palace. Nevertheless, the church remained closed due to the anti-religious propaganda of the socialist regime.[55] In the late 1970s, Ceauşescu decided to transform the palace into his private residence and added a wing to the existing structure. The church of the monastic complex was secretly demolished during the 1980s, because as architect Cristian Moisescu, who was in charge of the demolition, claimed, Ceauşescu had been informed by his advisors that the church was not an authentic monument.[56] While this was partially an effort by Moisescu to exonerate himself, it is conceivable that the misconception over the monument was deliberately circulated in political circles. Specialists surrounding Ceauşescu rarely dared to speak out concerning endangered monuments.

This was not the only instance of a monument dismissed as worthless. A similar account emerged in relation to another demolition, the Mihai Vodă Monastery, according to several witnesses. Virgiliu Z. Teodorescu, curator of the National Archives Museum, recalled a visit around 1985 by Ceauşescu at the National Archives, located at that time in the old Mihai Vodă Monastery. For a long time, the Mihai Vodă Monastery was intended to coexist with the planned House of the Republic nearby. Some architects involved with the reconstruction of the area, when visiting the monument, ensured Teodorescu that the monastery was out of danger. Soon after, Ceauşescu paid a visit to the ensemble and asked questions about its value

[54] Radio Free Europe acknowledged that the monument was not known, but does not consider this as a possible explanation for the weak resistance that the demolition encountered. See D. Ionescu, 'Monumente dărâmate la Bucureşti', chapter XXI: 'Mânăstirea Văcăreşti', *Domestic bloc*, 12 February 1985, RFE document, OSA, box 147. It is important to note that the demolition of another church, St Vineri, though less valuable as a historical monument, was well known and much loved by the inhabitants of the city, and the subject of greater resistance and symbolic mourning at its loss.

[55] N. Ionescu-Gura, 'Palatul Cotroceni de la resedinţă regală la palat al Pionierilor', *Bucuresti: Materiale de Istorie si Muzeografie*, 4, 2000, 205–18.

[56] Cristian Moisescu, now an expert on monuments at the Ministry of Culture stated that the director of the Bucharest History Museum at that time told this to Ceauşescu. See interview with Cristian Moisescu, AIOCIMS, tapes 1530, 1527 III, side B, 1590 II, side B.

and significance. Teodorescu confessed that he now regrets today that neither he nor anyone else was bold enough at the time to explain to Ceauşescu the significance of the monastery.[57] Apparently, Romanian preservationists considered that the fate of historic monuments depended upon the good will of a political leader charmed by isolated, providential specialists.

The Mihai Vodă Church was moved in 1985 some 227 metres behind a curtain of buildings in front of the House of the Republic. The entire monastery precinct was demolished. The buildings that made up the precinct belonged to different styles and different epochs, from the sixteenth to the twentieth century. According to the art historian Corina Popa, Romanian buildings that enjoyed a long historical pedigree were belatedly acknowledged as worth preserving. Arguably the demolition of the Cotroceni Church was attributable to an individual who described the monument to Ceauşescu as the result of a series of alterations to the initial structure, which may have led the self-educated president to think it was not a valuable monument.

An example of what happened when many specialists came together to work for the preservation of a monument is provided by the case study of the Sapienţei Church. In 1984, the plan was to move Mihai Vodă Church exactly to the spot where the small Sapienţei chapel stood. When the parish priest was informed about the imminent demolition of the church, he used all his connections to find help. Elena Budişteanu came to the rescue. Her late husband, architect Ion Budişteanu, had worked for decades at the Proiect Bucureşti construction company. Elena Budişteanu personally knew people in key positions who had worked and socialized with her and her late husband. In a *tour-de-force*, the priest and Elena Budişteanu gathered 13 signatures from important people in favour of preserving the church.[58] Backed and encouraged by this support, the chief-architect of Bucharest apparently contacted Ceauşescu with the suggestion to reconsider, and the church survived.[59]

Although this event is illuminating in the context of the 1980s, it should be noted that the Sapienţei Church is small and obscured from view, and

---

57 Teodorescu could have given the explanations, but he did not, probably out of fear or modesty. Ceauşescu came accompanied by important people; Teodorescu might have felt he was just a curator. Interview with Virgiliu Z. Teodorescu, AIOCIMS, tape 1531 I–V.

58 Interview with Elena Budişteanu, AIOCIMS, tapes 1586 I–II. Among the people contacted were: Grigore Ionescu, Dinu Hariton, Paul Focsa, Cristian Moisescu, Panait I Panait. Budişteanu is an old Wallachian *boyar* family. Also among those contacted, were members of the old elite, like Dinu Hariton. This case-study shows how the pre-war elite networks survived and actually functioned inside the socialist system.

59 I. Iancovescu, *Părintele Voicescu: Un duhovnic al cetăţii* (Bucharest 2002), 174–80.

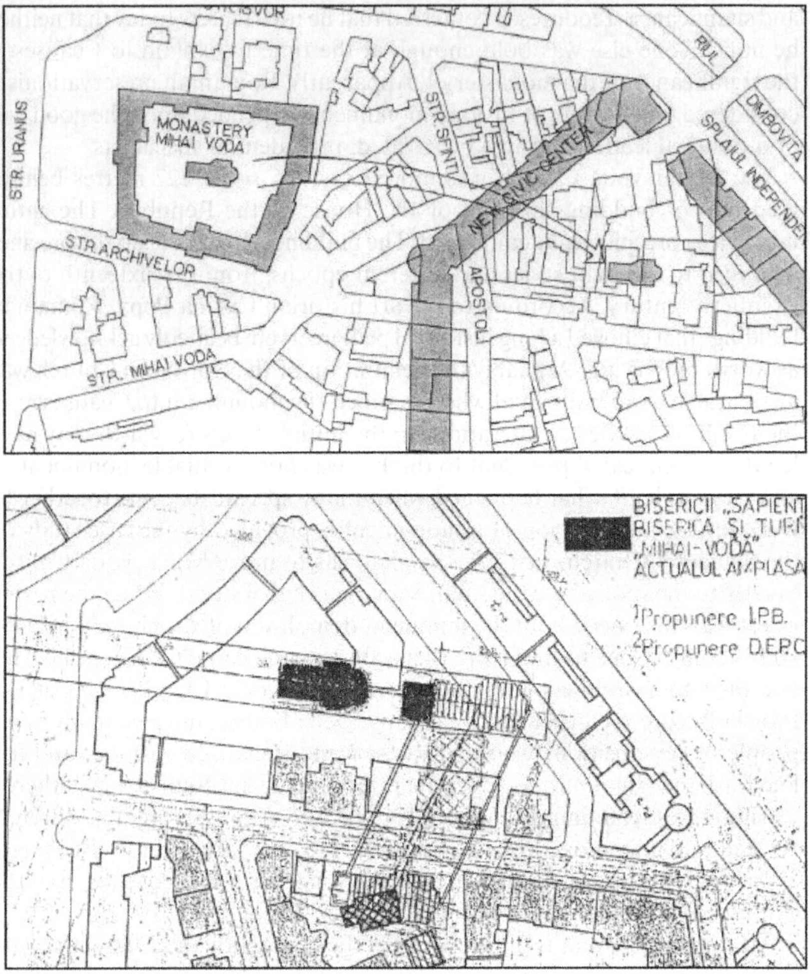

8.6 The new location of Mihai Voda Church

its reprieve might have depended upon convincing Ceauşescu that it was not visible from the grand environment of the new centre.[60] Thus, a strong network of specialists, appealing for the preservation of a certain monument through official channels of communication, was more effective than a few

[60] In a book discussing the survival of the church, it was hinted that Elena Budişteanu inserted photos in the file presented to the chief-architect, showing the church photographed from above to look small and insignificant behind the row of blocks of the new centre. See I. Iancovescu, *Părintele Voicescu*, 177.

8.7 Mihai Voda Church and bell-tower during the relocation process

letters of protest written individually, or by groups, and sent directly to Nicolae Ceauşescu or to high-ranking officials.[61]

To conclude, the lack of cohesion among the curators and historians, the lack of public knowledge of important monuments, as well as ambiguous preservation practices provided a general context that eased the way for the demolition of many historic buildings. In addition, art historians like Cezara Mucenic argued that history of architecture had been a neglected subject in Romanian academia, a subsidiary subject both at the Institute of Architecture and the Art Academy, with the exception of medieval religious monuments that were better known and studied.[62] Such diminished academic interest further weakened the voices of specialists scattered among several disciplines.

The perspective proposed here might appear to reinforce the popular understanding of the events of the 1980s as the result of a single historical agent, President Ceauşescu. Yet, the examples provided above offer a

[61] Protests have been written by a number of specialists for the preservation of Văcăreşti and Mihai Vodă. The term 'protest' is not always appropriate. In many cases, the letters sent to Ceauşescu were not protesting directly, but just 'bringing to the attention' of the president or other bodies that a certain historic monument was threatened by some state institution. See interview with Corina Popa, AIOCIMS, tapes 1590 I–II. One exception was the letter of Andrei Pippidi criticizing the demolition of Nicolae Iorga's house on Bucharest's ring road. His protest letter, though, was not accepted by a major magazine, 'Flacăra' and was broadcast in Romania only through Radio Free Europe in September 1986. See A. Pippidi, 'Despre o casă din Bucureşti' in *Rezerva de speranţă*, 5–7.

[62] Interview with Cezara Mucenic, AIOCIMS, tape 1585, I–II.

different perspective by revising the perspective of compliant and silenced professionals. In fact, Ceauşescu acted in a relative void of opinion not only because his repressive system silenced any protest, but because of the indifference of an educated elite toward these monuments, combined with a long tradition of Romanian paternalist submissiveness to the decisions of the political leadership. The revision that emerges from the oral testimony and from these examples suggests that sometimes Ceauşescu had room for manoeuvre not in spite of society, but because of it. The lack of cohesion among groups of specialists, the very lack of specialists, and a certain confusion regarding professional ethics and the value of the Romanian heritage contributed to the demolitions.

Oral history and the recent past

The analysis of the three dimensions presented here is by no means exhaustive. They do, however, challenge the current mainstream interpretations of Bucharest's recent past which tend to become more rigid moulds as the years go by. The use of oral history, as seen here, in uncovering the ambiguities, contradictions and muddling through of historical processes revises interpretations previously confined to the written literature. (See Figure. 8.8.)

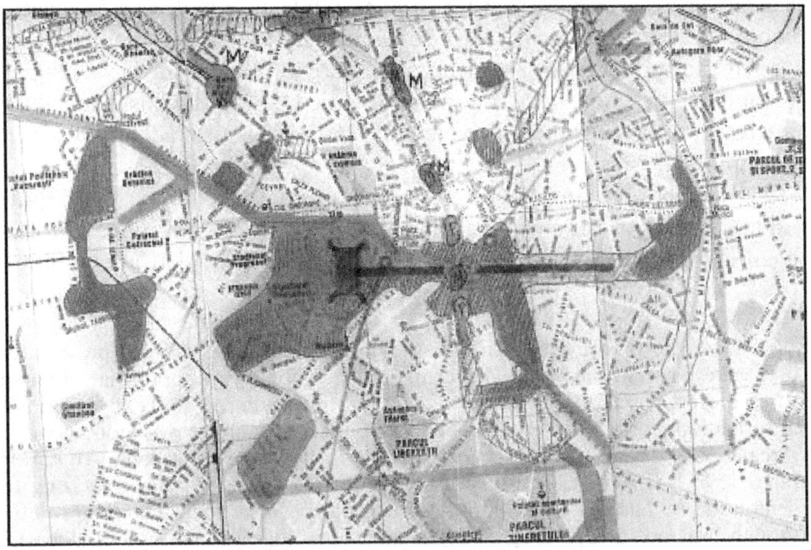

8.8 Mariana Celac's map of the reconstructed area

Recent scholarship warns of the dangers of playing psychological games of the type, 'What was going on in Hitler's (or Stalin's) mind?' or 'did he believe himself?' In this study, the same danger exists in Romanian literature. For the history of socialist Bucharest, the only historical agent usually acknowledged is the communist leader, Nicolae Ceauşescu. Many public intellectuals chose to avoid asking complex questions for fear of involving themselves or their colleagues in a long ethical debate. The opt out was to remember the socialist transformation of Bucharest as the result of Ceauşescu's maniacal drive for destruction. The assumption that the president was downright evil, despising the history of Bucharest and planning diabolical strategies of torturing the city and its inhabitants needs to be reviewed and the contribution of other individuals and agencies revised.[63]

The most succinct visual expression of this attitude is the common representation of the area transformed during the 1980s as a blank area, or as an area rendered in powerful, suggestive colours as red or yellow. These all-pervasive maps in the post-1989 cultural context of Bucharest fixed the idea that there is nothing else that one could possible say after looking at this map. The discourse and the map said it all.[64] (See Figure 8.9.)

---

[63] Slavoj Žižek similarly warned of the popular understanding that 'Hitler hated the Jews in his guts, viscerally, and his "theoretical" foundations were mere secondary rationalisations of this "irrational" attitude, which dominated him beyond his conscious control'. See S. Žižek, *Did Somebody Say Totalitarianism?* (New York 2001).

[64] The map of Bucharest with the blank area was first used during the 1980s as a political tool by exiles in Paris demonstrating against the demolition of historical monuments in Bucharest. (RFE document: Monica Lovinescu, 12 Aprilie 1985, 'About the demonstration in Paris against demolitions on the 1st of April 1985'). Dissidents from inside Romania smuggled out of the country various maps on which the area under reconstruction was carefully and accurately marked. (RFE document: Dan Ionescu, 'Monumente in pericol in Bucureşti: Turlele Văcăreştilor', 1985.) Later, foreign journals used these maps to disseminate sensational stories in the European mass-media. (RFE document: A. Dumitrescu 'Charte d'Athene', *L'Alternative*, 13 (February 1985); L. Duroy, 'Ubu architecte a Bucarest', *Architecture d'aujourd'hui*, February 1989, 13.) Finally, after the change of regime in 1989, the map travelled back to Bucharest and was used by the local architects when organising the first exhibitions about Bucharest both inside Romania and abroad. This map suggests the popular understanding of the entire communist period as a void, a blank in the history of the city, a period about which nothing can be said, beyond contemplating the disaster. Another suggestive image illustrating the popular metaphor presenting the city as suffering, as a cancerous body, is the cover of an issue of the journal *Arhitectura* discussing Bucharest. This cover shows a human profile having in the brain, as a tumour, the map of Bucharest with the reconstructed area painted red, as a brain tumour. See *Arhitectura*, 1–4 (1996), cover page. See also interview with Ştefan Lungu, AIOCIMS, tape II, side B. The cited RFE documents can be found in OSA, box 147 (812 Culture, Patrimonium 1985).

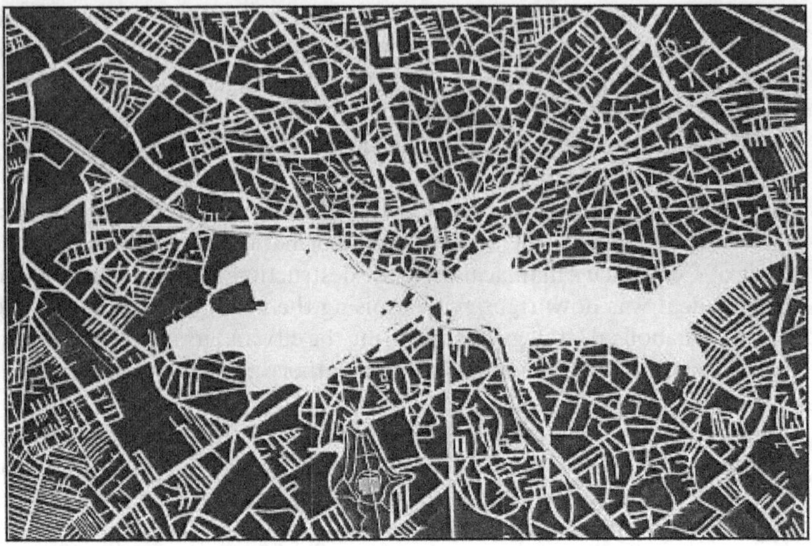

8.9 Map of the reconstructed area, 1989

With the entire recent history of the city thus fixed in the public consciousness by the use of suggestive metaphors, further inquiry was clearly blocked. Unless the veil of pseudo-psychological interpretations and metaphors is taken away, there is little that historical literature can do to advance knowledge on the subject.[65] De-mythicizing recent history opens up the subject for further scholarly interest, and oral history, as used in this study, is one way to accomplish it.

Once the events of the 1980s are freed of the baggage of inherited wisdom and suggestive metaphors, once the popular belief that there is nothing to be explained or worth explaining is rejected, the history behind the fixed, dystopian screen can emerge. As much as Ceauşescu's cult of personality can not be accounted for as something exogenous to local political culture and symbolic practices, the restructuring of Bucharest during the 1980s is an historical process deeply rooted within society.[66] Going beyond the popular

---

[65] Slavoj Žižek similarly argued that treating the Holocaust as an incomprehensible aberration of history discourages any attempts at studying, approaching or understanding the subject. 'The elevation of the Holocaust into metaphysical diabolical Evil, irrational, incomprehensible, apolitical, approachable only through respectful silence ... being outside historicisation, cannot be explained, visualised, represented, transmitted, since it marks the Void, the black hole, the end.' See S. Žižek, *Did Somebody Say Totalitarianism?*

[66] Adrian Cioroianu recently argued against interpreting the growing cult of personality of Ceauşescu's regime as a phenomenon outside Romanian society

interpretation of the project as the emanation of Ceauşescu's mind, oral history can unveil a multiplicity of motives, reasons and historical agents that contributed to, negotiated, or diverted the socialist restructuring programme from its planned course.

Abbreviations

OSA	Open Society Archives, Budapest, holders of the Radio Free Europe/Radio Liberty archive.
AIOCIMS	The Oral History Archive of the '*Memorialul Sighet*' Project, the Civic Academy Foundation, Bucharest.

Further reading

Anania, L., et al., *Bisericile osandite de Ceauşescu: Bucureşti 1977–1989* [Churches doomed by Ceauşescu: Bucharest 1977–1989] (Bucharest 1995).

Celac, M., 'O analiza comparata a limbajului totalitar in arhitectura' [A Comparative Analysis of the Totalitarian Language in Architecture], in L. Boia (ed.), *Miturile comunismului românesc* [the myths of Romanian communism] (Bucharest 1998), 285–306.

Choay, F., *The Invention of the Historic Monument* (translated by L.M. O'Connell) (Cambridge 2001).

Cioroianu, A., 'Cultul lui Ceauşescu, o surpriză?' [The cult of Ceauşescu: a surprise?], *Dosarele istoriei*, 8, 2002, 4–5.

Fawcett, J. (ed.), *The Future of the Past: Attitudes to Conservation 1174–1974* (London 1976).

Giurescu, D.C., *The Razing of Romania's Past* (London 1990).

Hall, P., *Cities of Tomorrow: An Intellectual History of Urban Planning and Design in the 20th Century* (Oxford 1996 edn).

Harvey, D., *Consciousness and the Urban Experience* (Baltimore 1985).

Hudson, H.D., *Blueprints and Blood: The Stalinisation of Soviet Architecture, 1917–1937* (Princeton 1994).

---

imposed on to it rather than eased by it. See A. Cioroianu, 'Cultul lui Ceauşescu, o surpriza?' *Dosarele istoriei*, 8 (2002), 4–5. Similarly, scholars argued that Stalinism could be seen, contrary to the historical mainstream, as a social force generated by the immediate social context. 'Stalinism could never have triumphed were it merely a force outside society; it was throughout its bloody history a constituent part of Soviet society.' See H.H. Hudson, *Blueprints and Blood: The Stalinisation of Soviet Architecture, 1917–1937* (Princeton 1994), 13.

Ioan, A., *Power, Play and National Identity: Politics of Modernity in Central and Eastern European Architecture. The Romanian File* (Bucharest 1999).

Leahu, G., *Bucureştiul disparut* [The Bucharest that disappeared] (Bucharest 1995).

Marcu, D., 'Centrul Universitar al capitalei', in A. Oprea (ed.), *Arhitectura: 50 de lucrari executate sau proiectate de la 1912 la 1960* [Architecture: 50 projects realized or planned] (Bucharest 1960).

Olsen, D.J., *The City as a Work of Art: London, Paris, Vienna* (New Haven 1986).

Petcu, C., 'Totalitarian city, Bucharest 1980–1989, semio-clinical files', in N. Leach (ed.), *Architecture and Revolution: Contemporary Perspectives on Eastern Europe* (London 1999), 177–87.

Petrescu, A., 'How I became the designer of Ceauşescu?', interviewed by Ivan Andras Bojar, *Octogon: Architecture and Design*, 1 (2002), 63–5.

Sezneva, O., 'Living in the Russian present with a German past: the problems of identity in the city of Kaliningrad', in D. Crowley and S.E. Read (eds), *Socialist Spaces: Sites of Everyday Life in the Eastern Bloc* (Oxford 2002).

Žižek, S., *Did Somebody Say Totalitarianism?* (New York 2001).

CHAPTER NINE

Resurrecting narratives: revitalization, ruins and modern cemeteries in the Brás district, São Paulo City, since 1970

Verônica Sales Pereira

When the East–West line of the underground passes by the Brás station in a long elevated leg, the passengers' gaze at the cityscape beneath is one of puzzlement. What could those hundreds of green numbered rectangles on the ground be? As they speed by, this question confronts commuters and visitors alike. Insulated by their railway carriage, they are unable to answer the question, but through an oral history of the district the puzzle can be solved.

The Brás, an extensive de-industrialized area of the city of São Paulo, is a district characterized by the ruins of derelict factories, vacant warehouses, and abandoned railway yards dating from the dawn of industrialization in the late-nineteenth century and active until the mid-twentieth century. The district was moulded by a populous, multicultural working class and what once was the home of factory workers and immigrants is today a neighbourhood composed of a large population making a living mainly as street vendors, scavengers, and illegal immigrant sweatshop workers who rely on the district's thriving clothing business. Many live and sleep in dilapidated tenement houses or sleep rough on the streets.

During the twentieth century, two processes adversely affected the Brás district. One was the relocation of industrial activity in the 1950s to the '*ABC*' region, the Greater São Paulo industrial cities of Santo *A*ndré, São *B*ernardo and São *C*aetano. Associated with this process was the gradual departure of many residents who abandoned the district in their attempt to move upwards socially. The second factor affecting the district was when, in 1976, the city started a series of demolition projects in the Brás designed to facilitate the construction of the underground line that today crosses the district, and which further accelerated the destruction and forced the eventual abandonment of the area. This extensive and widespread destruction of the district overwhelmed long-time residents, mainly Italian and Spanish workers and their descendants, and cast a long shadow over the future of the Brás.

As part of the underground project, the city of São Paulo, under the administration of mayor Olavo Setúbal (1975–79), decided to implement an ambitious urban renewal programme alongside the underground line, known as the Brás-Bresser CURA (Accelerated-Recuperation Urban Communities), that was intended 'to correct the scars brought about by the construction work'.[1] A considerable part of the district's history was erased both through the destruction of the built environment – 940 houses were demolished in an area of 260,000 square metres[2] – and by the displacement of 5,000 residents whose eviction severed important cultural, community and linguistic bonds essential to the vitality of neighbourhoods. The destructive effects were further deepened with the delay and incomplete execution of the project: it was ten years from when the underground construction began until the first middle-class housing projects (COHAB) were finished. In addition, urban amenities such as schools, crèches, churches, and commercial buildings never got off the drawing board. Unfinished, the renewal project generated dereliction as an enormous 'urban emptiness' between the new buildings and the underground line remained vacant, regardless of the city's efforts, over a quarter of a century, to reverse this urban blight.

This chapter analyses the role of narratives in the process of rebuilding the memory of an area of vitality subsequently consigned to 'urban emptiness'.[3] The focus is on how oral history rebuilds the urban memory of an area subjected to radical urban planning in the specific context of São Paulo[4], a modern Latin-American peripheral megalopolis, a city whose urban fabric temporality is marked by porosity.[5] As Walter Benjamin signalled, not only

---

1 Quoting Mayor Olavo Setúbal, *O Estado de São Paulo*, 11 October 1978, in M.P. Véras, 'O Bairro do Brás em São Paulo: um século de transformações no Espaço Urbano ou diferentes versões da segregação social (1890–1990)', Pontifícia Universidade Católica de São Paulo, unpublished PhD thesis, 1991.

2 Equivalent to 64,246 acres or approximately 161 square miles.

3 Quotation marks denote naturalization of the urban landscape, as if the latter were not the product of particular historical processes.

4 This intervention is studied by A.R. Martin, 'O Bairro do Brás e a deterioração urbana' Universidade de São Paulo MA thesis, 1984 and Véras, 'O Bairro do Brás em São Paulo', 1991.

5 Concept formulated by W. Benjamin (1987) in his writings on Naples in the 1930s, reflecting upon modernity in countries on the periphery of capitalism. On the current applicability of such a concept to address peripheral capitalist societies, see Wille Bolle, *A Fisiognomia da Metrópole Moderna* (São Paulo 1994), 33; G. Gillock, *Myth and Metropolis: Walter Benjamin and the City* (Cambridge 1996), 21–36, and S. Buck Morss, *A Dialética do Olhar. Walter Benjamin e o projeto das passagens* (Belo Horizonte/Chapecó 2002), 51–3.

does construction co-exist with destruction, but also abandonment and ruining spring up even before the completion of new buildings.[6]

Before exploring further the São Paulo case study, it is useful to consider some theoretical assumptions on the relations between history and oral history, and between memory, collective memory and individual memory, as these affect the way urban space is developed, consumed and remembered.

History, memory and urban space

Construction and destruction associated with urban segregation is not a recent process. In this respect, São Paulo shares some common characteristics with Haussman's Paris, and other capitals.[7] The continuous reinvention of urban form, therefore, including urban renewal and/or preservation, keeps neighbourhoods and communities in a state of flux, and São Paulo is no exception. On the other hand, since the 1970s, the revitalization of urban areas has generated considerable interest in the fate of those displaced and in their memories.[8] Segregation and displacement have prompted studies on urban processes in a global setting[9], studies that have resorted to memories and the important role they play in the reconstruction of urban areas.[10]

This 'culture of memory' also makes its presence felt in the humanities, especially in history, when the question of memory is incorporated with

[6] 'In such areas, one can hardly tell what is still being built from what is decaying. For nothing is ready, nothing has been concluded.' W. Benjamin, *Obras Escolhidas II. Rua de Mão Única* (São Paulo 1987), 145–54.

[7] W. Benjamin, *Obras Escolhidas III. Charles Baudelaire: um lírico no auge do capitalismo* (São Paulo 1991), 67–101.

[8] A. Huyssen, *Seduzidos pela memória. Arquitetura, monumentos, mídia* (Rio de Janeiro 2000), 9–40.

[9] For more on how this process came into place in North American cities, particularly in Baltimore, see D. Harvey, *Condição pós-moderna* (São Paulo 2000), 69–96, and in the European cities of Paris, Barcelona, Bilbao, Lisbon and Berlin, see O. Arantes, 'Uma estratégia fatal. A cultura nas novas gestões urbanas', in O. Arantes, et al. (eds), *A cidade de pensamento único. Desmanchando consensos* (Petrópolis 2000), 11–74. On the significance and intensification of patrimonialization processes in contemporary societies see F. Choay, *A Alegoria do Patrimônio* (São Paulo 2001) and H.P. Jeudy, *La Machinerie Patrimoniale* (Paris 2001).

[10] For information on Brazilian cities, and Rio de Janeiro in particular, see C. Vainer, 'Os liberais também fazem planejamento urbano? Glosas ao 'Planejamento Estratégico da Cidade do Rio de Janeiro' in O. Arantes., et al. (eds), *A cidade do pensamento único. Desmanchando consensos*, 105–20, and L.F. Vaz and P. Jacques, 'A cultura na revitalização urbana – espetáculo ou participação?', *Espaço e Debates*, 42–44, 2003, 129–40.

oral history.[11] Since its inception as an academic discipline in the nineteenth century, oral history has experienced an uneasy relationship with the history profession based on the resistance of academic historians to the use and meaning of oral testimony.[12] Faced with history's recurrent arguments with regard to the supposed fragility of oral sources,[13] the debate over memory has matured with the consolidation of the position of oral history within history.[14] The greater part of this debate is based on Maurice Halbwachs' sociology of memory[15] and will be further explored here with respect to the relationship between history and memory, as well as the relationships between individual memory and collective memory, and between memory and urban space. These relationships between history and memory, while of critical importance to the understanding of a variety of contemporary issues, are not without limitations as contributors to this volume have noted in other contexts.

Halbwachs' sociology of memory establishes a rigid division between collective memory and history, the latter being primarily written, systematized and presented as a rational critique of the past, while collective memory is presented as primarily oral, affective, and spontaneous. This rigid division implies a dichotomy that imposes obstacles to the perception of the intersection between history and memory in modernity.[16] A second feature of Halbwachsian sociology is the dichotomy between individual memory

---

[11] This is related to specific historical contexts as with the incorporation of the study of the new social movements in the 1960s and 1970s, and with the reports on the Holocaust in the 1980s. See, respectively, M. Ferreira, 'História Oral: um inventário das diferenças', in M. Ferreira, *Entre-vistas: abordagens e usos da história oral* (Rio de Janeiro 1996), 1–13 and Huyssen, 'Seduzidos pela memória', 9–40.

[12] For the relation between history and oral history, see M. Ferreira, 'História Oral', 1–13.

[13] The primacy of written documents based on the belief in their objectivity and reliability, and the dismissal of individuals' accounts for lack of representativeness and impossibility of generalization.

[14] This is due not only to a political reason, when the 'vanquished' of history are given a voice, but also for methodological and theoretical reasons: the consolidation of a history of the present time, handling live testimonies, and the recognition of the importance of subjectivity whose 'distortions' grant access to the universe of representations and, therefore, of the symbolic.

[15] Developed in M. Halbwachs, *Les Cadres Sociaux de la Mémoire* (Paris 1994) and *A Memória Coletiva* (São Paulo 1990), 131–43.

[16] Such dichotomy is reproduced in important authors of the French historiography as in Pierre Nora's radical argument diagnosing the end of memory in modernity, with memory taking refuge in history in 'places of memory'. On these relations between history and memory in the French and English historiographies, see J.A. Seixas, 'Percursos de memória em terras de história: problemáticas atuais', in S. Bresciani and M, Naxara (eds), *Memória e (res)sentimento. Indagações sobre uma questão sensível* (Campinas 2001), 37–58.

and collective memory. Initially, embracing a Durkheimian approach,[17] Halbwachs pointed out that even though it is the individual who remembers, it is within the group that s/he acquires, evokes, recognizes, and situates his/her recollections. Consequently memories reproduce the *point of view* of the group.[18] Subsequently, Halbwachs emphasizes the role of individual memory but recognizes that the individual only exists as a 'crossing of groups' – in other words, that the individual is the point where these groups, and their collective thoughts, intersect.[19]

Halbwachs also argues that relations between the individual/group and space are marked by a reciprocal determination: the space mirrors the group's image while simultaneously influencing it by virtue of its materiality.[20] Although, individuals/groups and space transform each other, the image that the space projects on to the group (and vice versa) is one of immobility and stability. Though spatial factors fundamentally affect the individual or group because of 'the inert nature of physical things', personal considerations are most important because of the relative stability of social groups.'[21] This durability is exemplified both by specific urban spaces – as in some old districts inside the modern city and in small towns where neighbourhood sociability is associated with stable local traditions[22] – and by the fact that the built environment is transformed more slowly by social relations.[23]

This is not to say that there are not radical transformations in a city: war, demolition, and reconstruction brought about by public works, among others, can each abruptly change the social composition of a district.[24] However, challenged by the transformations in urban space, Halbwachs goes on to single out the resistance of those groups embedded in a particular area and whose resistance is partially derived from the spatial arrangement

---

[17] For though it is the individual who remembers, it is within the group that he acquires, evokes, recognizes, and situates his recollections; in sum, sustains them. Halbwachs, *Les Cadres Sociaux*, VI.

[18] Halbwachs, *Les Cadres Sociaux*, VI; Halbwachs, *A Memória Coletiva*, 25–52.

[19] R. Bastide, 'Mémoire Collective et Sociologie du Bricolage', *L'Anné Sociologique*, 1970, 65–108.

[20] Halbwachs, *A Memória Coletiva*, 133.

[21] Halbwachs, *A Memória Coletiva*, 132. Halbwachs analyses the role of spatial images in collective memory based on the Comtean idea that psychological and emotional stability is rendered possible by the image of permanence and stability provided by the material objects with which we have contact in our everyday lives.

[22] Halbwachs, *A Memória Coletiva*, 135.

[23] 'Local habits resist the forces that tend to transform them, and that resistance better allows us to perceive to what extent, in such groups, the collective memory has its point of support on spatial images', Halbwachs, *A Memória Coletiva*, 136.

[24] Halbwachs, *A Memória Coletiva*, 136.

itself.[25] Insofar as that urban space is the objectification of the group, the strength of the group's 'tradition' and 'habit' stems from the space itself, of which it is the image.[26]

Thus, the group resists, and tries to adapt and keep its former equilibrium under novel conditions. Individuals/groups are islands of tradition and stability surviving amidst fundamentally transformed space. It is precisely the resistance of the group in the face of such profound physical transformation as the destruction of a neighbourhood that causes, in Halbwachs' view, nostalgia and banishment to be felt by long-time residents as strictly individual feelings.[27]

In this relationship between collective memory and individual memory, Halbwachs does not take into consideration nostalgia's social or sociological character, conceived as a strictly individual process.[28] The social dimension of resentment,[29] melancholy and mourning[30] cannot be comprehended otherwise in the unstable and fragile nature of modern urban space and its social groups, who leave barely any trace of their past on the urban landscape.[31]

This, then, is the context for understanding the redevelopment of the space associated with the Brás district underground station. Using inhabitants' oral narratives conducted between 1998 and 2002, both individually and in groups, numerous thematic and life-story interviews with individuals related

---

[25] 'If between the houses, the streets, and their group of inhabitants *there were just a relation entirely accidental and ephemeral*, men might destroy their houses, their block, their city, and rebuild others on the same site, according to a different plan; but if stones allow themselves to be carried, *it is not so easy to modify the bonds that stones and men establish.*' Halbwachs, *A Memória Coletiva*, 136. My italics.

[26] Halbwachs, *A Memória Coletiva*, 137.

[27] 'Such individual sorrow or uneasiness *has no effect because it does not concern the group* who, on the other hand, does not feel inhibited to demonstrate the collective suffering and outrage, and protests immediately. It resists with all the might of its traditions and this resistance is not ineffective.' Ibid, 137.

[28] V.S. Pereira, 'Brás: canteiros da memória na modernidade de São Paulo', Universidade de São Paulo PhD thesis, 2002, 28.

[29] P. Ansart, 'História e memória dos ressentimentos', in M.S. Bresciani and M. Naxara (eds), *Memória e (res)sentimento. Indagações sobre uma questão sensível* (Campinas 2001), 15–36.

[30] P. Ricoeur, *La mémoire, L'histoire, L'Oubli* (Paris 2000).

[31] Although widespread urban revitalization or preservation have outgrown the means of urban material destruction, the recovery of city images, made possible through reminiscence, is not immune to the trivialization carried out by the media, cultural marketing and tourism. And we also agree with Huyssen, *Seduzidos pela Memória*, 9–40, in that Halbwachs' sociology of memory cannot account for the contemporary processes involved in the constitution of collective memory, for the author works with relatively stable spaces and social groups.

a process of 'urban emptiness' or desolation, as just described.[32] Despite the diverse personal backgrounds and collective experiences, all groups shared one image of the district: that of the 'cemetery'. To understand the reproduction of this funerary image of the Brás district, commonly held among distinct groups and in various contexts, narratives associated with the demolitions that produced that 'emptiness' were collected and analysed. Analysis of these official interventions in spaces and areas formerly regarded as individually owned or owned by groups was based on the concept of 'anamorphosis', which hypothesizes that urban space is composed of different temporal layers operated by the memory and composed of buildings, gestures and discourses.[33]

Transmission of these memories, whether forgotten or rejected, fragmented or confusing, individual or collective, specialized or colloquial, is rendered possible by '*doxa*', or opinion. The urban 'doxa' is malleable, mutant, incessantly transporting clusters of memories, and its transmission implies a process of transformation: 'anamorphosis'. Operated by language, 'anamorphosis' is the work of time on space, which produces shifts in meaning between the images, allowing them 'to accommodate the different cultural strata and to keep record of the evolving past'.[34] By means of its symbolic element – which blends references of mythical and historical times, of fiction and reality, of fact and legend – attempts were made to understand each group's representations and form of appropriation of the city space: their refusal or acceptance of it, whether it should be destroyed or used. Summing up, how was meaning built out of 'urban emptiness' and historic debris?

The 'Future in Suspension': art and urban planning

In 2002, Arte/Cidades, a Brazilian non-governmental organization, reflected on the role of the city's East Side in the new global urban dynamics. In several districts of that area, the Brás district among them, the 'Artecidadezonaleste'

[32] These were categorized into Group 1 – long-time residents, who had had their houses appropriated for the construction of the underground, and Group 2 – those the demolitions had not affected including the street vendors and the residents of the housing projects. See Pereira, thesis, 2002.

[33] A. Cauquelin, *Essai de philosophie urbaine* (Paris 1982).

[34] Notion based on Erwin Panofsky's concept of pseudomorphosis, a process akin to the dream: condensation, replacement and semantic games transform the initial theme into another one which just barely holds any relation with the first. In it, 'The image, charged with multiple significations, deforms in the course of time, at the flow of events, following an external lifeline and, at the same time, fully preserving its internal consistence (its theme).' A. Cauquelin, *Essai de philosophie urbaine*, 46–53.

set up a number of installations. That 'urban emptiness' could not be ignored by artist Carlos Vergara, who intervened in that space through a work entitled '*Futuro em Suspensão*' [The Future in Suspension], by painting the ground red except for some question marks deliberately left in the texture of roughcast cement. According to its curator, Nelson Peixoto, the installation reflects the 'failure' of those urban projects associated with the building of viaducts and undergrounds.[35] In these areas, 'left to their own fate', a reflection of 'the urbanistic and social disaster', 'the future is in suspension'.[36] Unlike the urban planner, the artist 'produces an effect without knowing what the output will be'; 'the artist doesn't anticipate'[37]; he does not predict the reactions, the interpretations, or the uses of the work of art.

9.1 Carlos Vergara's *The Future in Suspension*

Source: Photograph: Marcelo Martinelli.

The work '*Futuro em Suspensão*' is intended thus as criticism and rejection of the urban planner's misconstrued assumption of time as emptiness and uniformity and of space as neutrality.[38] Hence, the interrogation marks of the artistic intervention in the area – 'what is it for?' – are also paralleled in

[35] N.B. Peixoto, *As máquinas de guerra contra os aparelhos de captura* (São Paulo 2002).

[36] Peixoto, *As máquinas de guerra.*

[37] Peixoto, *As máquinas de guerra.*

[38] Cauquelin, *Essai de Philosophie Urbaine*, 5–62.

the curiosity manifested by the underground users turned observers of urban space – 'what is it?' – and in the question posed by our work – 'what was it?' Future, present, past ... time itself is in 'suspension'. And the very same interrogations about the temporality of that site link the language of the work of art to the mute and anonymous interrogation of the underground users. To solve this time mystery, some answers arise through the oral narrative of the district's inhabitants.

A time of tradition: the Clock

José D'Angelo, aged 63, a small shoemaking businessperson, is a former resident who had his house expropriated. He recalls the memory of an old clock set onto the top of a building at the end of his street. The building was demolished, and on that site, they built the underground station. His narrative tells the history of the building and its clock, a replica of London's 'Big Ben', which served as a landmark for the neighbourhood.

> That building was constructed in the nineteenth century, 1880 ... perhaps before! Because this was the '*Casa dos Ingleses*', they imported everything, everything came from England. This building, this tower here is a replica of the Big Ben in London. As a matter of fact, when they were tearing everything down I had the pleasure of ... and now I am talking to you about that ... I photographed it because I thought this was *mankind's biggest waste of time*, that this *would be permanent history*. After the English people in came 'Wilson Sons', another English company, doing business in import-export, navigation, with their own ships. At that time, goods arrived [at the harbour] in Santos, came with the railway and were unloaded here, in this building you see right here [showing me the picture]. Then with time it ended, 'Wilson Sons' started selling their part, and the Jabaquara bus company moved in.[39] After the Jabaquara company, this building became city property and in came CMTC[40], which today is ... I can't remember the name. And here, next to it, this was let to the Viação Cometa[41]. Viação Cometa started here in this building. (...)[42]

José D'Angelo concludes:

> The older folks called it '*Casa dos Ingleses*' ... that would be my father, my grandfather ... But us, my generation, with the coming of 'Jabaquara', CMTC, we then called it 'The Cometa Clock', in my time.

39 Private bus company.
40 The municipal bus company.
41 Private bus company.
42 Pereira, *Canteiros da Memória*, 68–70.

9.2 Removal of the Clock during construction

Source: Personal files of José D'Angelo.

> But then again, if you take the other generations, they called it by yet another name …

José D'Angelo's recollection of the clock continues:

> I was born on this very street here, Campos Sales Street, quite near this building … I remember this picture [the clock's] … it's something that really touches me to be talking to you about … all the neighbours checked the time on that clock … All of them! There was no 'What time is it?' Today you pick up the phone to find out the exact time.

The memory of the clock is also cherished by other residents of the old neighbourhood who, when interviewed, recaptured moments of everyday life and the New Years' Eve celebrations. For more than half a century, the building and its clock expressed a link between a private and a collective temporality, that is, between the neighbourhood and the industrialization of the city, as well as across generations, which was only broken with the demolition.

The clock was the representation of a homogeneous and empty time (chronological time), but it also represented another temporality characterized by private and collective rituals. It is the image of Kronos, the devouring time, but also of Kairos, time apprehended and immobilized by individual memory as well as collective memory.[43] Therefore, from a historical perspective, the clock and the building both represent the city's (destroyed) industrial past crystallized in the architecture and, from the perspective of memory, the image of that group in time and space. They mark the presence of the past in the present, which, in turn, changes without breaking away entirely from the past. It is expressed in the correspondence between nomination and the life cycle of birth and death in a human context, and is replicated in the physical context of the building and its clock, or more generally in the building's recycled function. The replacements capture both continuity (in the sense of place and urban memories) embedded in transformation, and stability embedded in change, configuring a time of tradition.

Yet only the building was destroyed, not the clock, which was relocated. Its destination, according to José D'Angelo, was to be a farm, but it never arrived there for some neighbours started a campaign against its sale. Today it can be seen at Sé Station, the underground's central station. It no longer ticks the time of the old neighbourhood. Now it ticks for anonymous city passengers.

A time of rupture: The Second World War

Mrs Pascoalina Cerullo, 84-years-old and a retired housekeeper, recalls that, in 1948, she and her husband, a typographer, bought their old house in the same street, which also served as her husband's print works. The purchase was made without any guarantee because the selling party had gone to the war, abandoning the house. In order to settle the deal, they would have to wait for his return. However, the soldier never returned and that was how they bought the house and how they began their life there.

In another context, Ms Maria Carta, 79-years-old, a retired homemaker and former owner of a pastry shop, remembers the demolition in the context of the beginning of the construction of the underground in 1976. When

---

[43] Cauquelin, *Essai de Philosophie*, 40–46.

asked how she felt when she passed by the underground demolition sites, Ms Carta replied:

> Oh, there were people who cried tears that not even sheets could dry. I saw when they tore down those houses and the people leaving without even knowing where to, leaving those pretty houses, houses they had sacrificed to make, you see? And then suddenly to change everything, it's too strong an emotion, you know? Only those who watched and saw can tell you what it is to feel that … that emotion. Just like when the soldiers came back in 1945. So much sadness, so much. That's the year I was married, in '45. We'd cry just to watch them arriving. Alive, one with only one leg, another without … without the arm, another one injured, and still another … So we felt that … that sadness and to watch them take away the homes where the children were born and raised, after so many years, from one minute to the next, it's too saddening. It's sad, it's no joke, you see? There was a time when they were saying that they would demolish to open up an avenue … or something like that. And I started feeling sort of … Oh, my God, will I … But then it was all [a rumour].[44]

In the recollections, two temporalities are intertwined: personal history (the purchase of the house and the marriage) and collective history (the departure and return of the soldiers from the war and the demolition of the houses to give place to the construction of the underground). Collective history is not only a dimension of personal history, but also an image recovered by memory. The distant past (the war) is appropriated to give a meaning and a magnitude to the recent past (the demolition). Two different temporalities – that of the history of the war and that of the history of urbanism – are linked by recollection in order to comprehend the meaning and dimension of that 'urban emptiness', the collective mourning and trauma. It is a time of rupture. The image of the severing of the body becomes a metaphor for the neighbourhood, the severing of a part of its territory, and a metaphor for the subjectivity, the severing of the individuals in relation to their ties with the neighbourhood and the place.

Time Disciplined: the *Camelódromo*

Towards the end of 1997, the city government, headed by former mayor Celso Pitta (1997–2000), in association with commercial and financial capital, represented by '*Associação Viva o Centro*' turned its attention to the architectural heritage and urban design of the old city centre with the intention of implementing revitalization and preservation projects in the area. These included *Paulista* Avenue and the area of the 'Central Triangle',

---

44 Pereira, *Canteiros da Memória*, 78–9.

Direita, *XV de Novembro,* and *São Bento* streets. In preparation for the redevelopment, city authorities carried out a series of operations designed to expel the homeless and the street vendors, who occupied the thoroughfares of the Brás district such as *Largo da Concórdia* and its surroundings. During these '*Projeto Dignidade*' (Dignity Project) operations, the derelict area (urban emptiness) regained its function when local officials ordered the transfer of the street vendors, from a bustling downtown-like area, the *Largo da Concórdia*, to the new area. Dubbed the *camelódromo*,[45] the emptiness acquired a new function: that of segregating and confining informal street commerce. On the ground, green-painted rectangles exhibited the numbers that would identify each stall.

Consequently, the system that assigned a particular place for each stallholder transformed the anonymous crowd of street vendors of *Largo da Concórdia* and the surrounding area into an organized entity.[46] Thus demarcated and numbered by officialdom, the area sought to discipline the urban space and impose a rational configuration[47] to the *camelódromo*.

9.3 The Camelódromo

Source: Photograph: Verônica Sales Pereira.

---

[45] Derived from the Brazilian Portuguese word *camelô*, a popular name for street vendors.

[46] M. Foucault, *Vigiar e Punir: nascimento da prisão* (Petrópolis 1988).

[47] Foucault, *Vigiar e Punir*, 131.

The street vendors, however, resisted the relocation programme (from *Largo da Concórdia* to the 'emptiness' of the *camelódromo*) because they considered the space a deserted area. The project fell apart. Because the space assigned to stallholders was in an isolated area, where very few people circulated and retailing was limited in comparison with the main streets of the district, the image of death was explicitly evoked in the speeches of the street vendors. It was described by Afonso José da Silva, 34-years-old, and street vendors' union leader as a 'dead (commercial) spot' and as a 'cemetery',[48] reflections of the lifelessness that resulted from the earlier demolition programme.

Even the underground company could not remain indifferent to that 'urban emptiness' and, as early as the 1990s, installed several benches around the station in an attempt to transform it into a public square. Later on, the company itself removed them because the homeless, children and adults alike, dependent on the nearby shelters and social institutions, had improvised them as makeshift beds. Not even the abandoned police station of the *camelódromo* was left unscathed, as it, too, was occupied. The renewal programme for the public square had failed and all that was left of it was an urban blight.[49]

A time of legend: Tombs Square

Marcia, 40-years-old, a pre-school teacher and 11-year resident of the COHAB projects[50], describes the emptiness:

> It's full of tombs; I mean, we say they are 'tombs.' Because, you see, look at the shape of the squares, see, so now it's the Tombs Square, the one filled with little squares, where the city was going to set up stalls. But the street vendors united and didn't come here ... So it was abandoned again.[51]

The resistance of the street vendors to the disciplined urban space proposed by city authorities had transformed the area's streets, in the late 1990s, into a battlefield. At the same time, it imposed a new emptiness: the despicable official plots had had their meaning changed by language and the *camelódromo* is perceived as a cemetery by street vendors and residents of the COHAB projects.

---

48 Pereira, *Canteiros da Memória*, 254.

49 As this work was the product of a broader research, the local homeless were not interviewed though those from a neighbouring area were.

50 *Companhia Metropolitana de Habitação de São Paulo*: the São Paulo Metropolitan Housing Company.

51 Pereira, *Canteiros da Memória*, 228.

A tomb is a 'funereal monument erected in memory of someone over the place where he/she is buried'.[52] Death, monument, recollection: traces of the demolition of entire blocks –the emptiness – and of state-enforced spatial segregation – the *Camelódromo* – had transformed that space into a place of death, and, yet, of recollection (Tombs Square). But whose recollections? And of what?

According to Marcia, it is not rare for people to ask her if there actually is or ever had been a cemetery in the area. The funereal image itself revived unknown and anonymous urban memories, traces of which survive in the narrative as fiction and which, involuntarily, refer back to the principal image – the cemetery – and to the many mutated meanings that surround its name: Tombs Square.

Final considerations

Three crucial moments can be identified in the urban history of São Paulo, each associated with the various modernizations constituting the 'emptiness'.[53] At the turn of the nineteenth century, cheap land, marshland, along the courses of the Tamanduateí and Tietê Rivers made it possible not only to build railways and factories, but also houses for the working classes.[54] In the 1970s, planning was the tool used by the military regime's political project to modernize public administration and to intervene in a 'rational' and authoritarian way in the cities' configuration.[55] A conservative modernization cycle based on urban expansion, social integration and on the concept of project[56] had come to an end.

That cycle had barely finished and a new wave of modernization, based on the market-driven economics advocated by the neo-liberal ideology and

---

[52] A.B.H. Ferreira, *Novo Dicionário Básico da Lingua Portuguesa Folha/ Aurélio* (São Paulo 1995).

[53] In the discussion that follows modernity and modernization are distinguished by resorting to Gorelik's synthesis of Giddens' work: 'Modernity is therefore taken here as a time's most general cultural *ethos*, as the lifestyles and social organization that have become generalized and institutionalized uninterruptedly since their rational-European origin in the fifteenth and sixteenth centuries ... and modernization, as those core processes that continue to transform the world materially'. 'O moderno em debate: cidade, modernidade, modernização', in W.M. Miranda (ed.), *Narrativas da Modernidade* (Belo Horizonte 1999), 5.

[54] R. Rolnik, *A Cidade e a Lei. Legislação, política urbana e territórios da cidade de São Paulo* (São Paulo 1997).

[55] M.P. Véras, *O Bairro do Brás em São Paulo*, 526.

[56] A. Gorelik, 'O moderno em debate: cidade, modernidade, modernização', in W.M. Miranda (ed.), *Narrativas da Modernidade* (Belo Horizonte 1999), 55–80.

9.4 Tombs Square (The Camelódromo)

Source: Photograph: Verônica Sales Pereira.

extending into the 1990s, replaces it.[57] Today, in a globalized economy, urban space is cultural marketing's merchandise par excellence in the competition waged by cities to attract foreign investments. Abandoned or ruined architecture, and urbanism reminiscent of that first cycle, are valued and become the object of much dispute. On one side, we have the

---

[57] A. Gorelik, 'O moderno em debate'.

impoverished classes, who squat in them and improvise by living in the streets and working informally. On the other, the State, the elites and the middle classes, who seek to reoccupy them through renewal programmes, combining the historical architectural legacy of the old city centres[58] with social and spatial segregation in a widespread process of gentrification.[59]

On this 'urban emptiness', nurtured by the destruction of the city's history and the unfinished decay of its buildings, rise the ruins of urban modernity. According to Benjamin,[60] the temporality of modernity is most tragically clarified by its ruins, marked by the ephemeral and death. Commenting on Benjamin's interpretation of the nature of modernity in Baudelaire's work, Gagnebin remarks that 'Haussman effects the material bringing together of the old and the modern by manifesting the decrepitude of the present; to the ruins of the past correspond those of the present; death does not only inhabit the palaces of yesterday, but has taken possession of the edifices under construction. And it is this convergence of past and present in their future common form, death, which characterizes the temporal consciousness of modernity.'[61]

From a distinct theoretical perspective, Faoro concurs with the Benjaminian allegory.[62] He analyses the various modernization processes that occur throughout the history of Brazilian society and concludes that they characterize modernizations without modernity. Modernization processes, as promoted by a succession of self-appointed ruling elites, are not only abandoned before their conclusion but barely offer any real benefit to the majority of the population. According to Faoro, there is an accumulation of spectres and ruins, the result of an endless reiteration of failures. These modernizations 'are circumscribed to a *circular time* in which memory is conditioned to a precarious time, and last only until another wave is superimposed over the last, dissolving both ... History thus fossilized is a *cemetery* of projects, of illusions and of spectres.'[63]

If Benjamin conceives of the allegory of death and ruins, or in other terms, of the simultaneity between construction and destruction and between novelty and obsolescence, as constituting modernity, Faoro addresses the image of the phantasmagoric not as a founding element of modernity, but as representing the opposition between modernity at the centre of capitalism

---

58 Jeudy, *La machinerie patrimoniale*.

59 Harvey, *Condição Pós Moderna*, 69–96 and Arantes, *Uma estratégia fatal*, 11–74.

60 Benjamin, *Obras Escolhidas III*, *Charles Baudelaire*, 67–101.

61 J.M. Gagnebin, *Sete aulas sobre linguagem, memória e história* (Rio de Janeiro 1997), 150.

62 R. Faoro, 'A questão nacional: a modernização', *Estudos Avançados*, 14, vol. 6, 1992, 7–22b.

63 Faoro, 'A questão nacional', 19, my italics.

and in its periphery. Although not intending to focus our discussion on these two perspectives, it is worth pointing out that, despite their distinctiveness, both converge to the same image.

'Cemetery of projects'[64] and 'field of ruins',[65] the history of these modernizations that never catch up with modernity are expressed in the urban through the 'emptiness', recalled and symbolized by the inhabitants through the image of death.

Figuratively this modern cemetery, captured by oral history in the form of individual and collective memory, articulates many images: of the clock – the ephemeral in the disrupted transmission of the industrial, the family's and the neighbourhood's past; of the war – the individual's uprootedness and mourning; of the *camelódromo*, the emptied and segregated public space; and of the tombs, the legendary and anonymous memory of death.

Through this symbolic mediation, the ruined temporalities that characterize the urban history of the city of São Paulo are lived and represented in the inhabitants' experience. If the material ruins are signals of these historical strata, the oral narrative not only recovers the fragmented images of the past, but also, while articulating these images in the process of recollecting, updates them. The recollection thus attributes a meaning to that which, at first sight, appears as an empty area replete with interrogations and forgotten memories. But that is something the commuters journeying to work on the East–West underground line as it passes by the Brás station ignore.

Further reading

Bastide, R., Mémoire collective et sociologie du bricolage. L'Année Sociologique, 1971.

Benjamin, W,. *The Arcades Project* (Cambridge, Mass. 1999).

Buck-Morss, S., *Dialectics of Seeing. Walter Benjamin and the Arcades Project* (Boston 1991).

Cauquelin, A., *Cinévilles* Paris, 10–18, 1979.

Cauquelin, A., *Essai de Philosophie Urbaine* (Paris 1982).

Choay, F., *L' allégorie du patrimoine* (Paris 1996).

Gilloch, G., *Myth and Metropolis. Walter Benajmin and the City* (Cambridge 1996).

Halbwachs, M., *Les Cadres Sociaux de la Mémoire* (Paris 1994).

Halbwachs, M., *La mémoire collective* (Paris 1997).

[64] Faoro, 'A questão nacional', 19.

[65] Benjamin, *Obras Escolhidas III, Charles Baudelaire*, 86.

Huyssen, A., *Present Pasts. Urban Palimpsests and The Politics of Memory* (Stanford 2003).
Jaisson, M., 'Temps et espace chez Maurice Halbwachs (1925–1945)', *Revue d'histoire des Sciences Humaines*, 1999, 1, 163–78.
Jeudy, H.P., *La Machinerie Patrimoniale* (Paris 2001).
Mazzella, S., 'La ville-memoire', in *La ville des sciences sociales. Enquête/ numéro quatre* (Marseilles 1997), 177–90.
Ricoeur, P., *La Mémoire, l'Histoire, l'Oubli* (Paris 2000).
Todorov, T., *Les Abus de la Mémoire* (Paris 1998).

CHAPTER TEN

Uncommon threads: oral history, historical narrative, and public art in Los Angeles

Ruth Wallach

Urban redevelopment and public art

Los Angeles is a quintessential city of the twentieth century. It is a metropolis bleeding into the surrounding communities, with freeways acting as major transportation arteries. It is a city where there are few public spaces, and where the difference between public and private spaces is often ambiguous at best.

Since its inception in 1781, Los Angeles has undergone continuous changes. Some were due to demographic and economic shifts, such as the outflow of middle-class citizens into suburban and other communities after the Second World War. Others were imposed by urban planners and city government in an effort to reshape the downtown area. Still others had to do with displacements of particular ethnic enclaves, and had roots in a variety of causes. Examples include the displacement of Chinatown in the 1930s and of the Mexican-American working-class neighbourhoods in the 1950s in order to complete large building projects (Union Station, 1939, and Dodger Stadium, 1962, respectively), and the displacement of the Japanese Americans to concentration camps during the Second World War. The recent large-scale urban projects to revitalize the central urban core brought with them efforts to define urban space as desirable space for public life through rehabilitation of buildings, re-designation of use of spaces, gentrification, and the commissioning of public artworks to define public space and to add to the history of the city's urban narrative.

The question of what is public space is problematic in Los Angeles. It is a city of considerable geographical and urban diversity; there are many disparate places to see and in which to be seen, with no comprehensible way to link them into a holistic network that could be shared by many of its residents. The absence of public life is linked to the city's absence of genuinely public spaces. Public spaces that 'do exist can be difficult to gain access to and even to find'.[1] In downtown Los Angeles 'the few public spaces within corporate plazas and buildings tend to look private and can be hard to find out how to enter'.[2] Many of the city's pavements in the commercial districts bear an inscription stating they are private property, and that 'permission to pass over revocable at any time', hinting at a complex interrelationship between the public and the private spheres in this city.[3]

Los Angeles' city centre has experienced a variety of redevelopment efforts in the post-Second World War period, the majority under the auspices of the Community Redevelopment Agency of Los Angeles (CRA/LA). CRA/LA is a public agency with a mission to attract private investment into economically depressed communities. Its mandate is broad: 'to eliminate slums and blight; revitalize older neighbourhoods; build low and moderate income housing; encourage economic development; create or retain employment opportunities; support the best in architecture, urban design and the arts; and ensure broad community participation'.[4] As part of this mandate CRA/LA has implemented a policy on public art, funded through a levy of 1 per cent on the cost of development. According to the Agency's 1993 Public Art Policy, artists and the arts are primary resources in the revitalization of the city of Los Angeles. The policy calls for consideration of regional artists as important interpreters of community needs within Agency-initiated redevelopment projects, and as agents in bringing cohesion into public spaces.

> ... artists have taken a more active role in helping to define public spaces. The placement of large, frequently imported, artworks or objects on plazas has given way to statements by artists generated from the community experience. The artist as planner and designer seeks to create places which will attract people, offering them insight, repose, amusement, delight, or a sense of destination.[5]

Because Los Angeles is a very mobile, fast-paced city, a variety of circulation routes, such as streets, alleys, roads, tunnels, and public transportation stations have become loci for commissioning and displaying public art. It is public art that contextualizes circulation routes as public spaces. In this chapter, two such works are discussed, both sponsored by the CRA/LA mandated 1 per cent for art policy, and both located in downtown

---

1 J. Price, 'Life's a breach', *Los Angeles Times*, 15 June 2003, M2.

2 Price, 'Life's a breach', M2.

3 This language is taken from a small bronze inscription set within the pavement on Flower Street just north of the intersection with Wilshire Boulevard, downtown Los Angeles.

4 CRA/LA History, http://lacity.org/CRA/glance.html, last accessed April 2005.

5 CRA/LA Art Program, http://www.crala.org/arts/art/A2/1.htm, last accessed April 2005.

Los Angeles. These works, dating from the 1990s, commemorate two large ethnic communities important in the history of the city. In both cases, the artists relied on discussions with the local communities about how best to commemorate important events, and both artists used oral and/or archival evidence as an integral part of the visual aspect of the works themselves. While these are not the only public artworks in the city to use oral or archival elements, they have been selected for a variety of reasons: they commemorate communities with roots in East Asia that had somewhat similar histories in California and Los Angeles; both communities experienced geographical displacements important in defining their history within the fabric of the city; and both works are positioned within ambiguous physical spaces, neither private nor entirely public. They are interesting examples of contemporary commemorative public artworks, and use ephemeral records to fix strands of historic communal narratives. Both cases illustrate the contested nature of fixing communal histories in public settings, and that communal dialogues about historic memory are multi-layered and political.

Public space and the public

There is a longstanding understanding in western culture of what constitutes public space. The ideal public space has been historically seen as neutral and democratic. The concept of a neutral public space traces back to antiquity, and assumes a society holding a common view of politics and history, and a common belief in objective freedom. According to Hannah Arendt, the term 'public' means that 'everything that appears in public can be seen and heard by everyone and has the widest possible publicity'; it also 'signifies the world itself, in so far as it is common to all of us and [is] distinguished from our privately owned place in it.'[6] Traditionally, the type of public art commissioned for such a neutral, democratic space is commemorative and often contemplative. Most common types of public artworks for such an environment have been fountains, large statues and busts, and columns. These works define public space as distinct. Nevertheless, and in tandem with an increasing infusion of the personal into the public, in modern times the design of commemorative public art has changed drastically in the last century. One such example of a public art work that is monumental, commemorative, and contemplative, is Maya Lin's Vietnam Veterans Memorial (1982). It is located on the Washington, DC Mall, a huge green commons considered by many to be an epitome of democratic space, geographically connecting the concrete symbols of American democracy, the Capitol, the White House, the Jefferson Memorial, and the Lincoln

[6] H. Arendt, *The Human Condition* (Garden City 1959), 45, 48.

10.1 Maya Lin, *Vietnam Veterans Memorial*, 1982. This is one of the best known examples of an American memorial that encourages private reflection in a public space.

Source: Photograph: Ruth Wallach, November 2003.

Memorial: 'Between them all is space – empty space, poetic evocation of the New World and actual promenade for civilian gathering.'[7] Lin's memorial is large yet intimate, inviting the public to meditate on the lives of individual Americans who died in the Vietnam conflict, in close and private physical proximity to the monument itself.

A critique of the democratic interpretation of the public realm is articulated by Jurgen Habermas. He describes the public realm as a permanent structure of communication and authority that is state-related and controlling.[8] This notion particularly accounts for the rise of the nation-state and its control of discourse, aesthetics and space, although it speaks to political control in a wider historic context. Habermas offers another lens through which to interpret the place of public art in urban redevelopment. Thus, commemorative public artworks are not merely formal, valorized representations of particular historic events, but in their setting such works are often removed from direct engagement with the public, positioned as awe-inspiring, remote, and authoritarian. Many large commemorative statues, whether placed in public squares or on boulevard medians, are often elevated above the viewer; others are placed in locations that do not allow physical proximity. In any case, they rarely include the kind of direct physical interaction that the Vietnam Veterans Memorial invites.

Contemporary theoretical discussions of public space recognize that complete agreement on its meaning is impossible because the concept of the 'public' comprises many different sub-spheres, organizations, and institutions, each with many voices representing race, gender, ethnicity, sexuality, and class. The publics have different and often conflicting voices. For example, in her article on the politics of art and public space, Rosalyn Deutsche criticizes the political left's discourse on the boundaries of public space because it leaves out feminism, which the left construes as an example of the private sphere.[9] In art historian Thomas Crow's words, the public is 'nothing more nor less than a series of representations'.[10] Instead of consensus-building and monumentalizing, public art is seen as fostering public debate and dialogue about representations of the public realm. Discussions on what constitutes the 'public' have certainly affected art design. While many people still think of public art as display of formal sculpture, contemporary examples include functional works such as street lamps and bike racks, environmental works

---

[7] C. Knight, 'A memorial to forget', *Los Angeles Times*, 23 May 2004, E27.

[8] J. Habermas, *The Structural Transformation of the Public Sphere: An Inquiry into a Category of Bourgeois Society* (Cambridge 1989), 24.

[9] R. Deutsche, 'Art and public space: questions of democracy', *Social Text*, 33, 1992, 34–53.

[10] T. Crow, *Painters and the Public Life in Eighteenth Century Paris* (New Haven 1985), 102.

such as community gardens and landscaped plazas, public performance works, and works of the spoken word intended for public places. Many works of public art are temporary, such as installations in shopping windows or children's poetry posters on public buses, and some are ephemeral, such as artist-designed video works which alternate with advertisements on monitors displayed in commercial plazas.

Nevertheless, contemporary urban development and the processes related to the commissioning of public art incorporate a positivist concept of public space, viewing it as democratic at its core, but also as controlling of the public's relationship to urban space. To think otherwise would mean accepting that there is no 'there' to represent.[11] In essence, city planners and other agencies are trying to create a vital urbanity which is egalitarian, able to cater to a multiplicity of purposes, essentially modernist, where public space is 'that which is ultimately within the ownership and care of the people as defined in democratic politics'.[12] The current efforts for revitalizing the urban core are directed toward the middle-classes, who have for the past half-century avoided the city; living, working, and finding entertainment in the suburbs, ostensibly because they perceived that the city did not support accepted models of propriety and civility.[13] The middle-classes can no longer be treated as an all-encompassing economic and sociological lump, and are receiving somewhat more nuanced attention from researchers and urban planners.[14] However, many redevelopment efforts, which often partner city and private organizations, centre on a limited number of activities such as entertainment and high-end retail. In addition to the question of how the middle-classes redefine the notion of urbanity, an area that needs more attention is what art historians call 'the gaze', in reference to how members of a particular class relate to urban space and to an art work and shape that work's cultural reception and use. For practical purposes, public art is squeezed into a world rationalized by city planners for the various (mostly middle-class) publics and becomes a means of announcing and defining certain urban spaces. Public art may be self-referential as with formalist sculpture, that is 'art for art's sake', or it can be site-specific and, perhaps, utopian. It is a means to assuage and define our needs for a communal urban space and for a history of urbanity in general.

---

[11] This idea was advanced to the author by Robert Michelson in the summer of 2003.

[12] M. Gooding, 'Public:art:space', in M. Gooding (ed.), *Public:Art:Space: A Decade of Public Art Commissions Agency, 1987–1997* (London 1998), 19.

[13] E. Goffman, *Relations in Public: Microstudies of the Public Order* (New York 1971), 326.

[14] A good overview on the fragmentation of American society is M. Weiss, *The Clustered World: How We Live, What We Buy, and What it All Means About Who We Are* (New York 1999).

The idea that public space as primarily defined for use by the middle-classes is complicated by urban planners' and artists' interests in accommodating the social geography, the gendering of place, and the histories of all publics. Public art, as it moves into the twenty-first century has eluded definition. It could be said that 'public art' redefined the notions of 'public' and of 'art' within the context of specialized visual and intellectual activities. Contemporary public artworks, as formal and symbolic constructions, are a matter of compound experience, and attempt to draw the viewer into a discussion of beliefs and values.[15] Yet, works that demand a compound engagement contain histories and ideas that may not be easily comprehensible to the larger public, although they contain important meaning to the specific communities commemorated. At the same time, many works often blend into the busy every-day urban environment, demarcating and negotiating the complexities of public and private spheres. Such is the nature of the works discussed below.

Commemorative public art and oral and archival evidence

Two recent works of public art in the downtown area of Los Angeles that incorporate oral or archival evidence are considered in some detail. These works deal with specific non-white ethnicities that experienced great strides and great setbacks in the periods commemorated by the works. Little Tokyo's *Omoide no Shotokyo* (*Remembering Old Little Tokyo*) from 1996 celebrates the history of the Japanese Americans in the city from 1890 to 1945. The 1992 *Listening for the Trains to Come* in the Chinatown area pays homage to the history of the Los Angeles Chinese community from the 1870s to the 1920s.

Remembering Old Little Tokyo, *1996*

Omoide no Shotokyo, known in English as *Remembering Old Little Tokyo*, is a $95,000 artist-created pavement stretching along the commercial block of historical 1st Street, which encompasses 15 commercial buildings. The original $865,000 urban improvement project, of which this public art piece is a part, reduced the existing pavement width by two feet, to make it more to scale for human use. The call to artists was to commemorate and describe the history of the development of the Little Tokyo Historic District.

The pavement incorporates brass plaques with text and bears some images related to Japanese American everyday life. The artist, Sheila Levrant De

[15] D. Novitz, 'Participatory art and appreciative practice', *The Journal of Aesthetics and Art Criticism*, 52, Spring 2001, 160.

Bretteville, divided the entire length of the pavement into two sections. The first section extends to the building line, and consists of six timelines, each representing a decade from the 1890s through the 1940s. Pavement inscriptions in front of the building entrances identify the buildings' historical uses, the business names, and the goods and services offered to the community during these decades. Another pavement timeline recalls the internment of Japanese Americans during the Second World War.[16] De Bretteville chose stainless steel, visually a cold and hard material, for the painful record of discrimination, such as this one recorded on a dark pavement band: '1942 – U.S. Executive Order 9066 forces all Nikkei out of their homes and into internment camps at Amache, Gila, Jerome, Heart Mountain, Manzanar, Minidoka, Rohwer, Poston, Topaz, Tule Lake.' Events commemorating the more mundane aspects of Japanese life, such as '1903 – Seiichi Kito opens original Fugetsu-do candy store on Weller St.' are recorded in brass, visually a brighter metal set against the yellow pavement band.

The second section of the pavement lists short recollections from three generations of Japanese Americans who lived or worked in Little Tokyo. An example is this quote from Fumiko Tani: 'At Kyodo Grill we mixed up Japanese and American ingredients into "gacha" and "champon" – dishes that were our customers' favorite.' De Bretteville obtained the quotations by conducting more than 50 interviews and by reviewing books and old newspapers.[17]

In addition to inscriptions, this part of the pavement contains pictures of ceremonial wrappings (tsutsumi), designed by the artist Sonia Ishii, which wrap/illustrate people's memories. Such tsutsumi include a suitcase, denoting trips to America and to Second World War internment camps, a wooden bucket used to pickle delicacies, and an apple pie. The latter is a quintessential American symbol, and is embedded in the pavement in reference to an interviewee who told de Bretteville that he always felt as American as apple pie.[18] According to de Bretteville, herself a daughter of central European Jewish immigrants, 'I just wanted to give a taste, literally, of how a Japanese American is American and Japanese. I tried to get both in there … We are all combinations of things.'[19]

The dialogue that took place in the community during the development stages of the project was not an easy one, and created tensions among

---

[16] M. Several, 'Omoide no Shotokyo, Background Information', http://www.publicartinla.com/Downtown/Little_Tokyo/omoide5.html 1998.

[17] Several, 'Omoide no Shotokyo'.

[18] L. Gordon, 'Sidewalk art puts Little Tokyo's history on display', *Los Angeles Times*, 9 August 1996, 3.

[19] L. Gordon, 'Sidewalk art'.

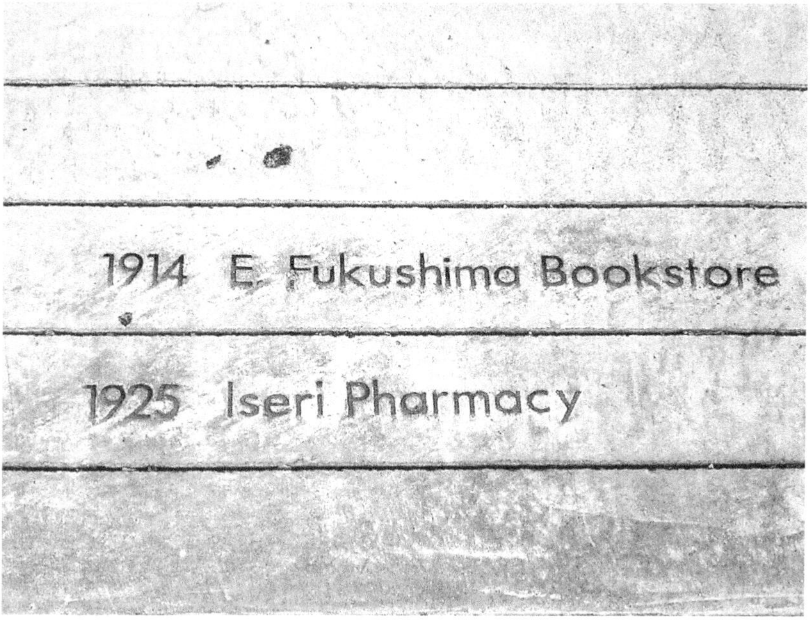

10.2 Sheila Levrant de Bretteville, *Remembering Old Little Tokyo*, 1996. Names of businesses operating in Little Tokyo from the 1890s to 1940, set into the pavement by the entrances to the buildings.

Source: Photograph: Ruth Wallach, January 2005.

generations of Japanese Americans, as well as disputes regarding several linguistic practices and the proper use of Japanese characters. Community representatives on the Little Tokyo Public Art Taskforce had differing opinions about the use of the quotations. Some were highly supportive of de Bretteville choosing recollections of daily life on the street, while others were highly critical, claiming that the recollections lacked drama. In a letter to a CRA public arts official, de Bretteville mentions that an active member of the Japanese American Community Cultural Center in Little Tokyo thought that the proposed quotes were appallingly banal and suggested more quotes about the Second World War internment.[20]

In another letter, defending herself from implications that she did not ask the right questions during the interviews and that she was not the right person to ask them, de Bretteville reveals not just what she sensed were

[20] Letter, Sheila Levrant de Bretteville to Mickey Gustin, 25 October 1994, Michael Several Collection, University of Southern California (subsequently USC).

10.3 Pavement section, Sheila Levrant de Bretteville, ***Remembering Old Little Tokyo*****, 1996. A section in the middle of the pavement, which incorporates reminiscences from oral interviews with pre-war residents of Little Tokyo, conducted by de Bretteville.**

Source: Photograph: Ruth Wallach, January 2005.

10.4 Tsutsumi of an Apple Pie, Sheila Levrant de Bretteville, ***Remembering Old Little Tokyo*****, 1996. Tsutsumi of an apple pie, set into the pavement amid several quotes from oral interviews conducted by Bretteville with pre-war residents of Little Tokyo.**

Source: Photograph: Ruth Wallach, January 2005.

important community memories, but also how her own sensibilities as an interviewer and artist were mixed into the process:

> As you know, the process I went through in getting these memories involved not only me but people who are themselves Japanese Americans who have lived and/or worked on this street asking the question 'What is it about this neighborhood that you want remembered by further generations?'... Of course, I feel these quotes are wonderful, and represent what the people want remembered and they touchingly evoke the neighborhood. I admit they are not dramatic but I heard many of these comments several times in one form or another – living in the hotels, the smells and sounds, the country people coming from afar and staying in the hotels, the organisations. Perhaps because my parents were immigrants and we lived with lots of family in a few rooms, making food that was half American and half middle European, in a neighborhood of a different ethnicity, but with some of the same features, I thought people would understand immigrant experience in general and a bit

> about hybridity, and the specificity of Japanese American history and culture in particular.[21]

Another major issue involved the question how the Issei (first generation Japanese Americans, many of whom started moving out of Old Little Tokyo into the surrounding communities in the 1920s and 1930s) wrote 'First Street' and 'Remember Old Little Tokyo' in Japanese script. What did the Japanese settlers name this area, and did they combine transliterated English terms and rendered them more Japanese-sounding?[22] Different linguistic suggestions reflected different attitudes on how the community saw itself and its relationship to the larger society.[23] One of de Bretteville's correspondents wrote:

> Doing work like this with a 'Japanese American' community is 'tricky.' In reading your letter I immediately thought about conflicting views which differing generations of Japanese Americans have held regarding 'Little Tokyo,' and 'ethnic enclave.' The Nisei,[24] in particular, are strongly inclined to reject any aspects of the 'Nihonjin-machi' ('Japanese Town') which might be tied to the past that they would rather forget ... The Sansei,[25] however, tend to idealize their ethnic heritage in the context of 'American dreams' and the notion that America is 'the sacred land of freedom and golden opportunities' and 'immigrants' paradise.' What views you would hold may restrict, or even decide, which events and dates you can emphasize in relation to the history of Little Tokyo.[26]

Another discussion ensued as the Japanese American National Museum, which anchors the Historic 1st Street on the east side, requested that the kanji characters[27] for the title of the work, originally planned to be included in the pavement there, be moved to another location. The museum felt that the inclusion of Japanese characters in such close proximity to its entrance suggested that it was a Japanese museum, rather than an American one.

---

[21] Letter, Sheila Levrant de Bretteville to Gloria Uchida, 17 August 1993, Michael Several Collection (USC).

[22] Letter, Sheila Levrant de Bretteville to Rinjiro Sodei, 24 December 1992, Michael Several Collection (USC).

[23] Several, 'Omoide no Shotokyo, Background'.

[24] 'Nisei' is a term used to designate second generation of Japanese Americans.

[25] 'Sansei' is a term used to designate third generation of Japanese Americans.

[26] Letter, Rinjiro Sodei to Sheila Levrant de Bretteville, 8 August 1992, Michael Several Collection (USC).

[27] 'Kanji' are Chinese characters in the Japanese alphabet.

As the Director of Community Affairs at the Japanese American National Museum wrote to the public artwork's project manager,

> Through our exhibits and programs, we provide educational opportunities for our visitors and the public alike to come to the understanding and appreciation that Japanese Americans and Asian Americans are not[28] foreigners, but contributors who have helped to build and shape this nation and will continue to do so. The Museum's daily challenge is to instill these messages to the busloads of schoolchildren who came in to the Museum, saying 'sayonara' and such, and adult visitors who assume that this is a museum about Japan. Please understand that the Museum is not opposed to the language of Japan or of the immigrant Issei community. The use of the Japanese language was lost to many Japanese Americans during World War II ... Racism against Japanese Americans and Asian Americans has been on the rise again ... Having 'kanji' (even with English translation) right in front of the entrance does not help us in this education process.[29]

De Bretteville described her project as an attempt 'to invent various ways for the contradictory multiple identities and complex generational different subjectivities to be represented.'[30] It is notable that the work, although designed by de Bretteville, also incorporated elements from designs by Sonia Ishii and Nabuho Nagasawa, two Japanese American artists whose proposals following the call to artists were highly cited by the jury. Ishii prepared the drawings for the memory wrappings, and Nagasawa prepared a homage to the photographer Toyo Miaytake, located on the pavement near the Japanese American National Museum. Miyatake was a significant member of the community:

> First-generation Japanese American photographer Toyo Miyatake (1895) opened his photography studio in Little Tokyo in 1923 and spent the rest of his life documenting his community's life on film. When Miyatake, his family and 120,000 Japanese Americans were unjustly incarcerated by the U.S. government during World War II, Miyatake bravely smuggled a camera lens and a film plate, considered contraband, into the Manzanar concentration camp in California. Using a secretly-constructed camera, he captured everyday life in Manzanar.[31]

Nagasawa's sculpture is a larger than life bronze replica of the Miyatake camera, designed to project slides of Miyatake's work onto the window of the original Japanese American National museum in the evenings. The

---

[28] Underlined in the original.

[29] Letter, Nancy K. Araki to Gloria Uchida, 13 March 1996, Michael Several Collection (USC).

[30] Several, 'Omoide no Shotokyo'.

[31] Text from the public plaque accompanying Nagasawa's work.

entire co-operative art endeavour takes as its mission to recall the historical development of the Los Angeles Japanese American community, the hardships and obstacles the community faced, and its success in securing its place in American society.[32] It is a product of fairly broad discussions by the community as to how its history and its relationship to a place should be represented visually and textually.

The history of Little Tokyo and of the Japanese community in Los Angeles is, of course, much more complex and fuller than what is represented on the pavement. The earliest confirmed identity of Japanese presence in the city was Charles Kame's opening of a restaurant on 1st Street in 1886. By 1900, two thousand Japanese were recruited by land baron Henry Huntington to lay tracks for the Pacific Electric Railroad. After the 1906 San Francisco earthquake, thousands of Japanese fled to Los Angeles. The Issei[33] left their mark on California and Los Angeles in agriculture, fishing, gardening, and retailing, despite the 1913 state Alien Land Law prohibiting Japanese nationals from owning or leasing land. While the 1942 presidential decree ordered an evacuation of all Japanese nationals and US citizens of Japanese background from the entire West Coast, some Nisei served as translators in the National Intelligence Service; still others served in the European war front in the famed 442nd Regimental Combat Team and the 100th Infantry Battalion. After the Second World War, Japanese Americans returned to Los Angeles, but few settled in Little Tokyo, visiting it primarily for dining and shopping. Some residential housing was built mostly to accommodate the elderly. Little Tokyo's population declined further in the 1950s when construction of the police administration building, known as Parker Center, destroyed housing for nearly 1,000 people and one-fourth of the district's commercial frontage.[34] As other urban redevelopment projects threatened historic Little Tokyo, the community established the Little Tokyo Redevelopment Project in 1969. Thus, since the 1970s, public art has been an integral part of redevelopment, and since 1991 the Public Art Task Force channelled community input to artists and developers. While such processes are inherently wrought with politics and power play – the Japanese American community is certainly not a uniform whole, with generational and gender issues intertwined with definitions of culture and history – it is important to note that the community established itself as a subjective agent in urban

---

[32] Several, 'Omoide no Shotokyo'.

[33] 'Issei' is a term used to designate first generation Japanese who settled in the United States in the late twentieth century.

[34] M. Several, 'Little Tokyo; Historical Background', http://www.publicartinla.com/Downtown/Little_Tokyo/little_tokyo.html, 1998.

redevelopment, and many members played a role in the design and execution of *Omoide no Shotokyo*.[35]

Listening for the Trains to Come, *1992*

The project in the Chinatown section of downtown Los Angeles, *Listening for the Trains to Come*, was executed in 1992 by May Sun, a Shanghai-born American artist at the cost of $22,000. It commemorates the achievements of the Chinese community between the 1870s and the 1920s, particularly memorializing the first Chinese labourers in Los Angeles. This 8-foot tall and 15-foot long work decorates a portion of a fence around the parking lot of a medical and business building. It was commissioned as an afterthought to the property development, since the Community Redevelopment Agency refused to sign off on the owners' request for a parking lot permit until there was evidence of compliance with the art requirement. The work is integrated into the parking lot fence, and has been at times defaced by a variety of business signs placed on the fence.

The work is composed of sculptural elements, with photographic negatives and text mounted on copper plates. The sculptural elements are bells, in reference to the ancient Chinese bronze bells, and pitchfork heads and shovels, commemorating the kind of work the Los Angeles community engaged in, such as building the railway. These objects, together with the rust on the fence, evoke a sense of age and blend into the colour of both the nearby brick building and the active oil pumps in the parking lot.[36]

It is the photographic negatives and the text plates that are interesting, as they are rich in historic content, and as such were contested territory for the representatives of the community. The four text panels are taken from several noted scholarly studies and from an oral history project. The English text has been translated into Chinese, which is printed next to the original. The photographic negatives come from the collection of the Chinese Historical Society of Southern California. The texts and the photographs correspond to each other thematically, but do not necessarily directly illustrate each other,

---

[35] There have been many excellent monograph studies of Japanese Americans in Los Angeles and California, as well as theses and articles, which have appeared since the 1970s. Of note are W. Masons *The Japanese of Los Angeles* (Los Angeles 1969), drawing on the collection of the Los Angeles County Museum of Natural History's archives and historic photographs; J. Modell's *The Economics and Politics of Racial Accommodation: The Japanese of Los Angeles, 1900–1942* (Urbana 1977), based on the author's doctoral thesis; and U. Sugiyama's *The Place-making of Little Tokyo: The Cultural and Historical Appraisal of the Urban Landscape*, Arizona State University MA. thesis, 1996.

[36] May Sun, interview by Michael Several, 27 May 1994, Michael Several Collection (USC).

10.5 May Sun, *Listening for the Trains to Come*, 1992. This work is part of a fence which surrounds a parking lot next to a medical and business plaza. To the right are several signs for the local business and religious institutions.

Source: Photograph: Ruth Wallach, January 2005.

nor are they directly related to the title of the work. The work pays homage to the Chinese workers who built the bed for the Southern Pacific Railroad,[37] yet there are no known photographs of Chinese railway workers from Los Angeles.[38] The 'Chinese Settlement in Los Angeles' text panel briefly describes the reasons for Chinese settlement in the city beginning with the mid-nineteenth century and is accompanied by a negative of a herb store in the old Los Angeles Chinatown, *c.* 1900. The text on 'Early Chinese women in Los Angeles,' which describes the dearth of women in the community in the nineteenth century and their economic participation, is accompanied by a negative of three seated Chinese women, also from around 1900. The text on the Chinese pioneer railway workers is accompanied by a negative of the vendor Chung Wong with his produce wagon in Los Angeles, around 1905. The segment on Chinese participation in California agriculture is accompanied by a negative of Chinese field hands *c.* 1898. This text mentions

[37] Letter, May Sun to Michael Several, 11 May 1994, Michael Several Collection (USC).

[38] May Sun, interview by Michael Several, 27 May 1994.

that the population was forced to move from old Chinatown to the current location in the 1930s to make room for the construction of Union Station. While the text provides information on the lives of Chinese in Los Angeles, it also places the lives of the first wave of Chinese immigrants within a larger historic context in California. Because this project reflects on a more distant past from which there are no survivors, the inclusion of negative images provides a startling visual layer. Negatives are ghostly images. They force us to peer closer at them to orient ourselves, disrupting our normal context and confusing us. Even upon closer examination we cannot discern everything on the negative plate. A negative requires a lot of attention, perhaps more so than a positive image. It also purports to be the first record of the object photographed. These negatives take us back to a period over a century ago, and as they are examined for meaning, the texts provide a context for 'reading' them. Yet, on closer examination, the negatives are separate and independent from the text, and give us additional context within which to contemplate the history of Chinese settlers in California.

To a certain extent May Sun had to work with sources which were available to her, and she also had to negotiate with the Chinese community on what historic events to include and how. For example, she wanted to include information about Katherine Cheung, the nation's first Chinese American aviatrix, who lived in Los Angeles, and about Union Station as a reminder that its construction destroyed most of the city's original Chinatown. However, the community advisory committee requested that anonymous women be used, and rejected a photographic negative of Union Station.[39] After Sun selected the text from archival and published sources, it went through many revisions to be rich in content, yet short, easy to read, but not too simple and not too detailed. Thomas McDannold, who wrote one of the earliest academic studies of Los Angeles' Chinatown assisted with text drafts, and pointed out the dilemmas inherent in using textual information in public artworks: 'I have rewritten the text for the panels of May Sun's piece … I attempted to keep the reading grade level at about the eighth grade. That is the comfort level for the general population … and seemed appropriate for the audience that will view the gate.'[40] Although the revised text was shorter and easier to read, it proved too simple.[41] This required additional rethinking of the textual panels. After the installation, some members of the community complained about the lack of clarity in the photographic negatives and the height of the placement of the text panels. The artist re-did

---

[39] May Sun, interview by Michael Several, 27 May 1994.

[40] Letter, Thomas McDannold to Julie Silliman, 2 October 1991, Michael Several Collection (USC).

[41] Letter, Julie Silliman to May Sun, 22 October 1991, Michael Several Collection (USC).

the image panels, so that the visual depth in the negatives changed with the angle of natural light.[42] Interestingly, the city's redevelopment projects, which deeply affected the lives of the Chinese before the Second World War are accorded very little place in this work, through the desire of members of the advisory community. While the most disruptive of these events, the eviction of the entire community living in the old Chinatown and the establishment of a completely new settlement is mentioned, much of the text concentrates on highlighting the developing demographic and economic conditions of the Chinese in Los Angeles and California.

As with the Little Tokyo project, or any public artwork commemorating people and events, *Listening for Trains to Come* is part of a complex history of an ethnic group in California and in the city of Los Angeles. While the first recorded appearance of a Chinese is in 1781, just as the pueblo of Los Angeles was established,[43] the Chinese started settling in the city in large numbers in the 1870s, many coming via northern California. They were hired as house servants, orchard hands, and railway construction workers. For decades the number of Chinese men far exceeded that of Chinese women. Through the later part of the nineteenth century, Chinese labourers were recruited into the city by Chinese contractors to work in virtual servitude for many years of their lives. They endured vicious racial hatred, were frequently barred from owning property, and faced restrictive federal legislation designed to force them out. With successive waves of immigrants, large Chinese communities sprang up elsewhere in the county, particularly in Monterey Park and Alhambra, east of the city of Los Angeles. A variety of economic incentives in the 1990s attracted large business investments from China, Taiwan, and Hong Kong. The Chinese communities in the Los Angeles area are as diverse as the Chinese-speaking populations are in Eastern Asia. Chinatown itself had several separate incarnations. The first Chinatown, coalescing in the tenements around the former Calle de los Negros (Negro Alley) on the eastern side of the pueblo plaza was a ghetto of mostly Chinese males working in food, laundry, and curio businesses. That enclave was razed beginning in 1933 to make way for the city's central train station, Union Station. At that time, several prominent families created the New Chinatown, northwest of the pueblo plaza, which is where it still is, albeit much larger and more diverse than when it was established in 1938. It is a bustling business and residential community composed mostly of recent immigrants, which experienced tremendous demographic and economic changes, especially as the centre of Chinese life shifted east of the city. In

---

42 M. Several, 'Listening for the Trains to Come; Background Information', http://www.publicartinla.com/Downtown/Chinatown/trains/trains.html, 1998.

43 T. McDannold, 'Development of the Los Angeles Chinatown: 1850–1970', California State University at Northridge MA thesis, 1973, 19.

the 1930s, an artificial Hollywood-inspired China-themed enclave, called China City, thrived for a while in downtown as a romantic tourist attraction. When it burned in the 1940s, the Chinese community did not attempt to reconstruct it, shifting all activities to the New Chinatown.

In the mid-1990s, the Chinese Historical Society of Southern California received 200,000 objects collected by archeologists during the digging for the construction of one of the city's metro lines. Most of the objects came from the area near Union Station, which displaced the original Chinatown. The objects and other finds in the digs provide rich evidence of life in the area and of the interaction between the Chinese and other populations living in the city at that time. Some of them have been incorporated into another large public artwork by May Sun, and installed in the renovated and expanded Union Station, that same train station that erased the old Chinatown.[44]

Conclusion

Described in this chapter are two recent commemorative public works that relied on oral histories and other historical evidence, artifacts, and archival materials. The works are not themselves instances of oral history. Sheila Levrant de Bretteville's interviews with 50 elderly Japanese Americans were intended to personalize her art project; May Sun's use of archival and published text contributed specific historical information to her work and infused it with the ambiguity inherent in time and space. The archival trail left by these projects of public art also illustrates the difficulties inherent in a display of public historic consciousness. Future studies on the communities can benefit from studies of how they see themselves and display their history through such formal means as public monuments. This complementarity in the use of sources to draw a larger historical picture is supported in Maria Popa's essay on the twentieth century architectural development of central Bucharest in this volume. In it she points to the importance of interviewing established architects on their role in Ceausescu's plans to refashion Bucharest's civic centre, because it adds considerably to what has already been written about the history of Bucharest in the twentieth century. In the case of Los Angeles, the communities involved in

---

[44] Among several informative publications, which document the everyday lives of Chinese immigrants in Los Angeles are L. Cheng et al, *Linking Our Lives: Chinese American Women in Los Angeles: A Joint Project of Asian American Studies Center, University of California, Los Angeles and Chinese Historical Society of Southern California* (Los Angeles 1984); R. Greenwood, *Down by the Stations: Los Angeles Chinatown, 1880–1933* (Los Angeles 1996); and I. Smith, *The Lonely Queue: The Forgotten History of the Courageous Chinese Americans in Los Angeles* (Gardena 2000).

contextualizing these works are complex, with a variety of power brokers influencing which images to use in May Sun's work or which personal reminiscences to quote in de Bretteville's work. All these instances show that the use of images and of text in public display is fraught with certain difficulties. Another issue that can only briefly be touched upon here is the question of what public it is thatthe works are displayed for and to whom the historical information is imparted. These works, as well as many other contemporary public artworks in the United States, while offering poignant historical testimonials, are set within an everyday environment so common that they are rarely consciously observed by the members of the public who use urban space. These projects require attention that can best be accorded by a tourist, the modern day *flâneur*, one whose knowledge of the history of the place is, perhaps, superficial, and who may view the city more in line with established historical narratives. It is possible to argue that such works also serve the needs of the local community to imprint itself firmly on the urban historical landscape. These works are a complement to what is already known about the communities through newspaper accounts, government documents, promotional and vanity publications, oral history projects, and academic studies. Their genesis lies in city regulations regarding urban redevelopment projects and use of private funds for public art, and in community leaders' sense of history and its preservation. In their content and geographical placement the works reveal a great deal about the communities. It is significant that de Bretteville's project encompasses the entire historical block of a street in the heart of Little Tokyo's commercial and cultural area, surrounded by restaurants, tourist businesses, and the Japanese American National Museum, while May Sun's work graces part of a fence in a parking lot out of the way of tourist activities in Chinatown. Because they are fixed in an urban public environment, these works also fix the image of each community in time and space. To re-use the notion of anamorphosis as described by Veronica Pereira in this volume, these works articulate urban historic complexities by re-signifying existing communal spaces, images and text. The two public artworks discussed mark the existence of the past in the present; they provide additional narrative to the urban space, which was previously articulated through oral discourse, some of it recorded and kept in archival collections. The description offered here of the works and their place in the narrative of the city's history is intended to add layers to what appear at first glance to be consensual markings of time and space. The question of methodological validity of both this analysis and of the original use of oral and archival resources is an open one. This chapter describes the use of historic text and image in public artworks in order to document the history of ethnic communities and to monumentalize their place-making within a complex fabric of the city. The works testify to the creative complexity of oral and archival evidence in simultaneously challenging and creating urban histories and 'myths'.

Further reading

Cheng, L., et al., *Linking our Lives: Chinese American Women of Los Angeles : A Joint Project of Asian American Studies Center*, University of California, Los Angeles and Chinese Historical Society of Southern California (Los Angeles 1984).

Davis, M., *City of Quartz: Excavating the Future in Los Angeles* (New York 1992).

Deutsche, R., 'Art and public space: questions of democracy', *Social Text*, 33, 1992, 34–53.

Hayden, D., *The Power of Place: Urban Landscapes as Public History* (Cambridge: Mass. 1995).

Klein, N.M., *The History of Forgetting: Los Angeles and the Erasure of Memory* (London 1997).

Maginn, P.J., *Urban Regeneration, Community Power, and the (In)significance of 'Race'* (Aldershot 2004).

Modell, J., *The Economics and Politics of Racial Accommodation: the Japanese of Los Angeles, 1900–1942* (Urbana 1977).

Nora, P., 'Between memory and history: les lieux de memoire', *Representations*, 26, 1989, 7–25.

Senie, H. (ed.), *Critical Issues in Public Art: Content, Context, and Controversy* (Washington, DC 1998).

Smith, I., *The Lonely Queue: The Forgotten History of the Courageous Chinese Americans in Los Angeles* (Gardena, CA. 2000).

Sugiyama, U.L., 'The place-making of Little Tokyo: the cultural and historical appraisal of the urban landscape', unpublished MA Thesis, Arizona State University, 1996.

Virilio, P., *The Paul Virilio Reader* (New York 2004).

Young, J.E. 'The counter-monument: memory against itself in Germany today', *Critical Inquiry*, 18, 1992, 267–96.

PART 4

MIGRATION AND METHODS

CHAPTER ELEVEN

Migrant voices in the contemporary history of Vienna: the case of ex-Yugoslavs

Wladimir Fischer

This chapter explores the most astonishing case of erasure of a large population – it outlines the reasons that have lead to that silencing, and finally sketches ways out of the dilemma. The chapter makes a case for oral history as the only historical method capable of contributing the experiences of migrants themselves to historical narratives. As in other chapters in this book, the use of oral testimony is vital because other sources, especially written testimony, are not available. The case of erasure in question concerns the migrants from the countries of the former Yugoslavia, who are the largest migrant group in contemporary Vienna. Nevertheless, they are invisible in public spaces and inaudible in the media – they are heavily under-represented in community structures and politics.[1] Their voices have hardly ever been heard in Vienna.

As this is an ongoing research project, methodologies and ethical issues are at the centre of attention. Many important issues in this regard, for instance the interactions between researcher and respondents from different social, ethnic and gender positions and the question of the selection of respondents, are considered by Herbert in Chapter 12.

A challenge is laid down here concerning an 'urban myth', the alleged unproblematic Viennese multiculturalism of the past and some special Austrian or Viennese predilection towards diversity. To include migrant experiences in the city's history instead of reiterating stereotypes regarding multiculturalism is, therefore, crucial, and this chapter seeks to engage with migrants' own standpoints, instead of relegating migrants to a position

---

[1] Other migrant voices are also worthy of study. This chapter deals particularly with ex-Yugoslav migrants because their situation seems to be especially pressing. Also other epochs need to be studied, such as the late nineteenth and early twentieth centuries, with migrants from Bohemia, Galicia, Hungary, and also the territories that later became part of a Yugoslav state.

congenial to mainstream historical stances. Such an approach should lead to the contemporary history of 'ex-Yugoslav' migration and its impact on perceptions of the city and interpretations of its past history, and to the reasons for the particular low public representation of these migrants.

The myth of multicultural Vienna

Clichéd accounts of Vienna's history before Fascism produce the impression that this was a multicultural city.[2] It appears as if this idyllic state was only destroyed by the national aspirations of the various peoples of the monarchy in the early twentieth century and finally by the Austro-fascists and the Nazis. By daring to look closer at how this historical cultural diversity is described, it is clear that the 'others' do not really figure as protagonists in these accounts. Any portrayal of diversity would logically involve an intense engagement with the history and culture of migrants in this central European metropolis. However, migrants do not by tradition figure as autonomous protagonists in historical accounts of Vienna, as the following explanations will show. If there is a tradition in the historiography as far as cultural diversity is concerned, it is a tradition of neglecting migrants. Rather, they are only mentioned on the occasion of their arrival to certain city quarters – what is left are Jewish, Bohemian and Hungarian 'cultural influences' in Viennese slang and cuisine, such as words and names, from the plum jam 'Powidl' and the Klobasse sausages to the frequent family names, Prohaska and Strnad. A glance into the Viennese telephone book reveals the historical ethnical composition of the population and provides a glimpse of the contemporary one. However, as Baumgartner and Perchinig criticized in a seminal article, the awareness of this fact has no impact whatsoever on attitudes towards diversity in Austria. Rather, it is part of a bland discourse designed to pacify existing conflicts and to repress memories of injustice.[3]

Such pacifying discourse is what remains of Vienna's historical ethnic diversity if questions of power, hegemony and dominance are not taken seriously in cultural and social historiography. Such discourse acknowledges influences of all sorts, beginning with the ancient Romans and ending with

[2] This multicultural myth has been summarized in the useful handbook on Austrian clichés – 'Multikulturelles Österreich', in S. Breuss, K. Liebhart and A. Pribersky (eds), *Inszenierungen. Stichwörter zu Österreich* (Wien 1995), 201–4. The Österreich-Buch, an Austrian government sponsored self-description issued after the Second World War may serve as an ideal type of this cliché. The book is available in an English translation: E. Marboe (ed.), *The Book of Austria* (Vienna 1958). I am indebted to Dr Cornelia Szabo-Knotik for this information.

[3] G. Baumgartner and B. Perchinig, 'Minderheitenpolitik in Österreich seit 1945', in H. Dachs and P. Gerlich (eds), *Handbuch des österreichischen politischen Systems* (Wien 1996), 678–89.

the Turks, including the Jews, but overlooks the various conflicts that have been typical for all these presences. Additionally important phenomena like the intersections and repercussions of several factors of exclusion and belonging, such as class, gender, ethnos, nationality and religion have not been dealt with to this day.[4]

An anecdote may illustrate the disjunction of migrant history from mainstream memory in Vienna. Mayor Karl Lueger, a 'founder' of modern Vienna, and his family lived in the same house as the family of the Vienna-based Serbian linguist, ethnographer and national hero Vuk Stefanović Karadžić (1787–1864). This coincidence went completely unnoticed both in Serbian and in Austrian/Viennese accounts of the period and about both men. The fact that Lueger gave a speech when Karadžić's body was exhumed and transferred to Belgrade in 1897, is only worth a footnote in Serbian historiographies.[5] Both men are emblematic in the respective historical discourses of Vienna and Serbia. This means that the disjuncture of mainstream and migrant's history is not limited to Austria but also to the so-called 'sending country'.

Migrants in Vienna's historiography

To be fair, in more recent accounts, immigration to Vienna has become more prominent. Many authors tend to describe the city as cosmopolitan, implicitly drawing parallels to North American urban imaginations. Though such descriptions are often well intended, they compound other problems by a tendency to metonymically concentrate on the achievements and contributions of elite migrants as though this was sufficient or in some way typical of all their countrymen. This approach was applied both by Austrian authors interested in tracing the multicultural past and by historians from migrant communities who intended to write a representative history of their respective community.[6]

Generally there has been a relative lack of research and publications on the subject of Czechs in Vienna. It is only in specialized accounts

---

[4] It should be noted that these evaluations hold for general historical descriptions of Vienna.

[5] K. Lueger, 'Govor na groblju Sv. Marka', in A. Gavrilović (ed.), *Spomenica o prenosu praha Vuka Stef. Karadžića iz Beča u Beograd 1897* (Beograd 1898), 38f.

[6] Compare, for instance, 'Wir: zur Geschichte und Gegenwart der Zuwanderung nach Wien', Sonderausstellung des Historischen Museums der Stadt Wien, 19. September bis 29. Dezember 1996, Wien 1996 on the one hand, with 'Auf den Spuren der Kroaten in Österreich: Katalog zur Ausstellung 1996/97. Tragovima Hrvata u Austriji' (Wien 1996) and D. Medaković, *Srbi u Beču*. (Novi Sad 1998) on the other.

that the Czechs, the best-known migrant element, have been treated as protagonists with their own agency in history. There are several professional historical accounts, although only three are comprehensive accounts, but date from before the Second World War or even the First World War.[7] Quantitatively the relationship between publications about these migrants and their numbers and relevance at the end of the nineteenth century is disproportionate. Arguably there is a causal connection between this under-representation and the virtual disappearance of Czech communities and their organizations during the first half of the twentieth century, although the majority of second- and third-generation migrants'remained in Vienna. There is a real possibility therefore, that migrants from the countries of the former Yugoslavia might be assimilated in a similar manner (see below).[8]

One population whose experiences of being excluded and persecuted as 'other' has been described in numerous accounts, are the Viennese Jews. More recently, a nostalgic interest in 'Jewish Vienna' has developed in broader discourses. Jewish *migrants*, however, are usually present only in general accounts of Viennese and Austrian history, and are not remembered as migrants but rather as a cultural presence. It is often forgotten that most Jews migrated to Vienna in the second half of thenineteenth century, just like the majority of Christians, but that many of them were forced migrants who had left the Russian Empire because of anti-semitic pogroms and poor living conditions. This migration context is often neglected in favour of essentialist images of 'the Viennese Jewry'.[9]

---

[7] See M. Glettler, *Die Tschechen in Wien um 1900. Strukturanalyse einer nationalen Minderheit in der Großstadt.* (München/Wien 1972); M. John, and A. Lichtblau, 'Ceska Viden. Von der tschechischen Großstadt zum tschechischen Dorf', *Archiv. Jahrbuch des Vereins für Geschichte der Arbeiterbewegung* (Wien 1987), 39f; V. Valeš, *Zu Hause in der Fremde. Tschechen in Wien im 20. Jahrhundert, Ausstellungskatalog* (Praha 2002); W. Winkler, *Die Tschechen in Wien* (Wien 1919). The Czech standard work is F.A. Soukup, *Česká menšina v Rakousku. Přehled vývoje české menšiny na území dnešní republiky Rakouské, zvláště ve Vídni* (Praha 1928). Another indication of the modest interest in Vienna's Czech history is the difficulty that a historical exhibition on the topic had in finding a suitable venue in Vienna while it was successfully shown in Prague and Brno. There was an official presentation of the exhibition in Vienna at the Czech Centre in 2002, although it was not shown there. Information on the exhibition is available at Wissenschaftsforum Tschechen in Wien: http://www.univie.ac.at/wftiw.

[8] See W. Fischer, 'Prominently absent. Problems of 'Ex-Yugoslav' migrants' representation in Vienna', *Paper given at the 8th International Metropolis conference in Vienna, September 2003.* Available on-line at http://www.civmig.balkanissimo.net.

[9] See G. Botz, *Eine zerstörte Kultur. Jüdisches Leben und Antisemitismus in Wien seit dem 19. Jahrhundert*, 2 edn (Wien 2002); K. Hödl, *Als Bettler in die Leopoldstadt. Galizische Juden auf dem Weg nach Wien, Böhlaus Zeitgeschichtliche Bibliothek* (Wien; Köln; Weimar 1994); I. Oxaal, *Jews Antisemitism and Culture*

Both histories, Czech and Jewish, would be logical candidates to receive increased historian attention in relation to their experiences of migration to and settlement in Vienna. However, this is not the case in equal measure in *general* accounts of Viennese history. What is also sadly missing are, first, accounts of the more recent centuries of immigration and, second, a foundation both in cultural and social history, including specialist knowledge of specific ethnic, religious and cultural backgrounds.[10] What is already available, despite the foregoing critique, are two chapters written in the 1980s on migration in relation to the economic and political history of Vienna. The contribution on political history shows, for example, that there was a Czechoslovak electoral movement in Vienna, which came third in the 1919 election (before the German nationalists), but plunged in 1923 to near irrelevance after the left wing of the movement had sided with the Austrian Social Democrats.[11] Slowly, migrant topics find their way into

---

in Vienna (London 1987). Due to the immigration from Galicia, Hungary and Bukovina, the Jewish population of Vienna grew massively in the late nineteenth century. See also S. Beller, *Vienna and the Jews, 1867–1938: a Cultural History* (Cambridge 1990). 'Essentialist approaches conceptualize 'identity' in terms of "unchangeable" human features, such as genetic inheritance, gender, birthplace, which are assumed to determine other human features such as personality, intelligence and social status. Essentialist discourses emphasize the fixity of identity on both individual and higher levels such as groups and social and political systems. Thus they offer a "scientific" justification on which a social order can be based, and on which injustice can be justified.' R. Bauböck, 'Preface', in H.G. Sicakkan and Y. Lithman (eds), *Envisioning Togetherness: Politics of Identity and Forms of Belonging* (New York 2005).

[10] Specialist research that should be integrated into future overviews includes J. Ehmer, 'Zur Sozialstruktur von Zuwanderern nach Wien im 19. Jahrhundert', in E. Francois (ed.), *Immigration et société urbaine en europe occidentale XVIe–XXe siècles* (Paris 1985), 31–45; Weigl, *Demographischer Wandel und Modernisierung in Wien, Kommentare zum Historischen Atlas von Wien 1* (Wien 2000); S. Hahn, 'Nowhere at home? Female migrants in the nineteenth-century Habsburg Empire', in P. Sharpe (ed.), *Women, Gender and Labour Migration: Historical and Global Perspectives* (London 2001), 108–26; M. John, 'Organisationsformen der Wanderminoritäten. Österreich 1867–1925. Thesen und Überlegungen', in B. Groppo and C. Schindler (eds), *Arbeiterbewegung und Migration* (Wien 1996), 105–19; A. Steidl, *Auf nach Wien! Die Mobilität des mitteleuropäischen Handwerks im 18. und 19. Jahrhundert am Beispiel der Haupt- und Residenzstadt Wien, Sozial- und wirtschaftshistorische Studien 30* (Wien [u.a.] 2003); S. Wadauer, and C. Putz, *Reisende – Mobilität und Erwerb im Österreich der 1920er und 1930er Jahre* (Wien 2003).

[11] G. Chaloupek, P. Eigner, and M. Wagner, *Wien. Wirtschaftsgeschichte 1740–1938* and M. Seliger and K. Ucakar, *Wien. Politische Geschichte 1740–1938*', each representing one volume of F. Czeike (ed.), *Geschichte der Stadt Wien* (Wien 1985, 1991), 2 vols.

more general descriptions of Vienna's history as new standard publications are being produced.[12]

It would be reasonable to expect that the history of the working classes and of their organizations does at least deal with migrants in the sense that most members of these classes in nineteenth and early twentieth century Vienna were migrants, mostly from the Slavic regions of the monarchy. Often, however, workers in these accounts are simply described as 'Viennese' or 'Austrian',[13] while their migration experiences and experiences of exclusion both socially and culturally, but also in a cultural-ethnic sense are largely ignored. Indeed, issues of ethnic belonging are usually neglected in the histories of workers' movements and only surface in the internal squabbles of the social democratic party. Even in sports history, despite the fact that many Viennese football players and members of the most successful volleyball team in Austria, Sokol, were from ethnic backgrounds outside mainstream politics, the issue of belonging has been sidelined. Similarly, the Jewish sports club, Hakoah, previously the largest in Europe, has had to struggle against establishment interests to have its Viennese sports fields restored to it. Sports historians themselves, therefore, have not focused on ethnic and cultural belonging; the 'other' was too seldom in focus as a result. Thus research that attempts to reverse the Viennese 'city imago' created at the time of Lueger, which 'constitutes itself through polarizing and excluding the respective Other – women, madmen, strangers, workers' is still rare and among the 'others' it is dealing with, there are few migrants with regional backgrounds. In sum, *other* places and cultures are too seldom in focus.[14]

---

[12] K. Vocelka and A. Traninger, '*Wien. Geschichte einer Stadt. Die frühneuzeitliche Residenz (16. bis 18. Jahrhundert)*' (Wien 2003); W. Öhlinger, *Wien im Aufbruch zur Moderne, Geschichte Wiens 5* (Wien 1999).

[13] 'Austrian' used to be a more complex term than today, as Austria included large non-German speaking territories. At that time, the German speaking Austrians were distinguished as 'Germans', while nowadays they would be called 'Austrians' in colloquial language.

[14] On the history of the marginalized classes see W. Maderthaner, and L. Musner, *Die Anarchie der Vorstadt. Das andere Wien um 1900* (Frankfurt/M. 1999). On the workers' movement, see for instance, J. Deutsch, *Geschichte der österreichischen Arbeiterbewegung*. 3rd edn. (Wien 1947); H. Hautmann, and R. Kropf, 'Die österreichische Arbeiterbewegung vom Vormärz bis 1945. Sozialökonomische Ursprünge ihrer Ideologie und Politik' in K.R. Stadler (ed.), 2nd edn., *Schriftenreihe des Ludwig Boltzmann Instituts für Geschichte der Arbeiterbewegung 4 (*1977). A detailed account is H. Mommsen, 'Die nationale Spaltung der Sozialdemokratie in Cisleithanien', *Die Bewegung – Hundert Jahre Sozialdemokratie in Österreich* (Wien 1990). On sports history, see M. Marschik, *Vom Herrenspiel zum Männersport. Modernismus – Meisterschaft – Massenspektakel. Die ersten dreißig Jahre Fußball in Wien* (Wien 1997); J. Bunzl, *Hoppauf Hakoah. Jüdischer Sport in Österreich, von den Anfängen bis in die Gegenwart* (Wien 1987).

More recent migrations, especially labour migrants from Turkey and Yugoslavia, have received considerable attention, however, mostly by sociologists, anthropologists and political scientists, rather than historians. An overview of migration to Austria in the twentieth century is therefore to be found in the Handbook of Austria's Political System and not in a history book.[15] There is valuable work on housing conditions, segregation and assimilation, consumption, and generational conflict (though less research into political rights and citizenship), and the beginnings of research into political (under-) representation of migrants and on cultural and political organizations.[16]

This chapter seeks to strengthen this relatively new strand of research and adds to it questions of culture in combination with social and political processes. It is also an attempt to introduce migrant viewpoints into the study of history in collaboration with authors from social and political studies. In particular, a new exhibition on forty years of labour migration to Vienna, the first one to try to present migrants' views themselves rather than others' views about them, has given new momentum to projects of 'historicisation as strategy'.[17]

Conspicuously absent

The under-representation of migrants in historiography is clearly connected to the non-representation of migrants in present-day public discourses. The disproportion between population numbers and their representation which was typical for Czech migrants in historiography is now also a feature for ex-Yugoslavs. Citizens from the countries of the former Yugoslavia are conspicuously absent in mainstream activities and also in specialized discourses and spaces. Ex-Yugoslavs account for ten per cent of the overall population and are thus the clear majority of Vienna's non-naturalized

---

[15] R. Bauböck, 'Migrationspolitik', in H. Dachs, et al. (eds), *Handbuch des politischen Systems Österreichs* (Wien 1997), 678–89.

[16] L. Bratić, 'Soziopolitische Netzwerke der MigrantInnen aus der ehemaligen Sozialistischen Föderativen Republik Jugoslawien in Österreich', in H. Fassmann and I. Stacher (eds), *Österreichischer Migrations- und Integrationsbericht. Demographische Entwicklungen – sozioökonomische Strukturen – rechtliche Rahmenbedingungen* (Klagenfurt/Celovec 2003), 395–409; W. Fischer, B. Herzog-Punzenberger, and H. Waldrauch, 'Migrants, minorities, belongings and citizenship: the case of Austria', in H. Sicakkan (ed.), *GLOCALMIG. Glocalization and Participation Dilemmas in EU and Small States 2* (Bergen 2004); A. Grasl, 'Sichtbar werden', *Wiener Hefte zu Migration und Integration in Theorie und Praxis,* 1, no. 1 (Schwerpunktheft Defizitäre Demokratie – MigrantInnen in der Politik), 2003, 141–52.

[17] Büro für ungewöhnliche Maßnahmen (ed.), *Historisierung als Strategie. Positionen, Macht, Kritik* (Wien 2004).

migrants. This is even more so the case if naturalized and non-documented migrants are considered. Given these numbers, ex-Yugoslav representation appears particularly low.

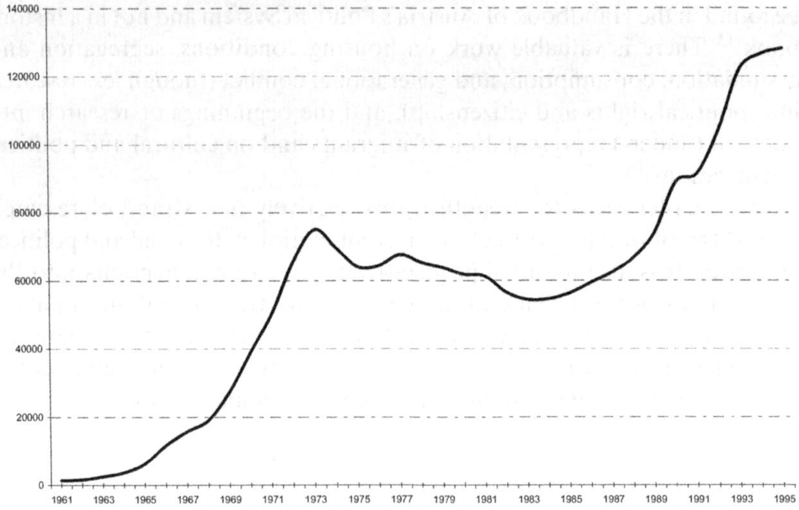

11.1 Ex-Yugoslav citizens in Vienna

Source: *Statistisches Jahrbuchder Stadt Wien, 1961–96*

As shown in the graph, from 1962 when the recruiting of Yugoslav workers started, there was a continuous yearly increase in their number.[18] At that time, foreign workers were still considered seasonal migrants, that is they were forced to return after a short period of employment in Austria. Hence the name *Gastarbeiter* (guest-labourers). In the late 1960s and early 1970s their numbers rose rapidly. With the economic crisis around 1973, the Austrian government changed its policy and tried to remove the labour migrants. The result was mixed. The average number of Yugoslavs decreased, but at the same time a stable permanent core-population developed. During the 1970s, Turks and Kurds became the second largest labour migrant element in Austria.

Because of Yugoslavia's severe economic and political crisis in the late 1980s, the number of migrants from the region rose again. In 1991, a series

[18] This section is based on a previous paper W. Fischer, 'Traveling tunes. Pumping up the volume of X-Yugoslav pop music in the diaspora', in S. Ingram, M. Reisenleitner and C. Szabó-Knotik (eds), *Ports of Call. Central European and North American Culturels in Motion* (Frankfurt/M. 2003), 221–47; see also Fischer, 'Prominently absent'.

of wars started, and forced a significant number of citizens who would normally not have emigrated to leave. Many came to Vienna. The result was an abrupt increase in the Yugoslav migrant population. Most were forced rather than labour migrants. The new arrivals changed the face of the diaspora profoundly. It fragmented and several new diasporas developed. Furthermore, the new migrants, with their various social, generational and cultural backgrounds, added new factions. The contemporary relations between several migrant groups can be illustrated with an image from the Vienna statistical department (MA 66, see Figure 11.2).[19] This situation has been typical for migration to Vienna in the last 40 years.

The majority, labour migrants from the countries of the former Yugoslavia were mostly working class with rural backgrounds. In contrast to other groups and communities, there is little elite formation, though many intellectuals from former Yugoslav countries arrived during the 1990s: These, however, typically kept their distance from the majority of migrants, either because they were of the 'wrong' ethnicity or because they were suspicious of them in an ideological or cultural way. Intellectuals imagined the *gastarbajteri* (Yugoslav labour migrants) as rural authoritarian personalities with chauvinist inclinations.

Although the diaspora was fragmented, it does have working class elites, which run organizations that limit their activities to sports, leisure and culture. These clubs and societies are very strong and numerous. There are national football leagues and national overarching organizations. Unlike Turks and Kurds, ex-Yugoslavs are, however, seldom to be found in organizations that deal with migrants and migration policy, such as the Vienna Integration Fund, now a department of the City Administration. Even rarer are they in Austrian political parties, let alone in representative bodies.[20] Correspondingly poor are the attempts of politicians to address migrants from the countries of the former Yugoslavia. Only in spaces of culture and art are there developments that might open up channels for ex-Yugoslav migrant voices into mainstream discourses. These are the spaces where a history of migrants in the city might take root and from where it could percolate into other areas.

---

[19] It should be noted that among the citizens of Serbia and Montenegro and of Macedonia, there are a substantial number of Albanians, Hungarians and Roma invisible in this statistic. Furthermore, among the citizens of Bosnia–Hercegovina, the three entities are not recognizable. Neither can the number of people who still declare themselves Yugoslavs be seen.

[20] The plan to grant those migrants resident for more than five years the right to vote on the district level was abolished by the Supreme Court. See Grasl. 'Sichtbar werden'.

Table 11.1 Non-Austrian citizens officially registered in Vienna (selected)

Country of origin	1999	2003	Composition of non-Austrians in 2003 (%)	Non-Austrians in Vienna population in 2003 (%)
Serbia and Montenegro	81,004	71,918	26.0	4.6
Croatia	16,510	16,664	6.0	1.1
Bosnia-Herzegovina	20,129	19,193	6.9	1.2
Macedonia	5,293	6,790	2.5	0.4
Turkey	43,343	40,192	14.5	2.6
Poland	17,251	14,504	5.2	0.9
Germany	12,776	16,014	5.8	1.0
'Post-Yugoslavs'	123,739	114,565	41.4	7.4
Foreigners	284,691	276,964	100.0	17.9
Entire Population		1,550,261		

Source: Vienna Magistrate, Section 66.

Data available at http://www.wien.gv.at/statistik/daten/bevoelkerung.html.

Reasons for non-representation

Basically, the reasons for under-representation reflect the particular problems of ex-Yugoslav migrants. These can be summed up as *assimilation, namelessness*, and *fragmentation*. Many observers have noted that in Vienna migrants from ex-Yugoslav regions, do not, if they organize at all, do this in public, nor do they try to engage in the community structures of Austrian society. A convincing interpretation of the situation points out that ex-Yugoslav labour migrants have assimilated into Vienna's working classes and therefore their access to other sectors of society is restricted. Furthermore, their organizations are limited to the fields of sports and culture and they focus on the 'internal'. Therefore these migrants are virtually invisible in the public sphere.

Since the wars of the 1990s, the collective name 'Yugoslavs' has been causing a dilemma for Viennese labour migrants. This name used to allow for a great diversity under its umbrella, but became discredited as the conflicts in Yugoslavia developed. The more specific names Croats, Serbs, Albanians, Macedonians, Roma, Vlachs and Hungarians had other specific disadvantages in such a way as to make *Tschuschen* the only remaining collective name. This however is highly derogatory and not a self-designation.[21] Self, thus, has become problematic and so the term 'ex-Yugoslavs' has been used here in quotation marks to denote the collective condition of people who are identified first and foremost as what they are *not*. Equally, problems with denomination have made it very hard to organize and to communicate 'ex-Yugoslav' migrants' presence to the public. Furthermore, on an individual level, all those who had never subscribed to one single nationality or those from so-called mixed marriages had completely lost an important term of self-designation. Namelessness was caused by and assimilation was aggravated by fragmentation of the communities in terms of organization, infrastructure and communication. These were infertile conditions for solidarity. Furthermore, as mentioned earlier, daily interaction with other migrants has become more problematic. But fragmentation was not only an ethnic one – another major dividing factor was the large generation gap between labour migrants and the socially different newcomers from the 1990s' war period.

Taken together, these dynamics have conspired, under background conditions of a very specific Austrian immigration and employment policy,

---

[21] As a prominent exception to this, the anti-racist group *Tschuschenpower* consciously adopted this name in 2000 (during the anti-government mass demonstrations), inspired by strategies of the gay movement and by the example of *Kanack Attack* in Germany. See http://www.topone.at/tschuschenpower.htm and http://www.kanak-attak.de.

to produce very low chances of upward mobility and higher education for the overwhelming majority of these migrants.[22] Although now, with the new arrivals since the wars, there are many well-trained and educated persons within the ranks of the 'ex-Yugoslavs', they are disinclined to communicate or even to write a history of those who came from the same region and who, in spite of everything, share similar problems. In a nutshell, fragmentation, namelessness and isolation have made a negative impact on historiography as well.

The 'Kolaric' effect

Besides these specific factors, there is also a discursive tradition of speaking and thinking *about* migrants from the countries of the former Yugoslavia. This is the history of a paternalistic attitude, which has been transformed into xenophobia in more recent years. Although discourses are conceptualized as contested and fluid, there was a remarkable shift in the late 1970s.

In the 1960s and 1970s, both trade unions and industry organizations were interested in creating a pacifying, paternalistic imagery of faithful Yugoslav helots who came from a poor country in order to fill the temporary gaps in the Austrian workforce and to return home thereafter. In the 1970s, particularly with the global economic crisis in 1973, the unions grew ever more sceptical of labour migration and, as mentioned earlier, the policy of the ruling Socialist Party was to make migrants return home. As this policy failed and the first Yugoslavs and Turks appeared in the employment centres followed by a second generation of migrants who surfaced in schools, these topics were increasingly discussed in combination with alleged Austrian 'fears' about *Ausländers* (foreigners). One strategy to deal with these fears was the Kolaric campaign of 1973. This was an advertising industry sponsored poster showing a stereotypical Yugoslav 'beast of burden' and a little Austrian boy asking him why he is called *Tschusch* (pejorative for migrants from the South and East) although they share the family name Kolaric (alluding to the Czech and labour migrant origins of the majority of Viennese).

This campaign set the tone for discourses on labour migrants in Austria, which consisted of a mixture of paternalistic and self-reflective elements. 'Kolaric' became a synonym for Yugoslav labour migrants. This image corresponded with the interests of the industry in cheap labour and at the same time with trade unions' policy who wanted to hold the influx of

22 B. Herzog-Punzenberger, *Die 'zweite Generation' an zweiter Stelle? Soziale Mobilität und ethnische Segmentation in Österreich. Eine Bestandsaufnahme*, Wien Kultur. Magistratsabteilung 7, 2003. Available at http://www.interface.or.at/Studie_2Generation.doc.

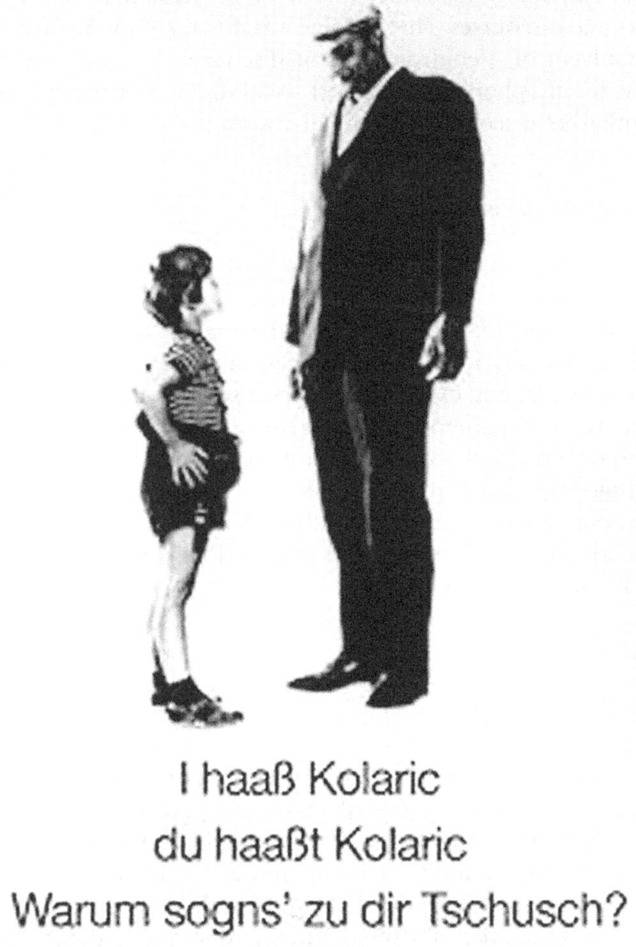

11.2 My name's Kolaric, your name's Kolaric, so why do they call you 'Tschusch'?

Source: U. Hemetek (ed.), *Am Anfang war der Kolaric. Plakate gegen Rassismus und Fremdenfeindlichkeit* (Vienna 2000).

foreign workers at bay while simultaneously protecting and controlling the *gastarbajteri*, as they were classical trade union clientele. This discursive strand came under pressure with the next global crisis in the 1980s when some Austrian conservatives, under pressure from the ever more right-leaning Freedom Party under new leader Jörg Haider, and in coalition with strong forces among the Social Democratic Party, dismissed the industry's policy of importing labour in favour of protectionist and xenophobic measures and discourses. The outcome was the end of the Kolaric consensus and the advent of a confrontation of discourses between anti-racist and mainstream xenophobia among most social strata and political camps, with a humanitarian discourse mediating between both.

Research goals and interviews

Strategic goals

In this complicated and hostile context, the research objective is to negotiate migrant narratives into public spaces, such as academic discourses, education, media, and exhibitions. Work already completed by colleagues, such as the recent migration exhibition *gastarbajteri*,[23] will be complemented with intensive research grounded on more migrants' experience. A series of semi-biographical pilot interviews serves as a preparation in order to create a comprehensive research strategy. The following is a description of the questions to be addressed in this process, that is, the problems, methods and ethics involved in this oral history project.

Thematic research topics

The first objective is to create a pool of contemporary history of and for 'ex-Yugoslav' migrants by undertaking interviews about their life experiences, turning points, and periodizations, thereby often touching on questions of belonging and conflict, as well as cultural practices. Issues such as the relationship between ideological discourse and everyday life in an urban setting, and of community building and community attachment, issues central to Valentina Gulin Zrnić's chapter in this volume, are contributing to this research as well. Caroline Varlet's approach to tune up the voices of 'witnesses who are seldom allowed to speak' also resonates with this methodological approach, as it relates to Vienna because it focuses on practices in ordinary places and captures the complexity of the social world by crossing sources and discourses in order to multiply viewpoints. What is to be avoided is yet another homogenized teleological history. Neither is this research intended to be representative – what is sought is the richness of different experiences or, as Ruth Wallach explained, to 'attempt "to

---

[23] The exhibition is documented in H. Gürses, C. Kogoj, and S. Mattl (eds), *Gastarbajteri. 40 Jahre Arbeitsmigration* (Wien 2004).

invent various ways for the contradictory multiple identities and complex generational different subjectivities to be represented".'[24]

There are two special focuses contained in this research: one is to describe individual experiences of migrants, the other is (re-) constructing collective experiences. As the history of migrants from the countries of the former Yugoslavia is characterized by several conflicts, totally collective experiences are not easy to find (*ethnic* as in Croatian, Serbian or Bosnian or *social* as in workers, urbanites, old and new migrants), and as collectivisms are normally contested by factors such as gender, generation, sexual orientation and lifestyle, then the fewer the assumptions about inferences the better. This means that the overarching research strategy is to allow for multiple and fluid belongings both during interviewing and in analyzing the material, so as to respect individual viewpoints and ways of life while simultaneously tracing collective imaginations and converging experiences.

Methods: Selecting interviewees

In order not to generalize from attitudes of specific socio-cultural groups, it is essential to reflect the socio-cultural composition of the migrants from the countries of the former Yugoslavia by including more working-class interviewees than middle- class ones. Of course, these categories are not strict ones, and the middle classes are not one 'lump' as Wallach notes. Social attachments have to be treated empirically and inductively, starting from the rough indicator of education levels and assessing their complexity during the interviews. A good example of how this complexity interacts with the step-by-step development of the approach to the respondents is one specific minority group of migrants, which has become visible only during field research. These are persons who came with the labour migrant waves of the 1960s and early 1970s, but with a different social background. These migrants were better educated and not aligned with the communists and often had a history of personal losses caused by the communist regime. In Vienna, they have had little contact with the other migrants and instead have followed a migration strategy of accepting a low- skilled job in the beginning in order to integrate quickly, hoping to achieve a higher income and education for their children in the long term.

Other considerations include gender, as sexual orientation is one criterion for selection. How this choice will affect the results remains to be seen. There are an equal number of male and female respondents. The regional focus is on migrants from Banat, Vojvodina, western Hercegovina and Slavonia, including a majority of Serbs, but also Croats, Hungarians and 'mixed'

---

[24] Quoted from de Bretteville, artist, in this volume, Chapter 10 by Ruth Wallach.

families, as well as Albanians, Bosnian Muslims and Roma, including both bilingual and poly-lingual persons. This selection reflects the regional-ethnic composition of the target group. Both un-organized and organized migrants are interview partners, including the leaders of migrant organizations. It turned out to be useful to interview two members of two generations from each family in separate sessions. Therefore, most respondents are between 25 and 40 and between 50 and 60 years, the so-called first and second generations of labour migrants. Interviews with arrivals from the late 1980s and those who came during the wars of the 1990s will be deferred for future research.

Selecting respondents sounds straightforward, but finding them is actually anything but easy. The reasons are the same as for the question why ex-Yugoslav migrants are so weakly represented in Austrian discourses and society, discussed earlier. Establishing contact with respondents works best via 'mediators' (as Herbert confirms), but it can be rather difficult to find working-class respondents. For instance, a metalworker refused to be interviewed because he said he did not want again to live through the terrible time he had had after he came to Vienna. Thus, from personal networks it is necessary to work further to find contacts in different milieus so as to discover suitable interviewees. The difficulty of this process, however, is rewarded with new insights.

Methods: Interview topics

The topics of the interviews are the migration experience, beginning with motives, arrival, work-life, leisure activities, family and education in Vienna, contacts with other migrants, links to the 'former' country including holiday practices, questions of return, and contacts with non-migrants. Interviews consist of two parts: the first a life history; the second a thematic interview. The first part deals with the respondent's biography, in an open structure, with an emphasis on life in Vienna, on strategies of placing oneself in an urban environment, on private and public places, friends and family, as well as travel and contacts with the place of 'origin'. In this part, questions of belonging and identity often come up spontaneously with the more educated respondents. In this first part, the question of belonging relates to the majority society, while in the second part belonging is about identification (or not) with a group of migrants.

The second part is more structured. In it, relations of the respondent to and involvement in community structures are essential as well as conceptions of diaspora, that is the way respondents conceptualize other migrants, and the role cultural practices play in this. Such cultural preferences reveal themselves in the conversation about musical practices (listening, performing, dancing) because music is not exclusive to specific migrant segments, is easily transportable and consumable, and loaded with cultural meanings in linking connections to oral traditions. Furthermore, music plays a central role in most of the cultural formations involved. There are over 50 ex-Yugoslav establishments with live music in Vienna.[25] Talking about musical practices opens up many ways of reflecting on the conditions of being present as a cultural 'other' in a metropolis. For example, one respondent from Vojvodina, a lady from the older generation, said that through her backyard window she could hear a man singing *Sevdalinke*, traditional urban Bosnian love songs. These songs have both a symbolic relevance for Muslim Bosnian identification, and for nostalgic feelings about belonging to Yugoslavia as it existed before the war. She had no idea who was singing and where, but it felt good, as she liked to listen to *Sevdalinke* in the old days, although she is not Muslim herself. The situation of hearing another migrant without seeing him, and attaching to the singing a kind of belonging, which might or might not coincide with the meaning the singer attaches to it, is highly symbolic for the cultural situation of ex-Yugoslav migrants, because they are isolated, and both divided and united by a common cultural repertoire.

The topic of cultural attitudes and judgments links with questions of belonging in the framework of (imagined) migrant communities. Therefore, participation in communal practices is at the top of the interview agenda, and includes passage rituals, celebrations, cultural and sports events, religious activities, political organizations, and courting. Systematic questions about what respondents think about how other migrants from the former Yugoslavia behave, tie these symbolic and ritual practices to concepts of community.

The second approach to collectivity concerns parallels in biographies. Here, the emphasis is on the turning points that exist in all biographies, both common ones, such as political changes, the war and new immigration legislation, but also 'scaled' turning points, such as the conclusion of the establishing phase, and the granting of an unlimited visa. What is essential in the search for collective narratives and judgments are the respondents' conceptualizations of their own histories and of migrant history, about 'what counts in life', as well as images of self and other.

Perceptions of urban space are discussed during the interviews with two focuses. First, respondents elaborate on urban places and what they usually do there and, second, they speak about everyday and special activities and

---

[25] Information provided by Dr Ursula Hemetek, based on field research conducted with Dr Sofija Bajraktarević.

where they perform these. So far, this thematic complex prompted shorter narratives than other questions, although the approach of combining places with practices in the questions seemed promising, as in Caroline Varlet's contribution in Chapter seven of the present volume, which emphasizes that people are more concerned with their close surroundings than with distant ones.

Ethics

Although not a member of the ethnic groups involved, despite a Slavic first name, it would be counterproductive to view myself on one side of a crude dichotomy of insiders versus outsiders, as Joanna Herbert points out in Chapter 12 of this volume. At this point, it should be mentioned that, although there are enough persons in Vienna with the skills to do a similar task as proposed here (a migrant background combined with training in history and interviewing), the manifold problems of this specific migrant population seem to prevent anyone from doing so. One colleague from Bosnia, argued, in contradiction to Valentina Gulin Zrnić's concept of auto-ethnography, that an outsider was better suited for the task instead of someone like her, because she would feel like 'a goldfish describing the goldfish pond'.

Having studied the languages and cultures of Yugoslavia is helpful in creating a positive and more balanced relationship during the interviews. Also, my first name makes me seem more familiar to respondents. Having at least one solid connection to the respondent's ethnic background is enough to provide a good basis for conversation. Social and gender differences are more difficult to bridge as Johnston and McIvor indicate. Male respondents from a working-class background, especially those who migrated from rural areas to Vienna, have differing concepts of masculinity. This often leads to an imbalanced interview situation, which is not the case with women in this respect.

Another problem occurs when respondents appeal to the interviewer to judge the responsibilities for the wars and war crimes of the 1990s. Here, it is often difficult to preserve a neutral basis for conversation, without siding with the respondent's inclinations to one or the other of the war factions. A proper response seems to be to insist on one's own experiences during the war period and to show commitment to war victims in general. However, the fact remains that this topic cannot be treated without emotion and neither without affecting the interview situation. The war has left deep impressions and wounds in the lives of the respondents and this impact on the research can only be dealt with by constantly reflecting it both during fieldwork and in its analysis and interpretation.

Conclusion

The central proposal of my research is to contrast diverging evaluations about comparable phenomena in the collective narrations, and bring these together with diverse life experiences in order to present the breadth of experiences of one specific migrant segment in Vienna.

Cultural inclinations, which might influence the standpoints of a respondent, are assessed during the interviews using as indicators attitudes towards cultural areas and activities. In spite of all efforts to capture the diversity of experiences and backgrounds among migrants from the countries of the former Yugoslavia, the study does not claim to be representative, but rather an exploratory investigation, which corresponds as closely possible to the experience of respondents. This, of course, makes it hard to generalize, though the breadth of migrant experiences in this historical situation should emerge.

It is a difficult task to publicly represent the contemporary history of migrations from South-Eastern Europe to Austria and Vienna. The major problem is that, because of the wars, many migrants are cautious about identity politics and there is little effort to organize publicly or to promote oneself, to 'become visible'. Introducing migrant narratives, self-conceptions, periodizations and a history of migrant cultural practices into the history of the city of Vienna, maybe even with reference points to migrants in earlier eras, such as the *fin-de-siècle*,[26] could be one strategy to encourage the development of migrants' own interventions in public discourses and histories.

In so doing, migrants might, as one of Maria Raluca Popa's respondents stated 'find a loophole in the system through which to slip into the mainstream'. That itself would be a worthwhile contribution to promote migrant voices.

Further reading

Clifford, J., 'Diasporas', *Cultural Anthropology*, 9, 1994, 302–38.
de Certeau, M. 'Walking in the city', in S. During (ed.), *The Cultural Studies Reader* (London 1993), 127–33.
Donald, J., *Imagining the Modern City* (London 1999).
Frith, S., 'Music and Identity', in S. Hall and P. DuGay (eds), *Questions of Cultural Identity* (London 1996), 108–27.

---

[26] See W. Fischer, 'An innovative historiographic strategy. Representing migrants from southeastern Europe in Vienna', in M. König and R. Ohliger (eds), *Enlarging European Memory: Migration Movements in Historical Perspective* (Stuttgart 2006), 155–62.

Gilroy, P., 'Diaspora and the detours of identity', in K. Woodward (ed.), *Identity and Difference* (London 1997), 299–343.

Gungwu, W. (ed.), *Global History and Migrations* (Oxford 1997).

Hall, S., 'Who needs "identity"?', in S. Hall and P. DuGay (eds), *Questions of Cultural Identity* (London 1996), 1–17.

Hoerder, D., and L.P. Moch (eds), *European Migrants. Global and Local Perspectives* (Boston MA 1996).

Lavie, S. and T. Swedenburg, *Displacement, Diaspora, and Geographies of Identity*. (Durham N.C. 1996).

Zhou, M., 'Segmented assimilation: issues, controversies and recent research on the new second generation', *International Migration Review*, 31, 4, 1997, 975–1008.

Negotiating boundaries and the cross-cultural oral history interview

Joanna Herbert

The process of researching South Asian communities, as a white English female, posed significant methodological and ethical issues.[1] The study took the British Midland city of Leicester as a local case study to explore the processes of, and responses to, the migration and settlement of South Asian migrants since 1950. My identity and social location, such as my ethnicity, age and gender, undoubtedly shaped the research process and posed numerous challenges and ethical problems. While ethical concerns have long been debated within the fields of sociology and anthropology, historians have been accused of overlooking these issues.[2] This chapter attempts to rectify this by reflecting on some of the most salient concerns. Was my ethnic identity a barrier to establishing trust and rapport? Were other aspects of my identity important? Were the respondents more willing to discuss particular issues? What were the dilemmas involved in representing and theorising sensitive experiences? It is argued that reflecting on the role of the researcher should not simply be dismissed as navel gazing but that it has fundamental implications for the interpretation of the narratives.

The research

Research was based on existing oral history archives with South Asians, in-depth interviews with white inhabitants, and my own life-story interviews with South Asians. The backgrounds of the South Asian participants

---

[1] 'South Asian' is used as shorthand throughout this chapter to describe collectively those who can trace their ancestry to the Indian sub-continent, namely, India, Pakistan, Bangladesh and Kashmir. This includes east-African Asians but does not encompass all south Asian countries and excludes the Chinese and Vietnamese. Although the term 'white' is also problematic, as it suggests an undifferentiated group, it refers to those who are of white skin colour and British origin.

[2] J. Sangster, 'Telling out stories: feminist debates and the use of oral history', in R. Perks and A. Thomson (eds), *The Oral History Reader* (London 1998), 93.

were considerably diverse and gender, economic status, place of origin, religion and education were just some of the facets of differentiation. The predominance of east-African Asians in the city is seen as a defining feature of Leicester's population and this was reflected in the sample of the respondents, as around half had migrated to Britain from east Africa, namely, Kenya, Uganda, Tanzania and Malawi. The oral history method was chosen at it enabled an exploration of the personal and collective experiences of South Asians who were otherwise absent from archival sources and it also provided a unique lens to view subjective, everyday experiences and to analyse the respondents' creative agency. Corresponding with the recent proliferation in biographical research, there is a growing acknowledgement of the merit and scope of oral histories to reveal not only the individual and collective histories of migrant groups, but also to explore migrant mentalities and identities.[3] The research was also informed by the awareness of how 'stories' are essentially constructed; thus, there was no whole picture or one authentic truth that the research sought to represent.[4]

Methodological issues

Feminist research has highlighted the unequal and intrusive power relationship between academics and the people they seek to study.[5] Accordingly, the academic occupies a privileged position as a white, middle-class professional. They choose the topics for the interview discussion, and edit and extract information from the 'stories' to correspond with their research agendas with the ultimate aim of producing an academic publication and furthering their own career. By contrast, the 'subject' of the study, provides the information, but has minimal gains or control over the outcomes of the research. From this perspective, the researcher is envisaged as possessing the power and the researched is deemed powerless. This structural inequality is seen as particularly problematic when the relationship between the researcher and respondent is cross-cultural. In the context of

---

[3] For an overview, see A. Thomson, 'Moving stories: oral history and migration studies', *Oral History,* 27, 1, 1999, 24–37. M. Chamberlain and S. Leydesdorff, 'Transnational families: memories and narratives', *Global Networks* 4, 3, 2004, 227–40. P. Chamberlayne, J. Bornat, and T. Wengraf (eds), *The Turn to Biographical Methods in Social Science: Comparative Issues and Examples* (London 2000).

[4] J. Clifford and G.E. Marcus (eds), *Writing Culture. The Poetics and Politics of Ethnography* (Berkeley 1986).

[5] D. Reay, 'Insider perspectives or stealing the words out of women's mouths: interpretation in the research process', *Feminist Review,* 53, 1996, 55–71.

post-colonial critiques, the authority of the West to represent and speak on behalf of other cultures has come under close scrutiny.[6]

The argument that whites should avoid researching minority ethnic groups came to the fore and was fervently debated in the 1980s when sociological 'race relations' research was heavily criticized for reproducing racism and stereotypes of minority ethnic groups, such as the typecast that all African Caribbean youths were under-achievers or inherently aggressive.[7] It was contended that white researchers would inevitably impose their own cultural norms and ideological position on the research and that they should turn their academic attention to the neglected issue of white racism, rather than perpetuating the view that minority ethnic groups were the principal problem. Other criticisms targeted whites for 'prying into the black community' and even acting as spies for the government.[8] Alongside this was the belief that because whites do not experience racism, they cannot empathize or understand experiences of discrimination and disadvantage. Attempts to overcome power hierarchies have lead to the methodological practice of 'matching' to ensure, for example, that only women interview women, and this is founded on the premise that the researcher and participants share a common social location and they can establish rapport and trust on this basis. In turn, it has been argued that this commonality will help to minimize the possibility of an exploitative power relationship.

Negotiating difficulties: the interviews

My research questioned some of these arguments. Although positioned as an 'outsider', throughout the interviews I was able to establish a degree of trust with the respondents and this was, to a great extent, due to the intermediaries or 'gatekeepers'. By contrast to an 'insider', who typically has expeditious access to potential participants, relations with the gatekeepers took a considerable length of time to establish and were cultivated throughout the research process through many informal meetings.[9] Some academics have

---

[6] E.W. Said, *Culture and Imperialism* (London 1993).

[7] See, for example, E. Cashmore and B. Troyna, 'Just for white boys? Elitism, racism and research', *Multiracial Education*, 10, 1981, 42–8.

[8] J. Bornat et al., 'Oral history and black history conference report', in *Oral History*, 8, 1980, 21–3 and J. Bourne and A. Sivanandan, 'Cheerleaders and ombudsmen: the sociology of race relations in Britain', *Race and Class*, 21, 4, 1980, 338.

[9] As Bourdieu has stressed, social capital must be invested in continually. See P. Bourdieu, 'The forms of capital', in A.H. Halsey, H. Lauder, P. Brown, and A.S. Wells, *Education: Culture, Economy and Society* (Oxford 1998), 52.

noted the influence of gatekeeper bias on the research since gatekeepers may actually hinder access to certain communities and attempt to influence the research.[10] Considering this, community male elders who would have a stake in portraying a particular perception of 'their community' were avoided and instead relations were sought with those who were simultaneously insiders and outsiders. For instance, one key contact originated from Kashmir, worked at a local community centre for over twenty years, and showed genuine sympathies and interest in the aims of the research. His occupation gave him access to a varied range of participants from different economic and social backgrounds, yet he also had an academic background in sociology and was, to an extent, set apart and detached from the local communities.

His role was vital as during the early stages of the research when attempting to contact potential participants on my own by arranging visit to local community groups, I encountered considerable suspicion. Despite my reassurances and proof of confidentiality through consent forms, the respondents were guarded and reluctant to talk due to fears that their interviews would be quoted in the media, such as local radio programmes or newspaper articles. However, my contact with the local community worker proved extremely fruitful; and he not only helped to arrange the interviews but also explained to the respondents the aims and importance of the research, ensuring that expectations were clear from the outset. As they viewed him as trustworthy, he proved to be crucial in gaining their confidence and establishing mutual trust. Consequently, the participants did not seem to resent the interview process, or view it as an intrusion; rather they warmly welcomed me into their homes with gestures of hospitality, such as offers of food and drink. Some invited me to community meetings and gave me tours of their local mosque, and many stated the importance and value of telling 'their story'.

Nevertheless, it would be naive to conflate rapport with absolute confidence or openness. Discussions with the gatekeeper revealed that there was a range of issues that the respondents were not willing to discuss in my presence. This included caste and the importance of caste associations within Leicester, stereotypes that different South Asian groups possess of each other, and less surprising derogatory views of white people, such as the commonplace perception that whites are dirty and unhygienic. Despite this, it was clear that my ethnic identity was not experienced as a fundamental divide, rather it was simply one marker of 'difference.' In reality, people inhabit multi-faceted identities based on gender, age, religion, sexuality and occupation

---

[10] R. Atkinson and J. Flint, 'Accessing hidden and hard-to-reach populations: snowball research strategies', *Social Research Update* (2001), http://www.soc.surrey.ac.uk/sru/SRU33.html.

and these differences constitute particular world views and subjectivities and are overlooked in a simple dichotomy of 'insider' and 'outsider'.

My younger age positioned me as a junior and enabled me to seem less threatening to the respondents. I was able to establish common ground and affinity with them, based on a variety of criteria, such as their education, knowledge of and experiences of living in Leicester, their interest in local sport and politics, or even sharing a similar sense of humour. When prompted by the respondents, I revealed details about my own life, rather than assuming a detached and objective stance and this may have also helped to generate a rapport. Many shared the same concerns of the white respondents and echoed their rhetoric of the 'good old days' by lamenting how the built environment had changed, how the city was once safer and free from crime and commodities were cheaper. It is important to appreciate that, compared to other ethnic groups, though the respondents were positioned differently in society, having lived in Britain for 30–40 years, they also possessed a shared history and were part of the same social milieu. As one respondent emphasized:

> I think what people actually forget is that all of us have a lot in common in many ways being human beings and we don't look at those common issues and we look at the difference and divide ourselves and fight on the differences, but differences are few and we can learn to live with differences.[11]

My gender had a paramount impact on the interviews. My relationships with the South Asian men were conducted on a friendly albeit formal basis, and my university status seemed to accord me with a degree of respect. There was a distinct sense, especially with the elderly male respondents, that I might perceive them as different and an 'other' and as a result; they attempted to emphasize the commonalties to make *me* feel more at ease. For instance, Mr Khan, a Muslim from Kashmir aged 75, claimed he was my grandfather and consistently stated 'I am not strange to you any more' and that 'strangeness is an evil'.[12] Another stated that I was like his child.[13] At one level, this compares to the experiences of South Asian academics who have observed how South Asian interviewees have used kinship terms with them such as 'Auntie' and 'Uncle' to signify a connection.[14] Yet, it could also be argued that in the context of my research, the male respondents employed these terms to reinstate their own patriarchal authority, which

---

11 Interview with Haq, 25 June 2002.

12 Interview with Khan, 4 July 2002.

13 Interview with Karim, 13 June 2002.

14 S.R. Dhooleka, *Where Are you From? Middle-Class Migrants in the Modern World* (London–Berkeley 2003), 14.

may have been threatened by the 'interviewer' and 'researched' relationship. The male elder respondents further bolstered this impression of authority by focusing on official histories. Entwined with details of their life story, such as their childhood, education and the journey to Britain were descriptions of political events, such as the independence and partition of India in 1947, the Africanization programmes in Kenya, Uganda, Tanzania and Malawi from 1968 and 1972, and the British immigration acts in 1962, 1968 and 1971.

Conversely, interviews with the female respondents were generally more relaxed and the women were remarkably open with me. Many launched into in-depth narratives of their private lives, and spoke spontaneously and movingly about tragic and pivotal events, family problems, and reflected on their feelings and emotions. This discrepancy between how the men and women narrated their stories reflects the influence of gender in the construction of life stories. It corresponds with other oral history studies, which have noted how men generally tend to locate themselves at the centre of public events, while women's stories are more likely to framed by their place within the family life-cycle and relate to familial concerns.[15] Yet the apparent ease and willingness of the women to openly discuss these issues was also related to my position as a woman. Some female respondents openly stated that they would talk candidly to me 'as another woman', and so although my ethnic identity may have been interpreted as a marker of structural oppression, I was simultaneously a woman with some shared interests and concerns.

My location as an 'outsider' also offered the women the space to criticize aspects of their own communities without fear of judgement or retribution. For instance, many were consistently critical of the extended family and equated it with 'a burden', 'no privacy', or 'no freedom', while others surmised, 'Indian community they never blame men, they always blame women.'[16] They revealed the ways in which their lives had been constrained by discourses of shame and honour, which defined the parameters of 'appropriate behaviour'. This resulted in rules pertaining to clothing or an exclusion from further education to prevent potential relations with South Asian male youths. Yet they also disclosed the frequently hidden ways in which they negotiated and subverted these restraints. Several women described tactics and strategies such as, as an adolescent, arranging to meet their boyfriend in non-Asian spaces away from the scrutiny of their neighbourhood, or by changing their appearance to correspond with different contexts. Mandy confided her experience of this in the 1970s:

---

15 Sangster, 'Telling out stories', 89. This was also noted in Gardner's study of Bengalis, in K. Gardner, *Age, Narrative and Migration: The Life Course and Life Histories of Bengali Elders in London* (Oxford 2002).

16 Interview with Devi, 24 June 2002.

> For me it was really strange because at home it was strictly Asian and when you were in town you were one of the kids you know so like the mini-skirts, I remember one day I forgot to get my skirt down because when you go out, you rolled your skirt up (laughs).' She claimed, '*we had* two extremes' and concluded 'we had to pretend a lot whereas the next generation doesn't have to pretend just to fit in.[17]

In these cases gender, as a social category, effectively superseded ethnicity as a basis for identification and rapport. The experience proved that my ethnic identity was not an insurmountable barrier or divide and that 'insider' and 'outsider' boundaries were not fixed or immutable but could be negotiated. Recent discussions on the problems concerned with insider research supports this. For instance, South Asian female researchers have remarked on the tendency for South Asian women respondents to treat them with suspicion and to view them as an outsider. This is as a result of various factors, such as their academic or feminist beliefs, their martial status, or their self-presentation through a combination of their clothes, make up and hair, which marked them out as different.[18] There is a emergent body of literature that reveals how contrary to expectations, 'insiders' may in effect become 'outsiders' and that a researcher may oscillate between 'insider' or 'outsider' status throughout the course of the research.[19]

Nevertheless, I was aware throughout all the stages of the research of the potential difficulties involved as a white researcher. I could not dismiss the possibility that South Asian participants would be unwilling to discuss certain issues for fear of causing misunderstanding or negative judgement.[20] In particular, would they be willing to discuss racism with a white interviewer who did not share these experiences and may not be able to comprehend them? Initially, direct questions on whether the respondents had experienced racism often provoked palpable unease. Some simply stated that 'racism was there' and were reluctant to elaborate further, while others insisted that they had never encountered racism. However, this defensive response was overcome by employing a more subtle approach and framing

[17] Interview with Mandy, 28 May 2002.

[18] For instance, Mirza noted that this perceived difference was based on her short hair and non-married status. M. Mirza, 'Same voices, same lives? Revisiting black feminist standpoint epistemology', in P. Connolly and B. Troyna (eds), *Researching Racism in Education: Politics, Theory and Practice* (Buckingham 1998), 79–94. See also S. T-Björkert, 'Nationalist memories: interviewing Indian middle class nationalist women', *Oral History*, 27, 2, 1999, 35–46.

[19] S. Acker, 'In/out/side: positioning the researcher in feminist qualitative research', *Resources for Feminist Research*, 28, 1/2, 2000, 189–208. Acker discusses J. Banks' typology of different insider/outsider relations.

[20] For discussion see S. Leydesdorff, 'Genres of migration', in M. Chamberlain (ed.), *Caribbean Migration: Globalised Identities* (London 1998), 81–91.

indirect questions to elicit information, such as asking them to describe their relationships with their neighbours or work colleagues. As a result, many respondents introduced the topic at their own pace and spoke freely and at great length about their experiences of racism and hostility.[21] Muslim women, in particular, gave extraordinarily frank accounts of their encounters with Islamophobia. These accounts provided a key insight into the extent to which anti-Muslim sentiment impinged on their daily lives and consequently served to question the prevalent image of Leicester as a harmonious city and a European model of multi-cultural success.[22]

It also became clear that the sample of respondents possessed varying conceptions and different levels of awareness of racism.[23] For instance, for one respondent their definition of racism may be confined to a physical attack, whereas others may be attuned to more subtle manifestations, such as disapproving or hostile glances from whites. In the words of one respondent, 'it's the undercurrents it's underneath. It's underneath the smiles, the politeness and all that.'[24] In contrast to Muslim women, who often used particular examples to emphasize how they were unequivocally the targets of racial and religious hostility, some Sikh and Hindu women were often ambiguous as to whether hostile behaviour was directed at them because of their ethnicity. So for instance, one Sikh woman recalled the verbal harassments her family received from her white neighbour in the 1970s, yet she did not interpret this as a manifestation of racial prejudice but instead simply viewed him as pathological. She claimed, 'We had a lot of harassment from the person next door: he was English he was like trying to drive us out of our homes I think', yet she reflected,

> It was just him, 'cause he used to row with his wife as well, there'd be pots and pans flying between the pair of them and I never thought it was a racial act. I just thought that's the way he is, a bit of a lunatic and when he's not fighting with his wife, he's having a go at us.[25]

---

21 This was also the experience of P.J. Rhodes, quoted in F.W. Twine, 'Racial ideologies and racial methodologies', in F.W. Twine and J.W. Warren (eds), *Racing Research, Researching Race* (Cambridge 2000), 12–3. Twine suggests the topic of racism may provoke unease regardless of 'race'.

22 See for instance, 'A British city finds that tolerance is good business', *The New York Times International*, 8 February 2001.

23 See R. Aziz, 'Feminism and the challenge of racism, deviance or difference?', in H.S. Mirza (ed.), *Black British Feminism* (London 1997), 74.

24 Interview with Nashia, 16 March 2004.

25 Interview with Mandy, 28 May 2002.

Hence, although racism may have motivated the neighbour, Balbir did not equate the hostility with racism.[26] As a result, these accounts effectively changed the course of the research. For although the initial focus of the research was the respondents' experiences of and responses to forms of exclusion, such as racism, it soon became evident that to concentrate solely on the issues of 'race' would have entailed the danger of racialising the respondents. I soon learned to prioritize their experiences and views, rather than rigidly pursuing my own research questions and stressed to the respondents the significance of recalling events that they felt had been important in their lives. This approach yielded significant findings. It showed, for instance, that class, gender and religion were key facets that shaped experiences of racism and for some respondents, racism was not a defining part of their lives; instead they possessed a different set of priorities and faced other problems which were of greater concern. Learning to listen and adapting a more flexible approach not only offered fresh insights and shifted the direction of the research but gave the respondents greater control over the interview and may have helped to shift the power imbalance between the 'researcher' and the 'researched'.

Issues of representation

My research experience showed that it was possible to negotiate some of the difficulties that arose during the interview process. However the greatest dilemma concerned the analysis and representation of the findings. Some respondents expressed derogatory remarks towards different religious groups or recent immigrants and claimed that too many immigrants were coming into Britain. For instance, one respondent, who was forced to flee Kenya in 1970, stated that he recently asked Somalis why they did not migrate to another country. He then added, 'I told them, I am the same as you but, this country is a small country.' I felt uncomfortable dwelling on these views in the writing up of the research but by excluding these issues I would have failed to capture the complex nature of racism or presented a romanticized and idealized view of 'community'. Academics have observed how this problem may be more acute for 'insiders' who may be less willing to criticize their own community, for fear of the ramifications, such as accusations of betrayal.[27]

---

[26] For further discussion of this issue, see D. Mellor, G. Bynon, J. Maller, F. Cleary, A. Hamilton, and L. Watson, 'The perception of racism in ambiguous scenarios', *Journal of Ethnic and Migration Studies*, 27, 3, 2001, 473–88.

[27] N. Islam, 'Research as an act of betrayal: researching race in an Asian community in Los Angeles', in Twine, *Racing Research*, 35–66.

Furthermore, western feminists have been criticized for presenting pathological accounts of monolithic 'third world women' who are inherently 'traditional'. A further stereotype is of the South Asian woman as a victim, possessing no freedom, suffering endemic disadvantage, and in desperate need of help and liberation.[28] It is argued that these accounts bear minimal resemblance to the women's real lives but are misrepresentations that stem from the Eurocentrism of western feminism. Consequently, South Asians have been judged against the West with little consideration for the histories and societies from which they originated. Since, the western nuclear family and romantic love are deemed 'normal', western women have been represented as enlightened and progressive, and any alternatives to this, such as arranged marriage, are viewed as deviant and backward. In response, black feminists have challenged the western feminist perception of the family as the main site of oppression by highlighting the prevalence of racism within the labour market, and emphasizing the ways in which the household acts as a site of resistance against white domination.[29] Muslim feminists have also added to the debate by underlining the honourable role women occupy within the home as mothers and domestic providers which, they contend, Western ideals of gender equality undermine.[30] However, a key issue throughout the life stories of the South Asian women was the constraints placed upon them within the household and a recurrent theme was the pressure to marry. For a few women, this pressure involved the threat of violence. For instance, Balbir described how her father arranged her marriage in 1972 as a punishment for her having male friends and said that, had they been living in India, he would have threatened to kill her and dispose of her body in the river. However, the more common experience was the immense social pressure to marry. Sophina's story was more typical.

---

[28] For recent comment see N. Puwar 'Melodramatic postures and constructions', in N. Puwar and P. Raghuram (eds), *South Asian Women in the Diaspora* (Oxford 2003), 21–41. See also H.V. Carby, 'White women listen. Black feminism and the boundaries of sisterhood', in Mirza, *Black British Feminism* 50. Mohanty is extremely critical of the stereotypes produced by western feminists, in C.T. Mohanty, 'Under Western eyes, feminist scholarship and colonial discourses', in C.T. Mohanty, A. Russo and L. Torres (eds), *Third World Women and the Politics of Feminism* (Bloomington 1991), 51–75.

[29] B. Hooks, *Yearning: Race, Gender, and Cultural Politics* (Boston 1990), 46; V. Amos and P. Parmar, 'Challenging imperial feminism', *Feminist Review*, 17, 1984, 3–19. See also G.T. Nain, 'Black women, sexism and racism', in S. Jackson (ed.), *Women's Studies A Reader* (Cambridge 1993), 220–22.

[30] H. Afshar and M. Maynard, 'Gender and ethnicity at the millennium: from margin to centre', *Ethnic and Racial Studies*, 23, 5, 2000, 805–19, F. Ahmad, 'Still "in progress?" – methodological dilemmas, tensions and contradictions in theorizing South Asian Muslim women', in Puwar and Raghuram, *South Asian Women*, 43–65.

> So I remember doing A Levels. I think I was virtually sitting for an exam and my mum and dad called me in the front room and they said that 'You are now getting old, you are nearly seventeen and we're going to marry you off, and here [he] is, you know, we would like you to marry him.' And he showed me the photograph and do you know what? I just looked at the photograph and threw it on the floor. And then my dad said, 'You do as you're told, you are my …' in those days we sort of said 'you are my izzat', a girl, a daughter is supposed to be an izzat, that means you can't, and you know you are my pride. You know the word izzat? You are my pride you cannot do anything wrong because I have to live in the community, I have to face everybody. So just think how much pressure I had to live with.[31]

The reference to 'izzat' shows how, as a daughter, Sophina was responsible for maintaining the family's honour. Sophina described how this pressure was also exerted through blackmail. That is, her father would allow her to pursue a teacher training course only on the condition that she would marry. She recalled,

> My uncle who was in Wakefield, my dad had obviously asked him to come and see me and I remember sitting outside the shop, he said: 'Marry him or else your dad is going to stop you from going to college, I am urging you to marry him.' And yes, I said 'yes' obviously. I was married off April 1969. To somebody I never knew. [32]

In these cases, the prospective husbands were not already resident in Britain but came from India or east Africa specifically to be married. The women described in great length and detail their initial reactions to the prospect of marriage and their feelings and emotions on seeing the photo of the proposed spouse. They detailed the journey to the airport to meet him, their initial feelings on their first acquaintance and the process of verifying with immigration officers, and signing declaration forms to confirm that they would marry. Some women also recalled the marriage ceremony and then discussed their changing relationship with their husband throughout their life course. During these in-depth accounts, the women frequently stressed the pressure they felt to comply with a marriage and this did not dissipate following the marriage ceremony. For instance, Sue recalled the warning from her father after she married, aged 19, in 1976:

> 'You never get separated or divorced, because none of my children do that. I'll never forgive you for that. If things get worse, we don't know what the family's like and if you can't take it commit suicide but you don't come into this house because I never want my reputation, somebody to point the finger at me that your daughter came back,' and

[31] Interview with Sophina, 3 April 2004.
[32] Interview with Sophina.

> it was a taboo it was a big time taboo, that you know if girls come back, it's always the girls fault full stop. So that was clear I was not accepted back, I had no choice but to put up with that.[33]

This pressure to marry was a dominant theme throughout the women's life stories, yet by focusing on these issues, was I conforming to a stereotype of South Asians as 'backward', 'traditional' and 'uncivilized', while also presenting women as passive victims? Was I judging the women's accounts in relation to a Western 'norm'? Would I also, unwittingly, contribute to the negative image of arranged marriages as intrinsically forced, as perpetuated by the media?[34] According to South Asian academics, these stories regarding arranged marriages have had very tangible and adverse consequences for South Asian communities in terms of directly contributing to racism and providing justification for post-war immigration controls.[35] At the same time, to censor and silence these experiences that had been a defining and important part of women's lives, also raised pressing concerns. The issues of representation, subsequently, posed an acute ethical dilemma.

Despite the concerns, these experiences could not simply be ignored and while acknowledging the diversity of marriage practices within different South Asian communities, I decided to include these examples but attempted to avoid conceptualizing them within a western, Orientalist framework. For instance, it was vital to highlight the agency of the women to avoid presenting them as essentially disempowered. This involved stressing their resourcefulness and creative capacity to adapt to constraints and develop long-term survival strategies. It was also important to situate these experiences within the context of the life cycle because this showed that certain constraints were not a permanent aspect of their lives, but were often transient. Likewise, it was significant to stress that, despite these experiences, these women did not reject the notion of the family and many respondents simultaneously praised their parents. For instance, Sophina conceded that, despite her father's attempts to bribe her into marriage, she did not blame him but was ultimately grateful as he helped her to complete her teacher training. Moreover, it was important to locate these women's stories within a particular historical period to avoid portraying their experiences as fixed

---

[33] Interview with Sue, 10 July 2002.

[34] See R. Penn and P. Lambert, 'Arranged marriages amongst south-Asians in contemporary Britain', *Pakistan Journal of Social Sciences*, 1, 1, 2003, 1–9.

[35] H. Ramji, 'Engendering diasporic identities', in Puwar and Raghuram, *South Asian Women*, 250. Recent research into forced marriages among the Bengali community in East London was accused of perpetuating racial and religious discrimination, with the hidden agenda of curbing immigration into Britain. Y. Samad and J. Eade, *Community Perceptions of Forced Marriage* (London 2003).

and universal. The women's experiences of marriage occurred in the 1960s and 1970s and research has shown that the younger generation of British-born Asians generally have more control over their choice of marriage partners.[36]

While I aimed to be reflective throughout the stages of the research, I became particularly conscious of the actual extent of the impact of my identity during the final stages of the analysis. Oral historians have stressed the need to reflect on the performative aspects of the interview, to decipher the meanings conveyed and to consider the messages the respondent is attempting to communicate.[37] In view of how the respondents presented themselves to me and the type of stories they decided to tell, it became apparent that many stories represented an attempt to educate an 'outsider'. That is, the interview may have served as an opportunity to contest the views of a white interviewer, who may endorse and reproduce racial prejudices and stereotypes. The older male respondents, for instance, typically framed their life stories, against the backdrop of political events and colonial history. For instance, Mr Karim's story began: 'My grandfather came from India to Kenya and went back again and he sailed with the British army in 1915, 1920 something like that and at that time it was known as the British Empire in India.'[38] He detailed how his grandfather worked on the Kenya–Uganda railway and outlined the process of Africanization and the consequent exodus of east-African Asians to Britain. Others explained how their father acquired a British passport and the implications of this in terms of their citizenship.

At one level, the decision by the elderly male respondents to detail the history and effects of British colonialism unveiled their acute awareness of how political events had fundamentally altered the course of their life.[39] Yet it is doubtful that they would have felt the need to explain the British Empire to an interviewer from the same ethnic background. Overall, the men's stories imparted the significant message that 'we are here because you were there'. It highlighted that although racism served to define South Asians as 'outsiders' and 'aliens' who did not belong, they were not only British passport holders with full legal rights to settle in Britain but they had played an irrefutable part in Britain's history. The interview, therefore, enabled the South Asian men to remind a white interviewer of the ramifications of the

---

[36] Ramji, 'Engendering diasporic', 232.

[37] R.J Grele, 'Movement without aim: methodological and theoretical problems in oral history' in Perks and Thomson, *The Oral History Reader*, 38–52.

[38] Karim, 13 June 2002.

[39] T. Lummis notes that respondents may detail public time, when events force a change in their own lives in T. Lummis, 'Structure and validity in oral evidence', in Perks and Thomson, *The Oral History Reader*, 278.

colonial legacy, to reinstate their integral place within British history, and to reaffirm their British citizenship.

Similarly, the female respondents may have constructed their life story as a means to confront and challenge the expectations of a white interviewer. Although the women's stories tended to focus on the suffering and hardships they had endured, the predominant and overriding message was the strength of the women to cope with and overcome these difficulties. This message was communicated through the particular aspects of their lives that they decided to reveal, such as their experiences of a negative marriage, but many women also stated their point explicitly. Balbir, for instance, detailed how, despite the opposition from the extended family, she ended her relationship with her husband because she refused to act as 'the *mere* woman'.[40] She added, 'I don't think of it like that, that doesn't cross my mind at all you know 'cause I've always been strong in myself. I mean even now I think to myself I'd rather be on my on my own than be with someone whose unsuitable 'cause I don't need a man. I'm quite independent.'[41] At the end of Sue's life story she asserted, 'I'm a *very very* strong woman now,' and as Sophina's interview came to a close she revealed 'I was talking to a colleague of mine, you know he's retired, and I was sort of telling him about my life, I said "I think I need to write a book." She reflected, 'the strength which women, you know, portray, it's phenomenal isn't it really?'[42] This emphasis on the fortitude of the women directly challenged the common stereotype of South Asian women as passive and submissive.[43] This demonstrates how the respondents attempted to negotiate the power imbalance within the interview and it would be erroneous to suggest that the interviews were simply characterized by the exploitation and appropriation of the 'researched'.

However, were the respondents' stories solely a response to my 'outsider' status and motivated by the desire to correct racial stereotypes? There are many factors which shape the construction of life stories such as cultural genres and the respondents' personal concerns.[44] This includes the need for composure and a coherent sense of self in the present, alongside sub-conscious emotions and desires.[45] Some academics have stressed how stories

---

40 Interview with Balbir, 8 May 2002.

41 Interview with Balbir.

42 Sue, 10 July 2002, Sophina, 3 April 2004.

43 See A. Rattansi, '"Western" racisms, ethnicities and identities in a "postmodern" frame', in A. Rattansi, and S. Westwood (eds), *Racism, Modernity and Identity* (Cambridge 1994), 68–9.

44 M. Chamberlain and P. Thompson (eds), *Narrative and Genre* (London 1998).

45 According to Roper, a rigid focus on the impact of the interviewer's identity negates the emotional aspect of the interview and unconscious dimensions. M. Roper, 'Analysing the analysed: transference and counter-transference in the oral history

are not simply spontaneously constructed during the course of the interview, but may have been told many times before and are already well developed.[46] Arguably, I was interpreting the respondents' stories in the context of my ideological framework and imposing my own expectations when reading the transcripts. These questions illustrate how the dilemmas involved in the cross-cultural interview are not easily resolved.

Conclusion

This chapter has reflected on some of the ethical concerns that arise while conducting cross-cultural interviews. Despite arguments that posit the dangers of whites researching minority ethnic groups, my experience showed that it was possible to overcome and negotiate some of the problems. As an 'outsider', it is possible to establish trust and rapport with the respondents based on various topics and through the vital role of the gatekeeper. The issue of rapport was also shaped by gender and it was evident that this aspect of the interviewer's identity had a crucial impact on the interviews. Through discussions of sensitive issues, such as racism, the importance of prioritizing the respondents' experiences was paramount and this yielded important findings that altered the course and focus of the research.

However, the interpretation and representation of the findings posed more intractable difficulties. The process of deciding which issues to include and exclude was most problematic, particularly with the contentious issue of arranged marriage, which has been described as one of the most 'exotic racist categories' in research on South Asians in Britain.[47] Gradually it became evident that although my ethnic identity did not prevent me from empathizing or establishing rapport with the respondents, my whiteness was far from unproblematic and may have had a considerable bearing on the type of 'stories' the respondents decided to tell. That is, the interviews not only offered a unique insight into the experiences of otherwise hidden groups but also revealed how the respondents actively used the interview as an opportunity to challenge dominant white perceptions and racial stereotypes. My experiences showed that the respondents were not simply powerless but were able to communicate their message and the perception that the researcher has the power and the respondent does not simply ignores

---

encounter', *Oral History*, 31, 2, 2003, 20–32. See also W. Hollway and T. Jefferson, 'Biography, anxiety and the experience of locality', in Chamberlayne, Bornat, and Wengraf, *The Turn to Biographical*, 167–80.

46 S. Schrager, 'What is social in oral history?', in Perks and Thomson, *The Oral History Reader*, 285.

47 S. Sharma, J. Hutnyk and A. Sharma quoted in Dhooleka, *Where Are you From?*, 107.

how power is relational. Finally, the process of reflecting on these issues did not produce definitive and unequivocal answers but ultimately raised further questions and served to elucidate the tensions and complexities involved in the cross-cultural interview.

Further reading

Afshar, H. and M. Maynard, 'Gender and ethnicity at the millennium: from margin to centre', *Ethnic and Racial Studies*, 23, 5, 2000, 805–19.

Ahmad, F., 'Still "in progress?" – methodological dilemmas, tensions and contradictions in theorizing South Asian Muslim women', in N. Puwar and P. Raghuram (eds), *South Asian Women in the Diaspora* (Oxford 2003), 43–65.

Björkert, S.T., 'Nationalist memories: interviewing Indian middle class nationalist women', *Oral History*, 27, 2, 1999, 35–46.

Cashmore, E. and B. Troyna, 'Just for white boys? Elitism, racism and research', *Multiracial Education*, 10, 1981, 42–8.

Chamberlain, M. and P. Thompson (eds), *Narrative and Genre* (London 1998).

Chamberlain, M. and S. Leydesdorff, 'Transnational families: memories and narratives', *Global Networks*, 4, 3, 2004, 227–40.

Chamberlayne. P., J. Bornat, and T. Wengraf (eds), *The Turn to Biographical Methods in Social Science: Comparative Issues and Examples* (London 2000).

Dhooleka, S. R., *Where Are you From? Middle-Class Migrants in the Modern World* (London – Berkeley 2003).

Grele, R.J., 'Movement without aim: methodological and theoretical problems in oral history', in R. Perks and A. Thomson (eds), *The Oral History Reader* (London 1998), 38–52.

Leydesdorff, S., 'Genres of migration', in M. Chamberlain (ed.), *Caribbean Migration: Globalised Identities* (London 1998), 81–91.

Mirza, M., 'Same voices, same lives? Revisiting black feminist standpoint epistemology', in P. Connolly and B. Troyna (eds), *Researching Racism in Education. Politics, Theory and Practice* (Buckingham 1998), 79–94.

Puwar, N., 'Melodramatic postures and constructions', in N. Puwar and P. Raghuram (eds), *South Asian Women in the Diaspora* (Oxford 2003), 21–41.

Sangster, J., 'Telling out stories: feminist debates and the use of oral history', in R. Perks and A. Thomson (eds), *The Oral History Reader* (London 1998), 87–100.

Thomson, A., 'Moving stories: oral history and migration studies', *Oral History*, 27, 1, 1999, 24–37.

Twine, F.W., 'Racial ideologies and racial methodologies', in F.W. Twine and J.W. Warren (eds), *Racing Research, Researching Race* (Cambridge 2000), 1–34.

Index